Virtuous Educational Research

Religion, Education and Values

SERIES EDITORS:

Professor Stephen G. Parker
The Rev'd Canon Professor Leslie J. Francis
Dr Rob Freathy
Dr Mandy Robbins

Volume 9

PETER LANG
Oxford • Bern • Berlin • Bruxelles • Frankfurt am Main • New York • Wien

Virtuous Educational Research

Conversations on Ethical Practice

Julian Stern

PETER LANG

Oxford • Bern • Berlin • Bruxelles • Frankfurt am Main • New York • Wien

Bibliographic information published by Die Deutsche Nationalbibliothek.
Die Deutsche Nationalbibliothek lists this publication in the Deutsche National-
bibliografie; detailed bibliographic data is available on the Internet at
http://dnb.d-nb.de.

A catalogue record for this book is available from the British Library.

Library of Congress Control Number: 2016932987

ISSN 2235-4638
ISBN 978-3-0343-1880-8 (print)
ISBN 978-3-0353-0831-0 (eBook)

This publication has been peer reviewed.

Printed in Germany

Contents

Preface

This is the first book of its kind about virtuous educational research, a book of researchers working in the UK (in England and Scotland), mainland Europe (Latvia, Russia and Spain), North America (Canada and the USA), and South Africa. They illuminate the lived reality of educational research – research on family life in rural South Africa, support for self-harming students in the UK, character development in the US and Korea, educational leadership in the UK and China, philosophical analysis of education policy, and much more. The book is built around a set of conversations. This way of presenting researchers is in part derived from the pattern set by Bryan Magee, in his conversations with contemporary philosophers (Magee 1971, 1978). The views of researchers are explored in discussion with me – a fellow-researcher. Although these could be described as 'interviews', they are more collaborative and therefore conversational than conventional interviews.

This book is for and about researchers themselves. Researchers work at the frontiers of our knowledge and understanding of the world, and frontiers can be dangerous places. How are the researchers' personal qualities – the virtues such as courage, honesty, and kindness – tested and exemplified in contemporary research? For all the work on research ethics in master's and doctoral degrees, and in the training of academic staff, researchers find that they face unexpected challenges – the challenges inherent in the process of research. Researchers talk about their experience of research and what qualities are needed – or wished for – to face the challenges of research. *Virtuous Educational Research* gives research a human face or, rather, a number of human faces: none perfect, but all prepared to explain what it takes to complete research. This book is an invitation to join a conversation of practitioners. There are many books that have lists of what to do and what not to do. Here, we find out what happens and why – and what it takes to keep going.

Contributing interest in the project, and contributing the majority of the conversationalists, is a set of networks each of which involves international conferences or seminars with which I have been involved. One network has been created by the *Value and Virtue in Practice-Based Research* conferences, held annually from 2011 at York St John University (<http://www.yorksj.ac.uk/value&virtue>). A second is the *International Seminar on Religious Education and Values* (ISREV, <http://www.isrev.org>), which has been meeting every two years since 1978, and has a concern with high-level research on some of the most challenging issues in education. The third of the networks is the *Social and Moral Fabric of the School* series, held roughly every two years since the early 1990s, led by the University of Hull, Seattle Pacific University, the Hong Kong Institute of Education, and York St John University.

I would like to acknowledge the considerable support from others involved in the project, including Mike Bottery (for commenting on drafts of several chapters, as well as his own), Leslie Francis and his colleagues (as series editors), Emily Morrissey (for transcription and for conversations about each transcription), participants in all the *Value and Virtue in Practice-Based Research* conferences (where I tested out some of my ideas), staff and students of York St John University (who commented on presentations of three of the conversations), and Marie Stern (who worked on the whole manuscript). Each of the 'conversationalists' made the book what it is, in the initial conversations and in correspondence and discussion before and since, and my biggest thanks therefore go to them. In the order in which we had our discussions (from September 2014 to September 2015), they are Chris Sink, Jean McNiff, Fedor Kozyrev, Mario D'Souza, Mike Bottery, Helen Lees, Ginger MacDonald, Jacqui Akhurst, Anne Pirrie, Helen Gunter, Morwenna Griffiths, Lāsma Latsone, Nel Noddings, Ron Best, Lynne Gabriel, Sr Agnes Wilkins, Shanaaz Hoosain, and Lander Calvelhe.

The book is dedicated to John, who won't read the book, and Marie, who did.

Julian Stern

January 2016

PART I

Remembering Virtue

It is easy to forget virtue. In professional work – professional research, professional education, or any other professional field – reason and regulation, codes of conduct and job descriptions, responsibilities and accountabilities, all give the impression of clarity and rationality. All give the impression that the work requires commitment and effort, but not – not so much – virtue. Talk of virtue makes people think of 'preachiness' and of being 'moralistic'. Defining it as 'the cultivation of a set of dispositions conducive to good character', and saying that 'human beings became good by consistently doing good things and avoiding bad things' (Arthur 2010, p. 3) may help a little, but then begs the question 'What do you mean by "good"?' This is described by Nel Noddings in Chapter 2 as part of an 'interminable discussion' of what makes people better. Even though the discussion will never terminate, we need to remember to join in the discussion. There is an expectation that work is done 'right', but we rarely argue over whether the people doing the work are 'good'. That seems just too intrusively personal, and too, well, *arguable*. So virtue is forgotten, goodness is forgotten: both replaced by performance measured in outcomes, obedience disguised as productivity, evidence presented as understanding. Remembering virtue means remembering that the character and the personal strengths of a professional *matter*. It means remembering that all the regulations in the world will not ensure that professional work is truly ethical, or will contribute to the good society. People will be more or less virtuous or vicious, and remembering this, and arguing about this, will encourage virtue and discourage vice, and remind people that they do – almost inevitably – want to make the world a better place.

CHAPTER I

Introduction: From Ethics to Virtues

Remembering Virtue

My brother-in-law, John D'Albert, is suffering from dementia as a result of Pick's disease. He didn't lose words at first, but decision-making skills. Gradually, many cognitive skills have left him, and now there are almost no words left. However, in his actions, in his physicality, he demonstrates so many of his continuing personal qualities, his personal strengths, including his kindness and his helpfulness. These are retained, even as he doesn't know how to do things, even as his physical control is disappearing. From John, I'm getting a very different feel about what his, what our, virtues are. His every action is kind and thoughtful, without him having the ability to talk about or understand what he is doing. How embodied virtues and personality are: it's striking. John's illness has coincided with the development and writing of this book, and he has contributed the idea that, whatever else may be forgotten, virtues are personal characteristics that can be retained. Virtues are more central to personhood than knowledge, and are more embodied than what might be stated as our values or beliefs.

I began the project that became this book as a way of describing research virtues in order to illuminate the process of research. It has become a book of portraits of people who do research, in which discussion of research illuminates the personal characteristics – the virtues and strengths, the temptations and challenges – of nineteen people, including me. It is a more personal book than I had expected it to be: 'personal' in the sense of exploring personhood itself, rather than personal in the sense of 'confessional'. And it 'voices' the conversationalists more than I had initially expected. Having completed a wide range of what is called 'empirical' research over the years (such as Stern 2009a, 2010, 2013a, 2014a, Stern and Backhouse 2011), I have made use of the voices of research participants, alongside voices of published authors, in my explorations of education. However, the more I worked on the transcripts of the conversations for this book, the more I realised that presenting each conversation in a dialogic form, the more the voices of each person shone through. I had avoided creating an edited book, with each chapter written by a different author, because of the challenge that this creates in achieving a coherent narrative. Yet by presenting the conversations in the way I have chosen for this book, I seem to hear the 'real' voices of the conversationalists – more real, that is, than I hear when reading their own publications. By 'real', I mean in part that I recognise the person I know, and in part I sense they are engaged in what Buber refers to as 'real' dialogue, in contrast to 'technical' dialogue (the exchange of information) and 'monologue disguised as dialogue' (Buber 2002, p. 22).

'By far the greater part of what is today called conversation among men [*sic*]', Buber says, 'would be more properly and precisely described as speechifying' (Buber 1998, p. 68). (When a quoted author uses non-inclusive language, I note it, with [*sic*], on the first occasion only.) In more conventional writing, I suspect, we 'clean up' what we say about research, 'speechifying', perhaps, and often write in order to exchange information – Buber's 'technical' dialogue. Not much of our selves remains. The French philosopher Michel Serres writes about how people in positions of power (including, especially, intellectuals) never see untidy things, messy things, as everything is tidy: 'whoever wields power … never encounters in space anything other than obedience to his power, thus … reason never discovers, beneath its feet, anything but its own rule' (Serres 1997, p. xiii). It is something like members of royal families thinking everything smells of fresh paint, and thinking everything is tidy and clean, as the visit of royalty makes people paint and clean. So this book is joyfully untidy, and smells, I hope, of people, not paint.

In such ways, remembering virtue means recognising that research is a deeply personal activity – for the researcher and the researched alike. Remembering virtue also means reaching through the all-too-often procedural 'tick-box' approach to research ethics and the practice of educational research, to find empathy, artistry, courage, humility, and the rest. That is the subject of the following section.

From Research Ethics to Researcher Virtues

For this project, my working definition of research is the one given by the UK's largest research funding body: 'research is defined as a process of investigation leading to new insights, effectively shared' (Hefce 2011, p. 48, also quoted in UUK 2012, p. 22). Research on education systems, and broader educational research, is a flourishing activity with a wide geographic spread and a relatively long history. Virtually all such research is likely in recent years to be covered by ethical codes: sets of rules that must be followed and must be *seen* to be followed. However, the ethics – exemplified by the various disciplinary codes – have been largely described and have operated in a procedural rather than a substantive way. Where substantive ethics and values are stated, there is often little reference to how researchers should account for their commitment to those values. The British Sociological Association (BSA), for example, says that research is a 'valuable activity and contributes to the well-being of society' (BSA 2004, p. 2). However, as the BSA says, their code 'does not ... provide a set of recipes for resolving ethical choices or dilemmas, but recognises that it will be necessary to make such choices on the basis of principles and values, and the (often conflicting) interests of those involved' (BSA 2004, p. 1). Specific values are described, such as the 'integrity of sociological inquiry as a discipline, the freedom to research and study', 'responsibility for the use to which their data may be put', and that 'research relationships should be characterised, whenever possible, by trust and integrity' (BSA 2004, pp. 2–3). Yet procedures for gaining ethical approval tend to require accounts of consent and confidentiality, with mention to be made of the methods used and – perhaps – some account of benefit and harm. More complex values are generally left unaccounted for, and unreported in publications resulting from the research. The British Psychological Society (BPS) justifies its procedural approach in terms of 'eclecticism': the 'underlying philosophical approach in this code is best described as the "British eclectic tradition"' (BPS 2009, p. 4), and the ethical principles of 'respect', 'competence', 'responsibility' and 'integrity' (BPS 2009, pp. 10–21) are each worked out in terms of behaviours and procedures. Similar lists and descriptions are common in disciplinary codes in many contexts (APSA 2008, ASA 1999, ASAUKC 1999, BERA 2011, BSC 2000, CIHR 2010). Procedures are checked; researchers' underlying values and philosophies – eclectic or not – are harder to trace and are much less likely to be tested or reported.

More recently, positive support for the virtue of 'integrity' has been offered, along with support for the education and training of researchers to enable them to be more ethical (UUK 2012), yet such work needs considerable 'bulking out' to make it meaningful to researchers. What is needed, I believe, is a more personal account of the nature of research and the ethics of researchers. For this, a broad virtues vocabulary can help. Virtue ethics has grown in influence since MacIntyre's *After Virtue* (MacIntyre 1981), or rather, it has regrown since the earlier virtue-based philosophy of Aristotle and colleagues lost its influence to the more impersonal ethics since Kant in the eighteenth century. It is the sense of virtues as personal (ethical) attributes, rather than ethics described in terms of rules, behaviours and procedures, that makes virtues worth exploring in the field of research. Along with a revival in philosophical interest in virtues, there is a growing interest in the psychology of virtues, notably in positive psychology where virtues are also described as 'character strengths' (Csikszentmihalyi and Csikszentmihalyi 2006), and in its application to schooling (Arthur 2010). When combined with an increased interest in personalist philosophy (of writers such as Buber and Macmurray) and broader issues of religion and values, connected to the failure of much of the 'value free' rhetoric of research, there is now an opportunity for exploring and promoting research virtues. Procedural ethical codes have started to recognise this, so '[e]ach ethical principle is described in a statement of values' (BPS 2009, p. 9), but there are limitations such as the use of 'whenever possible' in the BSA's claim, also quoted above, that 'research relationships should be characterised, whenever possible, by trust and integrity' (BSA 2004, p. 3).

Examples of research ethics policies and procedures, and of research ethics committee practices, are worthy of a major study. What is presented here, instead, is an account of the practices and virtues of educational researchers themselves. It was stimulated by an interest in sincerity in educational research. Sincerity was framed as 'more than not lying'. Guides to research methods tend to focus on questioning in a way that avoids confusing (over-complex or unclear) or leading questions. By avoiding misleading questions, it is thought that lying will be avoided and truth will emerge. However, reaching towards the truth, in educational research or in the rest of life, requires more than not lying. The 'more' was described as 'sincerity' (Stern 2001, p. 73, Stern 2006, p. 105, Stern 2007, p. 165). In the first of those projects, I wanted to gain the views of school pupils, trainee teachers and established teachers in a number of schools. (Throughout this book, I use the term 'pupils' for children and young people in schools, to differentiate them from 'students' studying in universities.) As I was also working with the trainee teachers (as their tutor) and working with the schools (supporting the student teachers placed there, and/or teaching in the school), I was concerned that responses to the research questions would be biased. The responses might attempt to please me (as tutor or teacher), or – for that matter – to displease me, and they might be ill-thought-through routine responses. I therefore framed the questions to try to elicit *sincere* responses.

Responses were elicited, for example, on the understanding that they would be used for the benefit of the respondents, schools, and so on. It was, indeed, a central aim of the research, to investigate the *use* of the views of members of a school community, to contribute to the development (or learning) of individuals and whole schools. As this aim was, in different forms, known or explained to respondents, there was a more or less explicit reason given for respondents to be sincere. For example, when a number of pupils, being introduced to the questionnaire by the researcher, were asked 'do you think you know, better than the teachers, how this school could be run?', the pupils answered in a loud and immediate chorus 'yes' (Stern 2001, p. 74). Their subsequent answers to survey questions, and the follow-up work on how the school could be improved, seemed to provide evidence of subtle, mature, well-thought-through understanding of how a school works and how it could be improved. They suggested, for example, specific types of training that teachers could be given, ways in which staff could be encouraged to follow the school ethos, ways of pupils putting their views forward to school managers, ways of balancing the interests of pupils and teachers, and so on.

Similar work was completed with trainee teachers and experienced teachers, with the research contributing to school development planning. It would be wrong to claim that such techniques would guarantee sincere, truthful responses. Nevertheless, the attempt to promote sincerity is a valuable contribution to methodological considerations. I used similar approaches in other large-scale research projects, such as those on spirituality (Stern 2009a) and on loneliness and solitude (Stern 2014a, Stern et al. 2015). Although sincerity is little studied in mainstream methodology textbooks, it is supported by philosophers from Wittgenstein to Habermas. Wittgenstein contrasts 'truthfulness' and 'sincerity', so that '[a] dog cannot be a hypocrite, but neither can he be sincere' (Wittgenstein 1958, p. 229e). That is, people and dogs can be truthful, but only people can be sincere – can exhibit the virtue of sincerity. Macmurray, similarly, contrasts 'negative untruthfulness' (i.e. lying) and sincerity, with sincerity being 'much more than' avoiding lying. Sincerity 'is positively expressing what you do think and believe', and '[t]o refrain from expressing what you think or believe or know to someone, if it is to his advantage or to someone else's advantage that he should know it, is positive dishonesty', that is, 'dissimulation – the suppression of the truth' (Macmurray 1995, p. 76). This is similar to the contrast in Habermas between 'truth' and 'truthfulness'. For him, '[w]henever we actually say something … validity claims are of three types … *Truth*: concerning facts or possible states of affairs about *the* material world – *Rightness*: concerning valid norms of behaviour in *our* social world – *Sincerity* (truthfulness): concerning *my* personal world of feelings and intentions' (Mingers 2009, p. 177).

'Sincerity' as an approach to research can also be related to the stress on 'ownership' of research tools, highlighted in the methodology of Dalin and Rust. They say that '[o]rganization development assumes that school personnel should have a maximum degree of ownership in the renewal process', as '[r]esearch on change indicates that successful implementation is highly correlated with a sense of ownership of the ideas, the process and solutions found' (Dalin and Rust 1983, p. 175). In this way, ownership can be seen as a way of increasing the likelihood of sincerity. Developing the theme of ownership, sincerity can also be demonstrated by valuing the *products* of research: research results can be given back to those researched, for their own use, then. An initial interest in sincerity became a more general interest in research virtues. For Pring, research virtues such as trust, courage, kindness, modesty, humility, truthfulness, openness to criticism, and respect (Pring 2004, pp. 257–261) should be promoted precisely because formal ethics procedures can never ensure universal good practice. '[N]ot every detail of the researcher's work can be checked', he says, so [t]here is a need for the researcher to be trusted – and thus to be trustworthy' (Pring 2004, p. 258). He asks:

> Have researchers the courage to resist the opposition of powerful persons when the conclusions are critical? Have they the modesty to recognize the tentativeness of their conclusions? Are they sufficiently trustworthy for us to accept both data and conclusions drawn from those data? (Pring 2004, p. 261)

Pring also asks whether researchers are 'members of a community where such virtues are respected and fostered' (Pring 2004, p. 261), putting research virtues in the context of professional and political communities, which may themselves be more or less interested in virtues. He notes how '[d]emocratic values (and the social and personal virtues which are associated with them) are difficult to sustain where policy and practice are increasingly controlled by government' (Pring 2004, p. 260). Such work complemented a range of more socially engaged activist research traditions – such as that presented by feminist challenges to pseudo-scientific approaches to research (Griffiths 1995), and the action research traditions of Stenhouse (1975), Elliott (1991), and McNiff (1993). And in recent years, the study of researchers themselves has developed, including their 'academic tribes' (Becher and Trowler 2001), their emotions (Neumann 2009, 2012), and their virtues (Macfarlane 2009). From Neumann's work, I take the approach of describing a number of active researchers, with all their personal characteristics and emotions; from Macfarlane's work, I take the emphasis on specific virtues (in his case, courage, respectfulness, resoluteness, sincerity, humility, and reflexivity).

Before I had any concern with virtues in research, I had a concern with research ethics, through justifying my own research (a process that started in ethics and ended in the virtue of sincerity), and through my awareness of the patently unethical experiments carried out in Germany in the 1930s and 1940s (Mitscherlich and Mielke 1949) and in many other countries before and since (Macfarlane 2009, pp. 9–19). An understanding of the ethics of research is crucial, and this book's subtitle ('conversations on *ethical* practice') reflects my concern with ethics. But there are limits to the value of more procedurally oriented research ethics, even where those procedures are vital in reducing the chances of the violent extremes of professional researchers in all-too-recent history. A virtues approach is more positively directed, rather than seeking to limit harm. It is also better able to take account of the personal nature of research (alongside other social activity), and the personal characteristics of researchers that may be promoted or discouraged. Researchers can be more or less virtuous or vicious. There are various ways of researching that are beneficial and that are harmful, as recognised in ethics codes. Finding out, exposing, and making public can make the world a better place, but can also be damaging, as 'social research intrudes into the lives of those studied', and 'the experience may be disturbing' (BSA 2004, p. 4). 'Even if not harmed', that guidance continues, 'those studied may feel wronged by aspects of the research process', especially 'if they perceive apparent intrusions into their private and personal worlds, or where research gives rise to false hopes, uncalled for self-knowledge, or unnecessary anxiety' (BSA 2004, p. 4). This is not a matter of truthfulness: the intrusion and the making public may be damaging, whether or not what is made public is true. Indeed, the truth may be more damaging than a falsehood: it is easier to deny a falsehood than it is to withdraw a truth. Hence the need for sincerity – going beyond 'not lying'.

Virtue is typically learned by example and by practice. As Aristotle said, although '[i]ntellectual virtue owes both its inception and its growth chiefly to instruction, and for this very reason needs time and experience', '[m]oral goodness ... is the result of habit' (Aristotle 1976, p. 91). Writing more specifically about academic research, Macfarlane makes a similar point:

> Most academics learn about the ethical dimensions of research through their 'appren-
> ticeship' as doctoral students rather than as a result of formal training programs. ...
> The observation of good examples of behaviors, whether knowingly or unknowingly
> set by role models, is the basis for learning virtue ... Similarly, bad examples can
> inculcate vice. (Macfarlane 2009, p. 155)

As a birthday card I once received said, 'If I can't be a shining example, let
me at least be a terrible warning'.

Methods Used

Having been interested in research virtues since the mid-1990s (published
in Stern 2001), in 2008 I moved to York St John University and was fortu-
nate to be able to work there with Jean McNiff, one of the most influential writers on research methodology. We discussed setting up a research
conference addressing our common interests. The first *Value and Virtue in
Practice-Based Research* conference was sponsored by BERA (the British
Educational Research Association, <http://www.bera.ac.uk>) and CARN
(the Collaborative Action Research Network, <http://www.esri.mmu.
ac.uk/carnnew/>), and took place in York in June 2011 (with the title in part
derived from Stern 2008 and Stern 2009a, p. 136, on 'the virtue and value
of research'). The conference was popular, and became a series of conferences taking place every summer since then. Both Jean and I have presented
papers at each of the five conferences to 2015, and a number of publications
have been generated by us and by many of the conference participants –
including edited collections on conference themes (McNiff 2013c, McNiff
2016), special editions of journals (*Educational Action Research*, 23:1, which
includes Stern 2015b), and individual articles and chapters (Stern 2013d).
Wanting to provide a more comprehensive account, I decided to work
on a book specifically addressing virtues. Balancing the advantages of an
edited book (gaining different perspectives) and of a monograph (creating a coherent narrative), I decided to try to get the best of both worlds,
using a model from the 1970s. Bryan Magee created a series of television

programmes from conversations with leading philosophers of the time. Transcriptions were made of the conversations and these were sent to the philosophers for further editing, and books were published (Magee 1971, 1978). They were dialogues, rather than interviews. Magee was himself a philosopher, and his contributions to the conversations were important in their own right. As a student of philosophy myself, in the late 1970s and early 1980s, I found the programmes and books useful in bringing philosophy alive. That approach to writing academic books was seldom copied outside the discipline of philosophy, notwithstanding large numbers of traditional interview-style publications. Within philosophy, Borradori completed a similar project, with some of the same philosophers taking part (Borradori 1994), and Osborne published a set of conversations more recently (Osborne 2013). Honouring the influence of Magee, the first two conversations presented in this book are with philosophers.

The choice of conversationalists might be described as an example of opportunity sampling, as all are known to me in one way or another. However, an attempt was made to have a variety of researchers: some very experienced, some relatively new to research; some philosophers, some psychologists, some working in policy studies, social work, theology or religious education, counselling, teacher education, and more; and researchers working in eight countries. Twelve of the eighteen are female – in contrast to the selections in Magee (twenty-seven men and one woman), Borradino (all nine male, although Borradino is female), and Osborne (six men, four women). All could be described as involved in 'educational' research, *promoting* education, though not all concerned with the *topic* of formal education. Of the eighteen people taking part in the conversations with me, all work or study in universities. Myself and four of the conversationalists have been active in the *Value and Virtue in Practice-Based Research* conferences (Mike Bottery, Shanaaz Hoosain, Lāsma Latsone, and Jean McNiff), seven have been active in the *Social and Moral Fabric of the School* conferences (Mike Bottery, Lāsma Latsone, Helen Lees, Anne Pirrie, Ginger MacDonald, Jean McNiff, and Chris Sink), and three (Mario D'Souza, Fedor Kozyrev and Lāsma Latsone) have been active in the *International Seminar on Religious Education and Values* (ISREV, <http://www.isrev.org>). Two conversationalists work with me at York St John University

(Lynne Gabriel and Jean McNiff), one is studying for a PhD at the university (Sr Agnes Wilkins), five have honorary positions at the university (Mike Bottery, Lāsma Latsone, Helen Lees, Anne Pirrie, and Chris Sink), and three others have previously visited or worked at the university (Jacqui Akhurst, Ron Best, and Lander Calvelhe). I have had contact with Morwenna Griffiths through the Philosophy of Education Society of Great Britain (PESGB, <http://www.philosophy-of-education.org>), Helen Gunter through the British Educational Leadership, Management & Administration Society (BELMAS, <https://www.belmas.org.uk/>), and Nel Noddings through collaboration on a special edition of the *Oxford Review of Education* on John Macmurray (Noddings 2012, Stern 2012) and *The Palgrave Handbook of Alternative Education* (Lees and Noddings 2016).

Seven of the conversations took place in my office in York, six took place by telephone (Mario D'Souza, Morwenna Griffiths, Helen Gunter, Shanaaz Hoosain, Ginger MacDonald, and Jean McNiff), two took place in the conversationalists' homes (Mike Bottery and Nel Noddings), two took place during conferences (Lander Calvelhe at ECER in Budapest, <http://www.eera-ecer.de/ecer-2015-budapest/>, and Lāsma Latsone at the *Value and Virtue in Practice-Based Research* conference in York, with the conversation itself being a public presentation), and one (Fedor Kozyrev) took place in the Queen's Foundation for Ecumenical Theological Education, Birmingham (<http://www.queens.ac.uk/>). Having spent many hours with the transcriptions of the conversations, I could not find any influence of the venue: there were no more 'personal' references in the conversations that took part in homes, and the telephone conversations had similar patterns of talk to face-to-face conversations. All took a similar amount of time, with the partial exception of the 'staged' conversation with Lāsma Latsone, where the overall time was the same as for other conversations, but the audience was drawn in to the discussion for the last fifteen minutes. As I had talked and corresponded with each of the conversationalists in other formats, prior to the recording, I assume this mitigated some of the possible influence of venue.

When arranging the conversations, each conversationalist was sent a guide to the project, which included the four questions guiding the conversation and the virtues vocabulary list (see Table 1). Each conversation lasted between sixty and ninety minutes, and started with an introduction, including discussion of the opportunity for the conversationalist to edit the transcript at a later stage. This was followed by questions:

1.   I'm interested in the practice of research, especially research that might be called, broadly, educational – having some influence on practice. Could you tell me a little about your own research in this area, and how and why you came to be doing it? (This first question could include, as appropriate, consideration of what 'research' is, why it is labelled as such, and any relationship of research to other aspects of education.)

2.   Can you describe one or two research projects (and the consequent publication/s), that demonstrate the way you go about research? (The publications might be added later, in correspondence with the conversationalist.)

3.   Can you give some examples of what you might call the main *research* challenges you faced, and how you dealt with those? (This question might also explore procedural ethics issues in the projects.)

4.   Can you give some examples of what you might call the main *personal* challenges you faced in this research, and how you dealt with them? (The issues raised in this question will often be related to the previous topic of discussion.)

Added to the fourth question would be follow-up discussion of the virtues vocabulary list (see Table 1). I also asked whether there are any other things to add, or any questions that the conversationalist wanted to ask or tell me about the project.

Table 1. Virtues Vocabulary

This virtues vocabulary list is adapted from Peterson (in Csikszentmihalyi and Csikszentmihalyi 2006, p. 45), with asterisked words added by Julian Stern.

Strength/ Virtues*	Absence	Opposite	Exaggeration
Disorders of Wisdom and Knowledge			
Creativity	Conformity	Triteness	Eccentricity
Curiosity/ Interest	Disinterest	Boredom	Morbid curiosity/ Nosiness
Judgment/ Critical thinking	Unreflectiveness	Gullibility	Cynicism
Love of learning	Complacency	Orthodoxy	Know-it-all-ism
Perspective	Shallowness	Foolishness	[None – there cannot be too much]
Disorders of Courage			
Bravery	Fright/Chicken Little-ism	Cowardice	Foolhardiness
Persistence	Laziness	Helplessness	Obsessiveness
Authenticity/ Honesty/ Sincerity*/ Truthfulness*/ Integrity*	Phoniness	Deceit	Righteousness
Vitality	Restraint	Lifelessness	Hyperactivity
Disorders of Love			
Intimacy	Isolation/Autism	Loneliness/ Avoidance of commitment	Emotional promiscuity
Kindness	Indifference	Cruelty/Mean-spiritedness	Intrusiveness
Care*	Carelessness*	Uncaring*	Worrying*
Social intelligence	Obtuseness/ Cluelessness	Self-deception	Psychobabble
Enstasy*/ Comfortable solitude*	Loneliness*/ Unable to be in solitude*	Needy*/Over-dependent on others*	Anti-social*

Strength/ Virtues*	Absence	Opposite	Exaggeration
	Disorders of Justice		
Citizenship	Selfishness	Narcissism	Chauvinism
Fairness	Partisanship	Prejudice	Detachment
Leadership/ Magnanimity*	Compliance	Disruptiveness/ Sabotage	Despotism
	Disorders of Temperance		
Forgiveness/Mercy	Mercilessness	Vengefulness	Permissiveness
Humility/ Modesty	Footless Self-esteem	Arrogance	Self-deprecation
Prudence	Sensation seeking	Recklessness	Prudishness/ Stuffiness
Self-regulation	Self-indulgence	Impulsivity	Inhibition
	Disorders of Transcendence		
Appreciation of beauty/Excellence	Oblivion	*Schadenfreude*-ism	Snobbery
Gratitude	Rugged individualism	Entitlement	Ingratiation
Hope/ Trust*	Present orientism	Pessimism/ Despair	Pollyannaism
Humor	Humorlessness	Dourness	Buffoonery
Spirituality	Anomie	Alienation	Fanaticism

Each conversation was transcribed, with the transcription (of between ten and thirteen thousand words) checked by me, with references added, to create a long transcription. This was then edited down to a medium-sized transcript of roughly six thousand words, taking out repetitions (including comments that I made in more than one of the conversations), explanations of the project, and discussion of issues that were not relevant to the book. The long and the medium transcripts were then sent to the conversationalist, to add, change, correct, or edit. It is the medium transcript that formed the basis of what appears in this book (and these are available online at <http://www.peterlang.com>). Reading through all the agreed medium transcripts, I made notes of the key themes and concepts.

I then paired up the transcripts, where there were complementary themes or concepts, and edited the transcripts further – cutting down to a short transcript of roughly two-and-a-half thousand words each (that is, about a quarter of the original long transcript). The principles of editing were to keep material related to my perception of the themes, and to keep strictly to the word-order in the medium and long transcripts. By keeping the same word order – even if I was able to cut out words – I could not, I believe, alter the 'voice' of the conversationalist. In previous research projects, I had used quotations from interviews freely – using them, as it were, to illustrate my own narrative analysis. Here, I do not interrupt or alter the order of words, and restrict my analysis to the brief chapter introductions and conclusions (in Chapters 2 to 10) and to the three chapters (Chapter 1, 11, and 12) which are free of detailed conversation.

The original plan for the book sent to the series editors had made assumptions about who would take part in the conversations (prior to anyone being invited to take part), and about what chapter themes might emerge. Of the twenty-one names initially put forward, eleven agreed, and seven new conversationalists were found. Of the ten broad chapter themes initially proposed, only two have been retained – Chapter 2 on philosophical research, and Chapter 6 on action/practitioner research. For me, the changes in the themes were indications that the conversations were driven by the voices and interests of the conversationalists, and not by any predetermined 'script'.

The Structure of the Book

The whole book is built around, and emerged from a consideration of, eighteen conversations, although this description of the structure of the book lists the emerging themes, not those who inspired them. Part I is a way of remembering virtue, with Chapter 1 describing the move from research ethics to research virtues. Following this, there are nine 'conversational' chapters, each containing two conversations. In Part II the conversations start, with researchers talking about a range of work on themes that also, coincidentally, started my own interest in virtuous research. From philosophical research (Chapter 2), the themes develop through integrity and sincerity (Chapter 3), and the 'insider-outsider' problem in research (Chapter 4). My own 'qualifying' research projects were for a research degree in philosophy (Stern 1982) and for a doctorate in education whose methodological originality was in its exploration of sincerity. The doctorate was also the first of my projects requiring a sound defence of 'insider' positioning in research (Stern 2001). Part III explores relationships. Chapter 5 considers how close research can be to therapy, either for the participants or for the researcher, whereas Chapter 6 addresses the relationship between research and professional practice. The researcher's relationship to their own research, and in particular the significance of timing, is explored in Chapter 7 on the theme of prudence and pacing. In the remaining conversations, in Part IV, the themes address the sustainability of research – and of researchers. How researchers can be sustained by others is the theme of Chapter 8, focusing on courage. Research will always involve hard work, and that is the theme of Chapter 9, whilst Chapter 10 is about the 'life of research' and the sense of legacy. Finally, Part V faces the future. Chapter 11 considers the significance of the conversations as 'portraits', and Chapter 12 the implications of all this work for the future of educational research in learning communities. This last chapter also proposes a theory of virtuous education research, a theory emerging from all the conversations.

PART II

Starting the Conversation

As a child, I was the quiet one, the one who listened carefully. Although I'm a little noisier now, I spent many years quietly listening, quietly reading, quietly watching the television. I was always busily in conversation – often enough, in my own head, arguing with characters in novels and (perhaps silently) debating social or political issues with the authors of books, with those on the television, and with family and friends. It might be that I was destined to study philosophy, in which, as I understood it, the essence of the discipline was itself thoughtful dialogue. I studied philosophy alongside social sciences, maintaining the sense of a conversation that included people who were not philosophers. (Even as a teenager, I realised how odd it would be to talk philosophically only with philosophers.) I continued as a student until, fed up with what I felt was studying for its own sake, I became a schoolteacher. At that point, I bumped up against one of life's 'stubborn particulars' (Cherry 1995). The people I taught in school were not quite like me or the people I was brought up with. They had their own views and ways of life, and were not necessarily susceptible to a powerfully rational argument about what was right and what was wrong. Brought up widely read and determinedly liberal and tolerant (as delineated by the left-of-centre *Guardian* newspaper), I realised as an adult how intolerant I really was. Intolerant of those with completely different world views to my own, and intolerant of those who did not succumb to the power of a clear rational argument. Although I thought I'd been listening all my life, I had been hearing ideas and arguments but not really listening to *people*. Over the next twenty years – as these things take time – I moved from a more 'dialectical' view of conversation (a progression of thesis to antithesis to synthesis, with every conversation having a definite conclusion) to a more 'dialogical' view of conversation – where differences remain and yet dialogue continues (Wegerif 2008).

I'm therefore starting this set of conversations with people who raise some of the issues that were 'starting points' for me: the nature of conversation in and beyond philosophy, the difference between naïve ideas of truth and understanding truthfulness, and the insider-outsider challenge for researchers – and for life.

CHAPTER 2

Conversation in Philosophy: The Rational and the Reasonable

Introduction

Philosophy is the founding discipline of the academy – the discipline at the heart of the original Academy in Ancient Greece. It is something of a concertina of a discipline, wider and narrower in turn, growing and shrinking, according to the approaches of different schools of philosophy over the years. Philosophers like Aristotle ranged across topics that are now regarded as well beyond philosophy – biology, theatre studies, constitutional politics, and more – whilst some of his contemporaries and others since have had a narrower view of philosophy as 'bounded' by, say, logic or linguistic analysis. Wittgenstein is sometimes described as at the 'narrow' end of philosophy, presenting, in 1918, the 'final solution' to all philosophical problems:

> the *truth* of the thoughts that are here communicated seems to me unassailable and definitive. I therefore believe myself to have found, on all essential points, the final solution of the problems. And if I am not mistaken in this belief, then the second thing in which the value of this work consists is that it shows how little is achieved when these problems are solved. (Wittgenstein 1961, p. 4)

'Anyone who understands me', he continued, 'eventually recognizes [my propositions] as nonsensical, when he has used them – as steps – to climb up beyond them', and the rest – all other issues – 'we must pass over in silence' (Wittgenstein 1961, p. 74). He later described his aim in philosophy as merely '[t]o shew the fly out of the fly-bottle' (Wittgenstein 1958, p. 87e). Combining a magnificently narrow conception of philosophy with a magnificently confident attitude to solving all philosophical problems, Wittgenstein found himself alone, a lonely solipsist ('I am my world', Wittgenstein 1961, p. 57), surrounded by silence (Wittgenstein 1961, p. 74, and see Stern 2014a, pp. 148–149).

Between Aristotle and Wittgenstein, all other philosophers take their place. However, even the narrowest of philosophers will be in – perhaps solitudinous – 'conversations' with those who have previously contributed to the long history of the discipline. Even Wittgenstein makes some reference to previous philosophers, and he enthusiastically 'philosophised' with – or at least in the presence of – his students. When considering educational practice, philosophers face the challenge of making the 'ordinary' life of education extraordinary, and making the all-too-often unquestioned, questioned. How is the depth of thought, required of all philosophy, retained, without sinking into self-referring technical virtuosity? How can philosophical researchers make sense to others involved in education?

The two philosophers in the following conversations are well thought of as philosophers whilst also having a broad view of what philosophy should be doing. Both are socially and politically engaged, and they do this *as* – not *despite* being – philosophical researchers. I was interested, in inviting them to discuss these issues, in whether philosophical (educational) research was distinct from what is often referred to as 'empirical' or 'social scientific' research. My own history, at the 'Aristotle' end of the continuum of philosophical breadth, is one in which the conversation is not entirely internal or solipsistic, and can and should reach well beyond other philosophers. But how do other philosophers see things?

Philosophy in Action: A Conversation with Morwenna Griffiths, University of Edinburgh, Scotland

JS: I am interested in talking to you partly because you've done such a
           wide range of research and writing on research across philosophy
           (Griffiths 1995, 1998, 2003, Griffiths and Troyna 1995) and action

research (Griffiths 2009, Griffiths and Woolf 2009), which some would see as very different types of research. I've written on what I would call action philosophy, which I think is related to action research (Stern 2015a), inspired by you in some of those things –

MG: That's nice to hear.

JS: and in the practice of research that's broadly educational with the 'al' on the end.

MG: I agree with that: I feel quite passionate about it. There's a big difference between education and educational: the field of education and being *educational* as a researcher.

JS: Would you like to tell me about your research and how you came to be doing that?

MG: I wasn't interested – when I was for instance doing my PhD thirty years ago – in action at all, except that I probably had the naïve idea that changes in theory changed how people acted – a naïve rationalism – 'Just tell them and they'll change'.

JS: Isn't that also Habermas's view of public sphere (Habermas 1974): they will end with a rational solution?

MG: Absolutely, and then it will be done because it's rational. If only! Coming towards the end of my PhD, I became interested in feminism. It was like the blinkers coming off. And feminism is inevitably trying to change things. I became involved in what later became the Society for Women in Philosophy (<http://www.swipuk.org/>), and I became interested in a movement on girls and science and technology (GASAT, now <http://www.unesco.org/education/educprog/ste/newsletter/eng_n1/gasatass. html>). Then I went to what was Oxford Polytechnic (now Oxford Brookes University, <http://www.brookes.ac.uk>), where they were putting in a teacher education programme based on action research and reflective practice. At the beginning, I was quite sceptical about action research, so I thought about it epistemologically. Discovering its roots in Dewey – reflecting on whatever I'm engaged in, and seeing that as a part of action research, and noticing the immediate impact of researching one's own practice on what one then did. And at the same time I was trying to

theorise all that, and bring a feminist perspective into it. Those
things came together, in trying to think about relations between
theory and practice, and in how my theorising might affect what
people did, and what I did. I was thinking what bit of research
would I talk about, and I thought probably the one where I was
involved in Creative Partnerships (<http://creative-partnerships.
com/>) in Nottingham. When the local Creative Partnerships
was putting together the proposal, they knew they wanted us to
do it – Nottingham Trent (<http://www.ntu.ac.uk/>) – and
they liked the person who would be working with us, because
she knew an awful lot about arts and arts in schools – Felicity
Woolf (Woolf 2004). We knew that I was going to work with
her because she wasn't very experienced in educational research.
I said, 'Look, if we just do an evaluation, that's going to do nothing other than have us tapping our research findings at teachers
who will look mutinously at us: much better to do it as a piece of
action research on how to do better what Creative Partnerships
thinks they're doing in schools'. They bought that. I was using
Jack Whitehead's 'living contradiction' idea (Whitehead 1989).
So we did action research, on bringing artists from drama, fine
art, sculpture, installations, landscape – anything that could be
counted as the arts and creativity – into schools so that artists
would work with teachers, for the benefit of the children. We were
keen to keep it as 'the arts are good because the arts are good, and
other good things might happen as a result'. We worked in detail
with six teachers on their particular experiences of working with
artists. We were able to talk across all the differences of university,
school, philosophy, action research, and the arts. We – two of the
teachers and myself – then presented that collaboratively at the
European Educational Research Association in Crete, which also
brought the teachers into conversation with educational researchers in a way that was really interesting for both of them. It seems
to me that virtue has an outcome that is virtuous, but it is also
how you conduct yourself personally and with others, as a virtuous person. Virtuous educational research is something that is

both personal, and also an outcome. With my values of justice, I should be acting justly.

JS: Some of the early forms of action research tended to see the university person as doing the real thinking and the teachers in school being very much research assistants.

MG: Yes. That was part of the reason I was so keen to take the teachers to Crete: it is their research. One of the six that I worked with was a very competent, assertive, infant school head – Judy Berry. When I said we were wanting them to do research, she got cross. 'We haven't got time to do that kind of thing; we'll help you with your research, but we've got other things to do, like educate these children.' But I kept asking her difficult questions about what she thought she was doing, and how she thought she knew what was going on, which she found interesting. And having told me she had no time, she and her deputy spent about an hour talking to me, working out as they talked the answers to my difficult questions about why they thought they were doing what they were doing. So it was a clarification, like a kind of self-study, about what they thought they were doing and how that fitted their values. The result of this collaborative working to your values was a 'proper' publication like the one I finally did, which was collaboratively written (Griffiths and Woolf 2009) and also leaflets for the parents, which they could also use for visiting Ofsted inspectors, to say 'This is why we do what we do'.

JS: I'd be interested in how you interview children. Do you see them, as well as the teachers, as researchers? Are they *objects* of research or are they *subjects*?

MG: One of the things that was important to Judy in that school is that you couldn't understand anything you were doing unless you had the children's perspectives on it, and respected them: it was absolutely central. So getting children's perspectives on what they thought was going on, what they liked about it, what they appreciated, was important to us.

JS: So they were clearly evaluators.

MG: Yes. How far were they subjects? Coming from a philosophical background most of what I would call interviewing, is in fact conversation.

JS: So you're not a philosopher at some point, and then an empirical researcher at another point.

MG: Exactly, yes.

JS: But you know that that confuses some people doesn't it?

MG: Yes. If you look at your philosophical heroes or heroines, one of mine is the early Socrates, who did everything in dialogue. And the early dialogues are ones where he doesn't come to conclusions – very different from the later Plato, where you're being led towards a conclusion. Instead, they go away both still a bit baffled, but feeling better for it.

JS: So, your example of action research, I'm guessing you chose that because it sits on the borders between the philosophical, the justice, the practice, the public, the inclusive –

MG: and brings in those dilemmas of being virtuous with truth and power, all the things we were talking about. Where we wanted to say 'our action research shows that these things are working well, and here things are not working so well', Creative Partnerships was reluctant to allow us to say that in any public forum. They felt it all ought to be positive. We said it won't be credible if it's all positive. This leads to an interesting moral dilemma. Almost every action towards research is filled with places where you have to judge what is difficult. I was struck early on by a phrase of Gayatri Spivak where she says we must negotiate with the structures of violence (Spivak and Harasym 1990, p. 138). There is no position of purity: you're forever negotiating.

JS: Can I just clarify: are researchers also a structure of violence?

MG: Yes. 'I'm coming to the school because I know that you've got money from Creative Partnerships, and so you've got to do something to get that money, and part of that is to co-operate with me, and do as I say.' There's a huge temptation to do that.

JS: I've described some research as a sort of smash and grab research, where you go in, get everyone interested and then you clear off and get a career out of it.

MG: Yes, exactly so.

JS: So the research challenges include those 'violence' things and you said there are also personal challenges – 'am I doing what I should be doing?' You have written a lot about justice – the justice drive is part of the research, that's one of the virtues you see as a research virtue?

MG: Yes, that's it exactly: I've written a paper on action research as and for social justice (Griffiths 2009).

JS: Could you be an authentic educational researcher who is *not* driven by social justice? Do you recognise researchers not driven by social justice who are still doing, if you like, virtuous or ethical research?

MG: Yes I do. I think you can do educational research into phonics, for example, which is improving the education of children and students and helping them learn to read but in ways that are not particularly driven by issues of justice in literacy. I think that there are a lot of different kinds of research that are also valuable.

JS: I put in the document that I sent you a list of virtues or strengths.

MG: I recognise them, but I start somewhere else if I'm trying to think about virtue. I'd never thought of virtuous research before, that's why I was thinking about the connection between personal virtue and research that would be virtuous in outcome. It was that that made me want to think, whereas if I'd looked at a list of words it just wouldn't help me.

JS: You are someone whom I think of as a philosopher who stretches, who stretches philosophy, and here you are talking about action research, as a philosopher. But what you're saying is it's all philosophical. Sorry, I'm putting words in your mouth.

MG: I was indeed saying that, yes – that's exactly what I was saying.

JS: You said earlier that these were challenging questions. Is it because people don't talk about these issues? Is it the nature of the writing:

is it that we write ourselves neat? Or is it that ethics committees have become procedural so we can't talk there?

MG: I think it's the performativity: we find ourselves having conversations about how to get more publications, how to get more money, how to get other people to write more publications at the right level, and then when we get out of that, we talk about the interesting things that we've seen in the research – but by then there's no more chance to talk about what it's actually like to do it. There's just this big performative pressure which is having some really corrupting effects on how people view themselves, and what they think they need to do. In the 1980s, there was some value to the then RAE (Research Assessment Exercise, the predecessor to the REF, Hefce 2011), because it allowed the former polytechnics to value research. But then the sharpness of the selectivity made the performativity go through the roof, whereas if the selectivity had been much more gentle, I think that the audit regime could be quite useful. Because the stakes are so high, it pushes people into the worst aspects of performativity, 'Look, I will pretend that I am doing this, and I will pretend really well'. And you have to collude with the idea that good educational research is world leading, when education is absolutely context dependent.

JS: One of the joys of philosophy is that sense of a longstanding conversation; the penalty of that is you're only conversing with people who are officially labelled philosophers, in a lot of philosophy.

MG: Yes: another reason to do action research!

Producing Better People: A Conversation with Nel Noddings, Stanford University, USA

JS: Can you tell me a little about your own research, and how or why you came to be doing it?

NN: When I graduated with my bachelor's degree, I had an emergency credential so I could take a sixth grade job (teaching students 11–12 years old). I taught the sixth grade for a year, and I loved it, I just loved those kids. At the end of the year we were asked if we would stay together for another year because the junior high was overcrowded. The kids had to agree and I had to agree. We stayed together through seventh grade, and at the end of that year we stayed together for another year. That was a life-transforming experience for me. We're talking about sixth, seventh, and eighth graders – kids that most people would rather never have anything to do with. It made me realise that continuity of persons is important, that time to talk about things other than a specific educational objective, is important. After that, I got my high school math teaching job and I spent about twelve years as a high school math teacher. Both those experiences were powerful in my later professional work. It made me realise that real education has a lot more to it than just teaching highly specified narrow learning objectives. There's a whole life. One of the kids was two or three years older than the others, because he had been held back. When he started high school, I was around for a month or so before I went to my new math job, and he came to me and said 'The teacher calls us punks'. What teacher would say that in front of the classes, 'Well, now, you punks are gonna do what I tell you to do'? It's even hard for me to talk about now: so awful, so awful.

JS: Bertrand Russell ran a school for a while, and Buber ran an adult education institute. Do you think there's something in the work of philosophers that's made distinctive by the experience of teaching people?

NN: Yes. It's that sense of joining in dialogue, finding common objectives and interests, and concentrating on the most important function of education which is to produce better people. That's the theme of the book that just came out (Noddings 2015). That's the idea: to produce better people. People say, 'Well, what do you mean by "better" people?' I say 'That is a question that should always be open', and they say, 'Well, you'd be in an interminable discussion'. And I say 'Yes, that's right, it would be interminable', which doesn't mean you never get anywhere. You become more and more enlightened, but it never ends. So the kind of experience that I'm describing convinces you that's what education is all about. How could anybody ever call that kid a punk?

JS: Going back to the beginning, you studied mathematics presumably?

NN: My undergraduate work was math, I don't think I had any philosophy. I taught math for twelve years. We pulled up roots here in New Jersey and went to California because my husband, an engineer, had this wonderful offer. I said 'Now, what am I supposed to do?', and he said 'Well, you've always wanted to get your doctorate, so why don't you go to Stanford and do it?' First quarter at Stanford, I took four courses. They all had to be at the right time of day because I had a house full of kids. I took two philosophy of ed courses to get them out of the way, because you were required. By the end of that term there were philosophy books all over the house, everywhere: I was completely captivated. Then I started taking courses in the philosophy department. Where had it been all my life?

JS: It sounds like it was there because you were looking at developing good people, as a teacher. For your own writing, do you separate the work that you do into 'this is research' and other things that are not research?

NN: I don't. There are things that interest me, and I work on them. As you know, I've produced an awful lot – always because there's something that interests me that I think is worth spending some time on. I can't imagine working any other way. In guiding young professors, I have tried to get them thinking that way. A lot of them think 'I've got to get out so many papers', 'I've got to be in such and such journals'. As soon as I hear that, I think 'You're giving up the heart of what you're doing', which is very sad.

JS: The sense of how research goes on, for you, is it the sense of communicating? Not just 'I'm interested in this', but 'I'm interested in *telling* people about this?'

NN: It's both. I can't imagine retaining my enthusiasm for the second – telling people things – if I didn't have this burning desire to find out something. The thing that now has me thinking: must a theory fall into a prescribed mind? We were talking about care ethics, to which I'm devoted, but must it now be codified? Must we have highly specified definitions? I know we need some: we need to be able to tell this from that. Specific principles that guide every step of the way? I don't know. It really is an open question for me, but you can see that I'm leery of it. I'm not sure that it would advance the cause, or advance anything really.

JS: What do you feel does advance the cause? Is it teaching the next generation, is it putting into practice? For your work, what *is* the cause?

NN: Certainly teaching the next generation and putting into practice, but especially putting into practice. What does it look like in real life? This is something I'll be talking about at the North American Society for Social Philosophy (<http://www.north americansocietyforsocialphilosophy.org/>). I think John Dewey was absolutely right: he said we can't make up a society out of our minds, and prescribe everything that should be done. John Rawls wasn't writing yet, but here Dewey was anticipating what Rawls called 'ideal theories'. Ideal theories are like mathematical systems, where you start with postulates and definitions and you build everything from that. That's what Rawls did in his *Theory of Justice* (Rawls 1972): he starts with an original condition which is nothing like the real original condition of people. Is it useless? No. There are some wonderful things in there. But it is ideal, whereas what Dewey was recommending was non-ideal. Care theory is non-ideal in the sense that it starts with actual conditions. Here are the way things are: we look at a situation, and we say, this is not good. On what grounds do we decide that? We talk about that. Do we have any good examples? Yes, there are good examples. We're looking at some problems in teaching, we compare them with families. There are some wonderful families that do wonderful things: here is an example in the real world. We don't have to copy it, but we can learn from it: we can try this and that from it. That's the whole idea of these so called non-ideal theories, of which care theory is one.

JS: Unusually for a philosopher, your examples sound like actual examples. They are not thought experiments – those, I did as a philosophy undergraduate, those odd games.

NN: I know, they're still there. The trolley game: the train is running down the track, and it is going to kill six people, say, and you can press the switch and put it on an alternative route where it will only kill one person. What do you do? I just throw my hands up and say first of all, I wouldn't know which switch to push. Why would I be anywhere near a switch? These things have no place in non-ideal theory, where we insist upon talking about the real world. These can be difficult and horrific enough, instead of making up these wild things.

JS: You've written so much on different aspects of education. How do you go about marshalling the material?

NN: I don't really know what to say on that except that it would be triggered by the current problem, the thing that I think really needs more thought. That's certainly what triggered this latest book on the American high school (Noddings 2015) – the fact that things have become so recipe-like, so fully prescribed in every detail. Another of the things that I'm working on now was triggered by some work like that of Cass Sunstein (Sunstein and Thaler 2008) and a number of writers who've noticed that we've got an increasing social gap in the US. It isn't just a financial gap, we've got that for sure, but a social gap. We can't seem to talk to each other across classes anymore. Some philosophers are writing about it. Elizabeth Anderson has done some interesting work on it (Anderson 2010). What is needed is we've got to talk with – with, not at – these people. After the Rodney King riots in Los Angeles, back in the nineties, a group of researchers went into the public schools in the area to see what was going on. The administrators told them 'We're doing this because we care about the kids'; when they talked to the kids they said 'Nobody cares here'. People weren't connecting.

That is the sort of thing that we're talking about now. Politically active, well-meaning people, who want to liberate this class of people, have decided what those people need and what should be done, but they haven't talked to those people.

JS: Turning that to research, one of the research challenges, I think, is to try to see how you can be in a conversation, and not simply getting the facts that you need to support your own argument.

NN: Yes. And that brings us back to the conversation we started earlier, my fear that by concentrating so closely on our own research, we get farther and farther away from the problem we started with.

JS: If I can ask about care – I can't think of anyone in the world better to ask about care – care, by its nature, has a certain hierarchy built into it. If I am caring for a person, there is some sort of power to be able to do that. In terms of research, we may be caring as a researcher, but it is still a power relation.

NN: Yes. That leads to a whole bunch of things to study and talk about it. We have to be careful to distinguish between caring and care-giving. Care-giving can be done without care. We have Nurse Ratched from *One Flew Over the Cuckoo's Nest* (Kesey 2002) as an example. While caring is certainly associated with care-giving, and we hope that it will be paramount there, it isn't always, and so they are different. How are they different? I – as you know – want to emphasise the relational character of caring. So if I meet with a stranger, it is equally likely that I will be carer and he cared-for, or the other way round. Both contribute to the caring relation. I'd emphasise that. But then you've got professional categories, and you can't ignore those either because there are certain responsibilities, expectations, that go with each profession. Then you have to ask yourself, if you're looking at caring and teaching, it's usually the teacher who's the carer, and the student who's the cared-for. But that doesn't mean that the cared-for doesn't contribute anything to the relation. As you know I'm very interested in what the cared-for does contribute to the relation. So that is the kind of openness, reciprocity, that I want to try to sustain. It isn't this powerful group of carers, care-givers, who decide what the other folks need and then they're generously going to give it to them – instead of meeting together and realising that both contribute to the relationship.

JS: I'm tempted to talk about careful as opposed to careless research – the sort of research that exhibits care, whether it's of dead people who have written hundreds of years ago, or of the children being researched in school.

NN: I think you make a very good point there. A critic who is careful is more likely to elicit a thoughtful response, and so between the two of you, you may advance the whole project. Whereas the careless, or just nasty, critic is likely to generate opposition – that does nothing to forward the project, but just get you mired in the fight.

JS: I sent a list of virtue words, and their opposites. We've talked about care. Are there other words that strike you either as things that you find particularly important or as things to be avoided? You talked about being troubled when you see new young researchers who are directed towards this journal or that journal. Is it a weakness, or a lack of sincerity?

NN: I look at this – loneliness, avoidance of commitment – it's something like that for them, that's promoted by a desire for recognition. Now where would that come up here – in the citizenship thing, selfishness, partisanship, compliance? But beneath that, compliance for what? Compliance to get ahead, to be recognised?

JS: It's interesting that you started with it as a loneliness and avoidance of commitment – it's not just bad for their research, it's bad for *them*.

NN: Yes. I recall an incident years ago. Young professor at Stanford: I asked him what he was really interested in and what he was going to pursue. He said, 'When I get tenure, I'm going to do what I really want to do'. Right then, I knew he wasn't going to get tenure at Stanford, because you don't work for tenure – well, I guess some people do – but the people who do the best in the long run are the people who work on what really grabs them, they really want to study and learn. The sadness is that so many of our

young people fall into that. They're losing out on the most important part of intellectual life. Elliot Eisner and I were colleagues for
many years, and he was deploring the state of educational research.
He said 'We've got graduate students wandering up and down the
halls saying "what shall I correlate?"'. I have no patience with that.

JS: Are there other things that you were thinking either I might be
asking you and I haven't, or that you wanted to say about the topic
now?

NN: Under philosophical research, the thing that I applaud is the whole
notion of conversations – not only maintaining those that we've
got going, but initiating conversations across social classes, across
ages, engaging conversations with kids. You can have wonderful
conversations with kids, but it means treating them as conversationalists, as co-speakers.

JS: There's a lot of what's called dialogic philosophy which is often
what I might call more dialectical – trying to solve and finish, a
Habermas style of intellectual public debate: everything gets neatly
tied up through reason, without the roughness of conversation.

NN: I agree. My emphasis would be on dialogue. That doesn't mean
you throw out the dialectic, because it has its uses: you try this and
you try the opposite, you work back and forth, not only with other
people, but with yourself. But you're doing that because you want
to promote this more basic thing, this dialogue – establishing relations of care and trust. Your project guide says 'How is the depth
of thought retained without sinking into self-referring technical
virtuosity?' It's awfully important. That is a question that I will
be posing to the Society for Social Philosophy (<http://www.
northamericansocietyforsocialphilosophy.org/program/>) two
weeks from now. Should I change what I'm doing and follow this
woman who's writing about the core of care ethics? She's making
it into a highly technical, almost Kantian project, you know – so
when I am responding to another, I would be asking 'what is my
duty in this case?' Well, shoot, I don't want that: that's not the
way I want to go. But if people want to argue that, I'm open to
listening.

JS: Do you feel you're being captured?

NN: Well I've been diverted somehow, yes. That temptation, of course, sinking into self-referring technical virtuosity, it doesn't even have to be self-referring. Just technical virtuosity: that's what I have seen happen to so many young professors. They give up what they were, what they might have been really passionate about, in order to prove that they've got whatever this quality they think they need to show – and people will recognise it, and their career will advance.

JS: And I'm aware that the word 'virtuosity' also refers to virtue, but for me it's a distracted virtue.

NN: Yes.

Conclusion

Both these philosophers started as schoolteachers, but that is unsurprising for people who have made such a contribution to educational philosophy. What is more interesting is that each of them see teaching – including school teaching – and research as essentially educational activities. As I see it, Nel Noddings fell sideways into philosophy, having understood teaching to be a way of producing better people, and finding educational philosophy a way of clarifying the argument – the perhaps interminable argument – over what is meant by a 'better person'. Meanwhile, Morwenna Griffiths fell sideways into participatory action research, having found – in researching with schools – the limits of the naïve rationalism of much philosophy. Such research is far from the comfortable undertheorised work as described by some of its detractors, for whom 'participatory research is not interested in developing theory, the goal of science' (Frideres, in Frideres 1992, p. 8). The development of participatory, engaged research, from Dewey and from feminist activism, is, instead, a way of (philosophical) being in the world. From a more conservative perspective, Oakeshott has also attacked naïve rationalism, and has highlighted the need for conversations rather than just 'reasoning' (Oakeshott 1991). As Alexander says, '[p]eople are subjects, not objects; to understand them we must endeavor to meet them in dialogue; to receive their thoughts, feelings, and desires into ourselves' (Alexander 2015, p. 85). Researchers have to negotiate with the daily realities of life. These 'realities' include the structures of violence – and research itself can be a form of violence. Justice is Griffiths' underpinning value, and this is achieved in dialogue – the genuine open discussion of the early Socratic dialogues more than the somewhat virtuosic and more conclusive arguments of the later Socratic dialogues. The enemy of such philosophical research is performativity: researching for the sake of gaining external rewards. How similar is Nel Noddings' view of performativity, albeit described in quite a different way. A 'burning desire to find out' drives the research which is a way of clarifying how to produce better people and a better society – whether through schooling or otherwise. Her preference is for open questions and non-ideal theories, rather than closed questions or the closed answers of more ideal theories. Dialogue is once again central – talking *with*, not *at*, people, across boundaries, whether those boundaries are academic or based on social divisions. If as researchers we end up only concentrating on our own research or on our own virtuosity, we will get further away from the problem we started with. If, in contrast, we perform for the sake of tenure or other public markers, we will no longer be caring about finding out.

The moment Nel Noddings describes as so upsetting – hearing of another teacher refer to a pupil as a 'punk' – is a fine illustration of her recognition of the difference between real dialogue and merely talking at one another. If teachers were to refer to themselves *and* their pupils as 'punks', trying to create a new way of looking at the world – as Beer does with his 'punk sociology' (Beer 2014) – then this would not be so insulting and might, like the punk music of the 1970s, be a sincere form of rebellion. But positioning oneself – as researcher or as teacher – as rebellious is not enough. Being a rebel or being conservative, being an outsider or being an insider: these are not moral positions in themselves, not least because it will depend upon what is being rebelled against, or conserved, or the qualities of the organisation of which you are 'inside' or 'outside'.

In the following two chapters, the issues of integrity and sincerity are raised by the conversationalists in rather different ways, as are, in the latter chapter, the insider-outsider issues.

CHAPTER 3

Integrity and Sincerity

Introduction

In Chapter 1, I described how I became interested in sincerity as a research virtue. It was a way of working with research participants that would – it was hoped – encourage them to be truthful, through having a good reason to do this. Convincing research respondents to be sincere, it was necessary to convince them that I, too, was being sincere: that I was wanting to help the schools to improve, and so on. However, it would be misleading to suggest that all educational research could be of this form, or that all educational researchers could be expected to have motivations so directly congruent with the motivations of the research participants. In the following two conversations, researchers describe different approaches to some of those same issues of personal integrity and sincerity. Both focus particularly on problems with schooling such that a researcher may not be in a position to seek common cause with those in the school. The challenges of educational research are not straightforward, and researchers may have to make decisions over competing claims of different virtues or principles.

'Research integrity' has raised its profile in recent years, as a way of describing some of the broader issues of research ethics and its governance. This is helpful in considering research virtues. The UK's *Concordat to Support Research Integrity* 'seeks to provide a comprehensive national framework for good research conduct and its governance' (UUK 2012, p. 4). Ethical and legal research issues need to be well governed, and research and its governance should be 'underpinned by a culture of integrity' (UUK 2012, p. 4). Many elements are relevant to virtuous educational research, and many are also mentioned in the following conversations.

> The definition of research integrity used in this concordat draws on a number of existing definitions in a way that is applicable to all areas of research. The core elements are:
>
> - *Honesty* in all aspects of research ...
> - *Rigour*, in line with prevailing disciplinary norms and standards: in performing research and ... in drawing interpretations and conclusions from the research; and in communicating the results.
> - *Transparency and open communication* in declaring conflicts of interest; ... in making research findings widely available, which includes sharing negative results as appropriate; and in presenting the work to other researchers and to the general public.
> - *Care and respect* for all participants in and subjects of research ... Those engaged with research must also show care and respect for the stewardship of research and scholarship for future generations.
>
> These core elements of research integrity are the values through which trust and confidence in research stem, and from which the value and benefits of research flow. (UUK 2012, p. 11)

In order to promote such integrity, there should be 'ethical guidelines and codes of conduct' and 'guidance', as might be expected, but also 'learning, training and mentoring opportunities to support the development of researchers' (UUK 2012, p. 15).

The *Concordat* mentions many virtues (integrity, honesty, rigour, transparency, care, respect, and trust), and this whole book – and the following two conversations in particular – describe how several of them are lived in educational research.

Competing Moral Principles: A Conversation with Ron Best, University of Roehampton, England

JS: Would you like to introduce your own research, and how or why you came to be doing that?

RB: My first piece of empirical research in the 1970s was to do with pastoral care in education (Best et al. 1977). I had not long finished a part-time course in sociology of education which was strongly influenced by Marxism and associated critical perspectives, and I wanted to look at the ideological content of school assemblies, but one of the other guys that I ended up working with said 'I have a better idea – pastoral care in schools'. As soon as he said it, I thought, yes, that's a much better topic. It started me off on a field of enquiry that hasn't stopped since, in which caring is very important. Over the years I've looked at aspects of pastoral care (Bell and Best 1986, Best 2001, 2007a, 2008b, 2014b, Best et al. 1977, 1983, 1989, Maher and Best 1984), personal social and health education (Best et al. 1995, Lang et al. 1994), up to the most recent pieces of empirical research, one focussing on people of secondary school age, and the other one dealing with university students, where the topic was how teachers and their institutions perceive and respond to students who deliberately harm themselves (Best 2005b, 2005c, 2006, 2007b, 2009). Along the way, I was put in charge of an educational research centre and in that way I ended up researching things that I never would have wanted to do, or felt equipped to do, such as two evaluations – one of a project to develop school libraries (Best et al. 1988), and the other a project to introduce a more creative approach to mathematics teaching in schools. In later years, the pressures of the RAE (Research Assessment Exercise, the predecessor to the Research Excellence Framework, <http://www.ref.ac.uk>, the UK audit of research) meant you'd got to be doing some research and you've got to publish it, so I was always on the lookout for something. The deliberate self-harm research for example: I can remember becoming aware by chance that there was a problematic bit of children's experience and behaviour that clearly was the sort of thing pastoral care should be helping with, that I knew nothing at all about, and, I realised, nor did many other people. It hadn't been looked at from an educational perspective, so my reaction was 'here's something that I don't know about, not many other people do either, I might be able to get some money for it, and I'll be able to publish articles that could go in the RAE'. One's motives are not altruistic in this regard.

JS: But wanting to find out about an area that hasn't been explored isn't selfish, is it?

RB: No. Here was something that I could do, and meet the requirement of my job, but it was also worth doing.

JS: But you have stuck with pastoral care. Is it that it's such a deep and complex area, that you keep finding new things to mine within that area?

RB: PSHE (personal, social and health education) gave way to SMSC (spiritual, moral, social and cultural development, as in Best 2000b) in (UK) curriculum documents and it looked to me as though, of the four, the one that was the hardest to nail down was clearly the spiritual. That led to the idea of a conference on spirituality. 'Education, spirituality and the whole child' we called the first one, and that stayed as the name for the next nine because we did one every year for ten years (Best 1996, 2000a). That's where that came from, a kind of practical motivation. But underneath that, it feels to me that there is something personal that I am actually trying to work through there, which is why, even now in retirement, the research that I'm doing is to do with spirituality in the work of Friedrich Fröbel (1782–1852). There's no need for me to do this now, other than as an academic – my academic activity is such a large part of my self-concept that not doing some research would be a loss of a bit of my identity. Stenhouse (1975) says that whenever you do a piece of research, there are two research agendas: the agenda of the body that's funding your research, and your own. But when it comes to something like the spirituality, I have no funding at the moment, so I suppose I'm released now from anybody else's agenda.

JS: Is another possible agenda, the potential readership?

RB: One agenda for the researcher as a writer, in education research at any rate, is 'How can I write this in a way that practitioners in classrooms and schools and colleges can understand it and apply it in improving what they do in schools?' With the report on deliberate self-harm in adolescence, I wrote two versions. One was published in the *British Journal of Guidance and Counselling* (Best 2006), and counted for RAE purposes. And I did another version for *Pastoral Care in Education* (Best 2005b), which at that time included as many articles as it could get which were about professional issues of use to teachers in schools.

JS: You talked about deliberate self-harm by young people. It is such a sensitive topic, a difficult area for many people to talk about, but also sensitive as a researcher. How do you deal with all of the difficulties?

RB: It poses all sorts of challenges. A practical challenge is to get ethical approval. But knowing, from reading around the topic, that deliberate self-harm can be a reaction to feeling under pressure, the danger of putting a child or young person under pressure in a research interview has got to be a worry. In the work with children of secondary school age, I made no attempt to get to speak to children who were self-harming. My focus (Best 2005b, 2005c, 2006) was how teachers and others, counsellors and school nurses, perceived self-harm, how aware they were of it, how they responded to it when they came across it, what they did to help. In the university case study (Best 2007b, 2009), I did interview a few undergraduate students who responded to an invitation which was at the foot of an anonymous questionnaire, indicating they would be prepared to come and be interviewed. I was aware, not just in terms of research ethics, but in terms of what I knew from my own work as a volunteer counsellor – aware of the vulnerability of these people who were coming to see me. I took every precaution I could in the way I introduced the interview and the questions I asked and so on, to make it as unthreatening as I possibly could. With the work in the university, there was an additional challenge that the members of staff that I was interviewing were themselves more or less emotionally affected by the disclosures made to them by students or discoveries they made about students' behaviour. In the jargon of therapy, I had to 'hold' their emotions, or contain their emotions, within the interview situation in a way not dissimilar to the way in which a therapist has to hold or contain the emotions of the client, or the clinical supervisor has to hold and contain the emotions of the therapist whom they are supervising. I had moments where I was saying to interviewees – lecturers for instance – who were distressed by the experience they were recounting: 'I'm really sorry; I didn't mean to upset you', only to have them respond 'I'm glad: at last I've got someone to talk to about this'. One of the findings of that piece of research was that the bulk of people in pastoral roles in universities do not have at hand opportunities for the kind of clinical supervision that counsellors, psychiatric nurses, social workers and so on have to have as an obligation and as a right. So in the end I never felt that I was putting a burden on people. I went away comforted by the thought that I might actually be helping them. Now, there is a knock-on effect of that, which is what do I do with the load that they've 'dumped' on me? Researchers don't typically have an equivalent to the clinical supervisor. They might have an academic supervisor, a director of studies, but they don't have this kind of thing at their disposal.

JS: The semi-therapeutic value of an interview, I've heard over and over, and I think that is a hugely valuable thing in itself.

RB: Yes: I don't remember it coming up before these instances with self-harm.

JS: What's the other research project? You said there was a non-empirical one.

RB: Well, that's on spirituality in Fröbel. It's not empirical, it's theoretical, to some extent it's historical, to some extent it's philosophical. I find in what I have written about spirituality (Best

2005a, 2008a, 2011, 2014a) – I don't know whether 'introspec-
tive' is the right word, or 'phenomenological' – but in it are
experiences that I have had, and I ask myself 'What is that experience I'm having, what am I feeling, what is going on here:
how could it be described?' So my own experience of certain
events is quite heavily in there. But with regard to looking at
spirituality in Fröbel, partly because I was in Froebel College
in Roehampton (<http://www.roehampton.ac.uk/Colleges/
Froebel-College/>), and became somewhat smitten with Fröbel
as a charismatic person, I was surprised that the spiritual or
spirituality doesn't get mentioned much with regard to Fröbel.
Could Fröbel be spiritual without being a Christian? Could he
be spiritual without being religious? That's where the notion
came in. The practical research-type problems for me are: not
being an historian, not being first and foremost a philosopher,
and not being able to read or speak German. Having read *The
Education of Man* (Froebel 2009), having read several books
about Fröbel including von Marenholtz-Bülow's *Reminiscences
of Fröbel* (von Marenholtz-Bülow 2015), you occasionally get that
he was a devout Christian, but there's not much explicitly about
spirituality or the spirit in any of these things. Some concepts
are clearly more contested than others, and spirituality is one.
In my experience it becomes contested mostly because people
are making a presumption that it equates with religion.

JS: You talked about problems with the Fröbel research, and you
couched it as non-empirical research. I'm increasingly puzzled
by the division between empirical and non-empirical research,
because it's the same language issues, the same interpretive issues,
with Fröbel as it is with Aristotle, as it is with a seven year old in
a classroom who talks about being lonely.

RB: I think that's a really good point. I make the distinction because
I think it would be readily understood by people interested in
the RAE for instance. I suppose it's a bit of fall-out from those
who see all empirical research as quantitative. Maybe everything
is empirical in the sense of getting data from something in the

world; even a philosopher is going to be making interpretations based on his or her experience of the world.

JS: I'm interested in that virtue vocabulary list. Some of the things we've talked about already, but are any other words relevant?

RB: One I would pick out would be authenticity, honesty, sincerity, and its opposite, deceit. People in the collaborative action research tradition often take the high moral ground because it's egalitarian, there's the notion of a critical friend, there's taking your interpretations back to the person who gave them to you so that they always have ownership of what they said, and so on. I think that that's linked to a presumption that people are basically honest, and well-meaning, and well intentioned, and you treat them with respect. But there's an inference some people draw from that, that if you're not doing your research that way, you are reducing other people to mere objects of study, and their institutions as quarries for your data. That you're going to be honest, sincere and authentic with the people you're researching, or you're some kind of intellectual predator. But that is naïve. I was influenced by a book by Douglas called *Investigative Social Research* (Douglas 1976), in which he argues that the social researcher, at least for certain sorts of topic, needs to be like an investigative journalist or a private detective. A good mental set is of distrust of this person and what they tell you, what they give you as an account of their behaviour. Douglas says that what people may be giving you may be an alibi, not the truth. That pessimistic view of humankind was there in the early research. It's become much less so as I've got older, or done more, but at that time one was always engaged in an act of deceit, in the sense that the researcher deceives the interviewee by presenting themselves as 'a person you can trust, I am objective, impartial', whereas the researcher is actually viewing you as somebody who's probably lying and protecting yourself. So there is a kind of deceit built into that. Can the pursuit of truth ever justify reducing other people to mere objects, and using them for your purposes, and deceiving them, if not by telling them lies, at least by not telling them the whole truth? Showing that things may not be as they seem, and that people may not always be motivated entirely by a commitment to the welfare of the pupil, is a good thing to do. You couldn't do that if you didn't start out with a suspicion that not everything is good in the world and not everybody is telling you the truth all the time. So it has some strengths, but it feels uncomfortable beside the feeling that one ought to be sincere, honest, open and so on.

JS: I can see that you're uncovering professionals' self-deception. I don't see how it required deception on your behalf.

RB: Well it's not being transparent.

JS: I understand that, but there is a sincerity in trying to find out the reality of assemblies or pastoral care or counselling. There's a difference between that and being deceptive in what you're doing

RB: Yes, I think that's probably true. Like all moral dilemmas I suspect we're talking about clashes between competing moral principles: the search for truth being a good thing, comes into conflict with other principles – confidentiality, or other commitments you might make to people about what they tell you.

JS: There's not an easy way through that. What qualities are there, especially when you talked about newer researchers and supporting them, that you think 'Actually this is the one that really is important'.

RB: For me, it's about persons. If you don't have some sense of care for persons when you're researching them, you're likely to do them damage with your research. So being caring, having the capacity for empathy. I guess judgement and critical thinking have got to come high on the list for the reasons I've already given – that wherever you've got some tension between competing moral imperatives, such as treat people with respect but get at the truth, then you have to engage in critical thinking and make informed judgements about what's possible. You have to be able to engage in moral reasoning, critical thinking. No code of ethics, or research ethics, can get you off the hook of having to make a judgement at the end. Critical thinking ought to involve a scepticism which means you don't just take things at face value. However, I would rather plump for hope and trust these days. I have realised that, except when I consciously set out to adopt this sceptical, pessimistic view of the people I was researching, most often I'm impressed if not bowled over by the goodness of the people, particularly in the case of looking at self-harm. It's ennobling. It's a privilege to have access to seeing that, and a good slap on the wrist for the much more sceptical, pessimistic, suspicious person that I probably was when I started researching.

JS: Some of Marxist theorising where everything is done for the sake of capitalism, or the Foucauldian 'You may think you're being kind, but actually this is a power game that you're playing', I think both of those work against that positive approach. Thank you so much.

RB: Well, I've enjoyed it.

Thinking Myself Into the World: A Conversation with Helen Lees, Newman University, Birmingham, England

JS: Do you want to start by saying a little about your research and how or why you came to be doing it?

HL: I ended up being a researcher it seems quite by chance, but looking back, I had no choice, it was just *the* thing that was right for me. I had no idea – and we're talking 2003 – I had no idea that there was such a thing as research. It shocks me, because that's not that long ago. I didn't really understand anything about research when I was an undergraduate, I was too busy being a journalist. I didn't do a particularly academic or scholarly undergraduate degree. But then left university with a desire to never stop reading, never stop learning. I was just thinking myself into the world. I was pursuing that line in poorly paid jobs, and then I thought, well, I'm too poor: I'll be a teacher. I went back to the school where I'd been a secondary school student. I couldn't make sense of what this school had done to me, and I realised then, that the school that I'd been to as a student, eleven to eighteen, had formed me, had attempted to mould me in a way that was totally contrary to what I believed to be the truth. That was the driving force of those ten years of thinking: I was trying to undo the work of the school. At the same time, I picked up A. S. Neill's *Summerhill* (Neill 1985), and I thought 'this is the blueprint for how a school should be'. This makes sense, this allows freedom of the self, this is what I should have experienced. And that same week I was in a university library, and I saw these little thin books in an A4 folder, and I said 'What are they?' I picked one out and it happened to be a copy of *Educational Review* and on the back cover, the contents list had Clive Harber's *Schooling as Violence* (Harber 2002). I read that phrase 'schooling as violence' and I said 'That's it: that's what it is'. I then read the article, which was the first research I'd ever read in my life, and I thought 'That's amazing, that people can write like this – I had no idea this genre existed – I want to do that'. I came to understand that in order to do that kind of thing, you needed to get a PhD, so I thought, get a PhD to get the skillset to do that kind of work.

JS: It's unusual for people to be attracted to research via the genre of academic articles.

HL: The irony is, I haven't really written that many academic articles yet: I've still got this ambition to fulfil because I've focused more on books to start with (Lees 2012, 2014, Lees and Noddings 2016, Trotman et al. 2016). An article has the kind of impact, the singular idea, that affects me more often than books.

JS: You are a journal editor (*Other Education: The Journal of Educational Alternatives*, <http://www.othereducation.org>), and have edited books. That's an odd career, to be stimulated by an article, to do a doctorate so that you can be doing that, to be writing books, but editing journals more than writing journal articles.

HL: It's just that the writing of the journal articles is a craft, and I haven't
        got to the point just yet where I know that craft. Being an editor is
        like being a teacher of others, and the best way to learn something
        is to teach it.

JS: What do you mean when you use the word 'research', other than
        a genre of academic peer review journal article?

HL: My vision of research is work that offers new conceptual path-
        ways that lead to a better world. Even though it's heavily philo-
        sophical, it does for me involve an empirical element, it does
        involve talking to people: I think that's really important. I'm a
        philosopher of education who, to do philosophy, wants to talk
        to people, to find things out. Participants in research are phi-
        losophers in their own right. I trust that their voice has mean-
        ing. My research is mine, it's not theirs, but by involving them in
        my research, I'm offering them a platform for their voice to be a
        part of the presentation, and I don't interfere with their voice.
        The things that they say matter in the academy. So I would call
        myself in that sense a translator, or an emissary. I'm like a post
        person carrying things from one place, the non-academic world,
        carrying those letters, those messages, parcels, whatever it is that
        I get given, into academia, so that then they can have impact on
        academic terms.

JS: So tell us about some of the research you've done. I know you've
        done work on both silence and non-school-based education. The
        people whom you've been talking with, in both of those projects,
        are mostly adults.

HL: Yes, I've not yet talked to children. I think adults have a responsi-
        bility to know, so that's where I focus my attention. I'm interested
        in adult conversations so that we can lead a world in a way which
        allows children to flourish and have voice.

JS: So it's the adults' responsibilities, more than their voices? It's
        not that adults have voices and children have only half-made or
        imperfect voices.

HL: That's a good way to put it. Although I've never articulated this
        before, what I'm probably doing is trying to achieve a world where

adults can shut up, and then children will have the space to speak and we will have the space to listen. It would be a lot more authentic. If we could be silent, if we could be quiet, we would notice children more, we would hear them better, and we would see much better how beautiful they are, and how much they have to teach us.

JS: A history educator, John Fines, writes that 'I have in the course of my teaching career learned many hard things but the hardest of all has been to shut up' as '[t]he instinct to lecture children is profound and we have to chain it, and to learn to listen' (Fines, in Fines and Nichol 1997, p. 231). There is an irony, of course, in voicing people as part of a campaign to get people to shut up. Is that the power of silence? Is that about the power relation?

HL: Yes. The power relation is the end goal. In silence there's an equality and a democratic naturalness of self, with self and with other. It's not about people shutting up in an oppressive or coercive sense, it's about them volunteering to cease to use voice for ego purposes, and to choose to Be, with a capital B, with others. If we had more of that in education, it would enhance education.

JS: The main research and personal challenges, you've talked about some of those already. But in the research you have done, what would you say that the main research challenges are?

HL: I've pitched it ahead of its time, so the challenge is to make it conceptually familiar. The research is challenging because it affects people's mentality, and they have to suffer their own dissonance when that occurs. So I suffer on account of not being instantly popular, or instantly recognisably understandable. But it's a price I'm willing to pay.

JS: I often start one of my presentations by saying I hope to be disagreeable, because frankly if you all agree with me already, there's not much point me being here. A lot of journals are conservative in the sense they want agreeable items, they want things that agree with what's already been said, even in that one journal, and that just say it a bit newer.

HL: Don't you think that's a problem with education as it's currently
        configured?

JS: Yes. It's a problem with education when it's pre-determined. So
        'intended learning outcomes' in higher education are great in
        terms of equity and people knowing what the curriculum might
        be, and why they might be doing it, but are appalling if they set
        the limits to what is learned. A doctoral student who withdrew
        said she was 'torn between conformity and originality' (Graham-
        Matheson 2012).

HL: I had the same situation when I did my doctorate, but I was so
        determined to get to the place of power where I had the skill set
        to write like that article of Clive Harber, I was prepared to listen,
        and bend myself to this moulding force, to get through and be
        rubber-stamped with the PhD award. Playing the power game in
        research is bending like a reed in the wind. There are a few char-
        latans, people who call themselves original. I would say that if
        they have the privilege and the power to do research, they have a
        responsibility to ensure that they are genuinely doing new original
        work of great importance, not that they are tweaking the envelope.
        But if I'm going to say that it's possible that some researchers are
        charlatans, I think that is something that we are all in danger of,
        and to give credit to those charlatans. Most of them know: it's
        just that they have a comfortable job that's hard to give up. They
        probably suffer on account of the lack of veracity of the vocation
        that they find themselves in. It has to be a vocation of some depth,
        and charlatans in research probably know that they're not really
        doing what they could do.

JS: So it's the issue for research, as with adulthood: it's responsibility.
        It's that you have a responsibility to do something with the power
        that you have.

HL: Yes. It is an important responsibility, one that makes the researcher
        suffer. I think huge responsibility is a load of suffering that you
        bear, because it matters.

JS: Like parenthood?

HL: Yes – or leadership.

JS: And the fourth group of questions is about the personal challenges of research. You describe the suffering of the charlatans, where they realise they're successful but unfulfilled or unhappy.

HL: I have some compassion for them, because that could be me. I'm lucky: I feel like I'm leading an existence as a researcher that is worth doing, without changing my pathway. That's why I can't leave academia: I feel like I have to be here, even if I don't want to be. It's what I've been called to do.

JS: The word 'calling' connects to vocation that you mentioned.

HL: For me it's a calculation. From whenever I can remember, I was calculating 'how can I have most impact?' Quite early on – say about aged eighteen – I thought maybe books – anything that's published that's read. If the research work, through a book or presentation or journal article, allows someone to suffer less such that they say 'thank you', then you've done some work.

JS: Research or learning is a human and inter-human activity. William Hanks says 'learning is a way of being in the social world, not a way of coming to know about it' (Hanks, in Lave and Wenger 1991, p. 24), which is a nice idea. It is a way of being.

HL: Yes, it's not instrumental. Going back to your thing about responsibility, I think there's a real pleasure involved in research. There's such a drive, a pleasure drive I'd call it, in knowing more things, and becoming an expert in a particular area. That's so pleasurable, and to be able to converse then with other experts in the area, and have meaningful conversations. It's a privilege and a pleasure, and that comes back to the responsibility. If you're given those kinds of highs, you've got to give back

JS: I've got a list of character strengths or virtues and their absences, opposites and their exaggeration. We've talked about quite a few of these already. Are there any others that you would think are particularly relevant to research?

HL: Bravery.

JS: Courage goes with the responsibility and the hurt: you do it, even if it's painful.

HL: But I've also just talked about the pleasure of the job, so I would say there's less pain than pleasure.

JS: Why did bravery strike you then?

HL: Because being a woman in academia, doing the kind of 'other', in inverted commas, research that I do, takes guts.

JS: What do you mean by 'other'? You mean because it's not mainstream or conventional?

HL: Yes. And surviving takes guts.

JS: Any other strengths there that you haven't already talked about?

HL: Self-regulation is a hugely important thing in research. There is so much solitude and so much freedom, and nobody really knows what you are doing, unless you're in an interview like this, so to get the work done, needs a huge amount of self-regulation. I'm in this game, or battle – I think both words apply for me – to win. So it's about trying my best to do that. I think other people should be braver. There is so much conservatism.

JS: What does lack of courage do to people?

HL: It makes for boring conversations. If I'm talking about other people being braver, I'm talking about the bravery involved in thinking differently and taking risks, and translating that into the world through publications. That makes them vulnerable because they could be attacked on account of their difference, rather than being safe. I think that people should be risk-takers. You have to look back and be able to say 'At least I did it according to what I thought'. I don't think you will ever be a failure if you have done it on your own terms. And so all educational researchers have a responsibility to not fail.

JS: I think that's a wonderful place to stop this conversation Helen. Thank you so much.

Conclusion

Many academics will be familiar with teaching students that the 'critique' needed for research and the 'critical theory' of Adorno, Benjamin or Habermas, are not the same as being 'critical' in the ordinary language sense of fault-finding. However, what Ron Best describes, alongside the necessity of critique, is a set of qualities – scepticism, a detective-like suspicion, and perhaps even mistrust – that could be interpreted by research participants as negative in the 'ordinary' sense. What is more, there is a risk that the researcher will also lose out, and find it harder to exhibit hope and trust. Virtues are not neat and tidy. Even if they were, re-casting any one approach to research – such as collaborative or participatory action research – as the most virtuous approach, or one virtue – such as sincerity – as having priority over others, is unlikely to be accepted beyond a relatively narrow group of researchers. A number of legitimate agendas may be recognised by researchers, including those set by employers or research auditors, without necessarily making the research less virtuous. And a number of competing moral principles are always present. Ron Best suggests – in the light of a long research career characterised both by continuing interests and by changing practices – that critical thinking, when combined with care and empathy, can help guide a researcher through these competing principles. He hopes that this will recognise and exhibit hope and trust. But that will require a lot of support for researchers, notably in the form of the kind of supervision typically offered to counsellors, therapists and social workers.

Meanwhile, Helen Lees was stimulated into research through trying to understand school. In this way, and in describing herself as a philosopher who needs to talk with people, she has a similar position to that of Nel Noddings. Research is just 'right for me', and more of a way of life than a separate activity – having been 'thinking myself into the world' in the build-up to becoming a professional academic researcher. As with Ron Best, school research may be approached with a considerable degree of suspicion. Indeed, her self-recognition as a researcher started from reading Harber's account of schooling as violence (Harber 2002). Harber himself describes his position on schooling as unusual, saying (in a book following the earlier article) that 'rarely is the role of the school itself seen as problematic in any systematic way' (Harber 2004, p. 2). To the extent that violence is the dominant characteristic of schooling, any researcher positioned as working with the school might be regarded as complicit in the violence, and so the kind of sincerity achieved through establishing a 'common cause' with those in school may prove impossible. Wanting to make a better world is not the same as promoting schooling, and adults in schools may be 'voiced' as part of a longer-term attempt to help them be more silent. Although 'risky' research may involve suffering, on balance there is more pleasure through completing worthwhile work and having a positive impact on the world. This is compared to parenthood and leadership: challenging but worthwhile work.

Both conversationalists talk of the specific genres of research writing, and the various readerships for any such writing – academic peer reviewers and auditors, professional educators, or others. In different ways they both describe well some of the challenges of a research career, and researchers' need for support. They see themselves in some ways as 'outsiders' in schools, although Ron Best describes moving closer to being an insider over the years. In Chapter 1, I described myself as being more of an insider. In the next chapter, therefore, there are two conversations that illustrate even more explicitly the challenge of both insider and outsider positions.

CHAPTER 4

Inside Out: Orthodoxy and its Alternatives in Educational Research

Introduction

This third set of conversations, completing Part II of the book, explores what has been referred to as the 'insider/outsider' problem in humanities research. Insiders may have special knowledge and access and understanding, yet their position may bring with it bias and a failure to achieve critical distance. Outsiders may have independence and critical distance, yet their position may bring with it an inability to understand. Researchers have written widely on these issues (McCutcheon 1999 on religion, McDonald 1989 and Crossley et al. 2016 on education), on how outsiders can become temporary insiders through setting aside their assumptions (as in phenomenological epoché) in order to understand 'as an insider', and on how insiders can avoid some of the potential biases (through the use of external reference points). Being 'orthodox' in the ordinary sense implies being something of an insider, holding 'currently accepted opinions' (OED 2005). In Peterson's list of virtues, it is contrasted with a 'love of learning' (Peterson, in Csikszentmihalyi and Csikszentmihalyi 2006, p. 39). This is interesting, but a little odd: must the orthodox be rejected by all learners?

Complementing the insider-outsider metaphor, there might be a heavy-light metaphor. Research is a serious business: it can weigh heavy on researchers. Academic roles typically have a high social status, and successful researchers may be expected to be powerful figures exhibiting gravitas, 'the gravitas of dignified thinkers' (Pirrie 2015, p. 535). To the extent that this is true, it carries with it the dangers of power and of weight. Power can tempt people to believe they are inevitably right (and others are inevitably wrong); weight can make it harder to travel, to cross boundaries. An alternative approach to research is therefore to exhibit lightness, lightness of touch, lightness of being. Researchers can untie themselves, they can float across boundaries and be travellers: 'troubadour' intellectuals (Serres 1997).

This chapter presents two conversations which explore the virtues, and the challenges, of insider and outsider, of orthodox and light, approaches to research. Notwithstanding the different approaches taken, these conversations are presented as complementary, and not – or not primarily – as contrasting. We should remember that being an 'insider' somewhere means, of necessity, being an 'outsider' somewhere else. At different times in our lives, we have different positions, and the positions we have – as researchers, professionals, or in the rest of life – can always surprise us. Sometimes there is a greater 'shock' in the critical position of an insider than there is in a more predictable critical position of an outsider. Sometimes we find ourselves unexpectedly 'included' in a group – and we may object to inclusion as vigorously as we object to exclusion.

Am I Just Hiding Behind a Tradition?: A Conversation with Mario D'Souza, University of Toronto, Canada

MDS: My primary area of interest in research is the philosophy of education. I did a doctorate on Jacques Maritain's philosophy of education, but I have become more interested in questions of the intersection between philosophy of education and religious education, and wider questions of the role of philosophy of education, and indeed the roles of philosophy and of education, in the context of religious and cultural diversity today. I see myself in a sort of transcendental Thomist stand (like Lonergan 1974), and a personalist school of philosophy of education. I would see my interest within the context of religious and cultural diversity and plurality (D'Souza 2000).

JS: You are interested in what might broadly be called philosophical research, but not as it were for the sake of philosophy as a disembodied practice apart from life, but as a practice related to life, as you say, of religious and cultural diversity, the way in which people live amongst and with different ways of life.

MDS: I think you are absolutely right. I'm not interested in philosophy per se, but a philosophy of education as an applied discipline – the principle of philosophy applied to education and to other areas as well – to extricate a broader understanding of what the meaning of life is today, and how people frame and conceive the meaning of life.

JS: Some might see applied philosophy of education meaning seeing how different philosophies were worked out in practices, and doing what might be called empirical research on that. I don't see you as going down that line.

MDS: No, I don't have an empirical mindset, I'm not good with statistics and numbers and graphs and percentages of changes, etc., so I've not gone down that route. Because I don't have those skills, I don't have an interest in it. My approach over the years has been to use a philosopher of education as a foundation. I see the advantages of that foundation, but also maybe some of the weaknesses, and then try and relate that. So for years I used Jacques Maritain (1962, 1971) as a foundation for my theories, but not exclusively, and then over the last six or seven years I've encountered Bernard Lonergan (1974) and then the German philosopher Josef Pieper (1966). I say to my doctoral students that it can be beneficial to begin one's academic and scholarly career by basing your thoughts on a philosopher – Aristotle or whoever. I think it gives people a good anchor. It's certainly given me a good anchor. So whether or not I'm making any individual contribution, my contribution is really to read my interests of today through the lenses of specific philosophers of education. I am carrying on a conversation, saying 'This is what these philosophers are saying', and 'Is what they are saying of use or some relevance to contemporary society?', and 'Can contemporary society be read through the lenses of these philosophers?' It's not just my experience, or my opinion, it is more a Catholic approach to philosophical work in philosophy of education and Catholic education. These are what the documents of the church might say, these are what the church's teachings are on education or the implications of its teachings on culture and ecclesiology. The documents are written progressively, they keep coming out with the documents, so the response is not simply a response to a document written forty years ago, but to further documents that have been written over the years, and continue to be written. It's an ongoing conversation with documents that are alive and dynamic, as is the thought of philosophers and the position of the church.

JS: Do you see yourself as an interpreter of the documents and of Maritain and Lonergan (as in D'Souza 2014)? You've said you are continuing a conversation, but what are you actually doing with them? Are you witnesses for them, or are you doing some hermeneutics?

MDS: Yes, I think there is a hermeneutical process going on. One never comes to anything without one's own stance, or one's own position, or one's own interpretation. So interpretation goes on, in an intentional manner, but you're reading the context, or the document, or a book, or a conversation, through your own stance. The important thing in that is to make sure that your own stance is not becoming a bias, and that it's not becoming an oppressive form of subjectivity. You certainly bring your subjectivity to it, but it should be a critical, dynamic, form of subjectivity. You're aware of your own limitations and biases in interpreting the situation, but you're also being fair to what's being read or what's being conversed with. My reading both of Maritain and Lonergan have taught me this, that you bring your own subjectivity to the conversation or to the text, but while you're doing that, you're keeping an eye not only on the text, but on yourself as you're doing the interpretation.

JS: A lot of today's writers are more as you say oppressive – pressing their own position more strongly.

MDS: Yes, I find it difficult today with many writers using this approach.
       This is what has inspired me to write my forthcoming book
       (D'Souza 2016). It's all very well for you to say what you think
       Catholic education is about, and how one should go about it.
       But the important thing is to know first of all what is the church
       teaching about Catholic education, what are its documents saying,
       and what are its philosophical presuppositions – and how, in my
       case, one may use Maritain and Lonergan to be in conversation
       with these philosophical approaches. Too much has been going
       on in Catholic education not necessarily to shun Rome, but to say
       'Well, yes, but you know we are in Canada or we are in the UK
       and our matters are so particular, and so concrete to this situation
       that they have very little to say to us'. I'm not interested in that
       kind of conversation, because I think that becomes solipsistic and
       egocentric.

JS: Is this the main research challenge for you?

MDS: Yes, I think it's both a challenge and a frustration, at least in the
       Canadian context. In my field of Catholic education people are
       very blinkered. I think religious education is a subset of philoso-
       phy of education, and it cannot come to define or describe or
       delineate the whole field of Catholic education. So the challenge
       I have is that I take the sort of philosophical, anthropological,
       theological approach to Catholic education, and I don't find
       many voices, at least in the Catholic tradition. There are a few
       in England – Terence McLaughlin (McLaughlin 2003) was a
       Catholic and he was very philosophical. Catholic philosophy
       of education has a say about the overall nature and purpose of
       the school and the curriculum, and religious education is one
       very important subject certainly of the curriculum, but just one
       subject.

JS: Many of the church documents – as I read them – are not nar-
       rowly school-based, but are about upbringing and coming to live
       a good life.

MDS: That's right. My frustration is precisely that Catholic educators
       are speaking in the name of the church, while the church doesn't

narrow education. They seem to be able to talk only about religious education and then they say very little about the other intellectual and learning dimensions of education in the school or university. That's what I've found to be wanting. The principal challenge I find – and I hope this doesn't sound too haughty and too self-satisfied – is that I find a decidedly anti-intellectual approach by practitioners. Practitioners constantly speak about 'the real world', as if the real world of the school is a series of concrete daily surprises, whereby the intentionality and the planning of the educator and the teacher has no say. I realise that there are daily challenges at a school that a teacher might face, that a school might face, or Catholic schools would face in York that are not necessarily the same in Toronto or Bombay. I recognise all that, but that if education is an intentional activity, is a planned activity, you know what you plan to do, you know why you are doing it, and you know who is involved with the process – the teacher and the student – then it's not a series of surprises in the sense of not knowing what's happening. (It *is* a series of surprises in the sense of the student's responses to what the student is learning.) So the approach by practitioners and a lot of people in the field of Catholic education, especially Catholic school education, is decidedly anti-intellectual.

JS: When you say there is an anti-intellectual approach of many in Catholic education, some might think that that would be because it veers into faith-based, or spiritual and less worldly, senses, whereas actually what you are saying is the anti-intellectualism is a retreat into the concrete and the immediate, not into the spiritual and other-worldly.

MDS: That's right.

JS: We are getting on to the personal challenges you've faced in this research.

MDS: I wonder from time to time whether what I saw as a strength, earlier in our conversation – that I base my research and thought on a couple of philosophers as my anchor – I wonder sometimes whether I should be saying something that is so thoroughly unique, and should be so thoroughly my own, that I am not beholden to the thought of Maritain, or Lonergan, or the church documents, or Joseph Pieper, or whoever. While I used to worry about that when I was younger, and from time to time I think about it, I don't know how I would go about it and what would this unique contribution be. I frame Catholic education from this kind of philosophical, anthropological, epistemological cognitional approach of the education of the whole person. Should I be making some sort of unique contribution which is not linked to Lonergan or Maritain or the documents or whatever? I don't know how I would go about it, and it would require a fundamental change of paradigm. To put it crudely, the only way I could see that paradigm changing is if I changed – if I were no longer Roman Catholic, or possibly no longer a Christian. If I converted to another faith tradition outside the Christian tradition, my world view would necessarily change, and as a result of that world view changing, so would an approach to education. But even that I am not sure about because my approach is more philosophical, and the thing that I am arguing in my current book is that the contribution of the Catholic approach to education is precisely because it is philosophical, and that it is universal.

JS: And you wouldn't be unique in being a non-Christian or a non-Catholic, anyway, so you wouldn't be leaping into unicity by leaving the church.

MDS: I've never thought about that. But you're quite right that even if I were to change to a faith tradition that were not Christian, that would hardly be unique, and I'd hardly be alone. It would require me to think of a new faith tradition of such staggering difference that I could then make my contribution. So, while I think about these things with you, I have to say that at the stage of life that I am at, I am happy and content with the approach I take in my research. I may be preaching to a choir that has long gone home, but at this stage in my life, I'm not sure how I would approach the philosophical questions of education, other than the way I do.

JS: Could you say what you're doing is exhibiting humility? You are
          not someone to blow your own trumpet. When I've seen you give
          talks, and write, the shock of what you say is all the more power-
          ful because you are not trying to press it as shocking. You are not
          trying to press it as your original idea: you are saying this is simply
          building on traditions that are well established. And yet what you
          say has huge significance for everything that happens in schools
          – not just Catholic schools, but schools in general. The sense of
          intentionality, the sense of purpose, the sense of the meaning of
          life, is all there, and is distinctive.

MDS: When I speak I come across in some sense as self-confident. I'm
          just saying what the tradition is saying: I make no excuses for it and
          say 'This is what it's saying and I'm not making this up, and now
          you need to respond to what's being said by the tradition'. That
          gives me confidence, but I wonder sometimes, am I just hiding
          behind a tradition? But then again I am not: I believe in it, and
          I hold to it, I agree with it, with its philosophical position and its
          intellectual progression.

JS: You are saying what you think – you just think that this is a con-
          tinuing conversation from other people. Are there any of these
          virtue and vice words that strike you as something of interest for
          you?

MDS: I certainly have a love of learning, and I suppose critical thinking.

JS: Peterson, who did most of the words on the virtues list, has the
          opposite of 'love of learning' being 'orthodoxy'. I find that an odd
          contrast, and particularly for you as you've talked about being
          orthodox in the sense of working within and believing within
          and practicing within a particular tradition.

MDS: Well, precisely. I find that to be somewhat disturbing.

A Bit of a Nomad: A Conversation with Anne Pirrie, University of the West of Scotland, Ayr, Scotland

JS: Could you tell me a little about your own research, and how or why you came to be doing it? I am interested in research in its broadest sense.

AP: I have diversified in recent years. Often there's a latency period when you're doing funded or time-bounded research that has a 'deliverable'. The intellectual work carries on well beyond that. I came to be doing research through a series of contingent events. I slid into it. I started off editing research reports in an independent research outfit after I'd quit my school teaching job and gone to Italy. I'd done a bit of translating there, and I had done a lot of editing of English as a second language, so that got me into the role of editing research reports, and then I gradually became involved as a researcher. You are drawn into discussing 'What do you mean by this?', 'What happened here?', and 'Why did you do it that way?'. Basically being curious and willing to get involved. To go further back, I think the fact that I studied foreign languages influenced the way I am as a person, and a scholar. It's made me more adventurous. I don't expect to have complete mastery of an area, but I go in and make the best I can with my resources. I dwell in my incapacity, in a sense, and that doesn't scare me because that's what it is like to speak another language.

JS: It means you are, as it were, a foreigner as a researcher, you are an outsider?

AP: Yes, and you depend on being in relation in a very fundamental way. When you run out of words you wait for your interlocutor to give you them – you wait for them to come, or they don't come and that doesn't matter. The story goes way back to when I was about fifteen, when I was developing a facility for and a love of speaking other languages. That's the beginning of my research career.

JS: Do you think every discipline will have its route to research?
         Do you think engineers think, 'Well, I've spent my life trying to
         construct things, and so I was constructing an argument'?

AP: Yes, absolutely.

JS: It is an interesting picture of research as like entering a foreign
         country.

AP: The willingness just to venture out and see what happens.

JS: Does that affect the empirical research differently to how it affects
         the other research that you do?

AP: I think it affects both. The other research I do, I describe to people
         as 'Working alone with dead people, in the pages of a book'. I've
         always been attracted by boundaries and I think that dates right
         back to when I was doing my PhD. I see myself as a bit of a nomad.
         This engenders enormous insecurity that is sometimes quite disa-
         bling, because I think 'Where is my disciplinary home?' Perhaps
         I don't have it and I'm experiencing a horrible form of second
         language loss, and quite soon I will be begin to babble and I'll be
         finished – because I don't have a secure disciplinary base.

JS: And a discipline is also a community, and so it's also about not
         having a community to which you either identify, or feel you
         belong, is it?

AP: Yes. I remember when I was an undergraduate in the German
         department where I studied, and a big name came from America.
         Somebody asked a question. The response from the speaker was
         'You are not a Germanist'. It was a blank refusal to respond to a
         question that was not asked by a Germanist. I remember thinking
         'Well, I don't think I'm a Germanist either, in that case'.

JS: So you describe yourself as a nomad, and of course nomads can
         only exist when the field is left for them to move. Actual nomad
         communities tend to be destroyed by farmers, whom you might
         describe as disciplinarians, people who build fences. Is your fear
         the fear of farmers, as it were?

AP: When I think about how it is that I work, often I feel that there
         are things that just jump out at me that I have to pick up, like
         somebody might pick up a shiny stone on a beach. So it's a kind of

collecting of things and carrying on with them, and then bringing them into relation to other things. There's something that starts telling itself, and I simply have to follow it.

JS: It's an unusual combination, to have a mode of work that's in some ways like a contract researcher or an editor or a translator, and in other ways like an ongoing intellectual project.

AP: As I move further on in my career, I see that there's this incredible intertwining of strands of enquiry that look quite different, and the same themes come through again. I am still thinking about some of the things that I have been thinking about for years – they never go away. There is a paper that I wrote, called *Tripping, Slipping and Losing the Way* (Pirrie and Macleod 2010). It was about a particular research project after the research project had finished. I had to write about it. Something must have triggered this – it was a process of coming to terms with things that had happened in the course of the project, things that hadn't gone to plan, and documenting with hindsight the realisation that things not going to plan was actually one of the most important findings from the research. It was an enormous catharsis when collectively we realised that. Talking about that illustrates three things. It illustrates that I problematise – to use a horrible word – that mode of enquiry which is serendipitous, risky, uncertain, and evolves over time, and often extends way after the life of a particular project. Secondly, the way of writing, which is simply to start, and then the writing has its own life. Often my task is just to attend to what it's saying, as if I hadn't written it. The third point, is that it illustrates my eclecticism, my magpie-like tendencies. It's just hitting upon something that helps me see something in a particular way. It's this unpredictable coming together of a particular set of circumstances.

JS: Is there a specific sense in which the writing, as it were, brings out the things that have been troubling either you or a situation?

AP: Yes: it's troubling that troubling, I suppose: that is what the writing's about. I was involved in a literature review for the government, looking at the relation between engaging in some form of sport and attainment and achievement. They didn't like what I had said, that there was no causal relation. I think I put in the phrase 'running around and pinking up is a valuable experience for young children in itself, and it doesn't have to be justified by any putative impact on their attainment scores'. The review was not published by the government. Then I wrote an article called *Spoilsport* (Pirrie 2003), in which I discussed what had occurred, what I'd researched, and my engagement with the Government. I wouldn't want to imply that I cynically produce the deliverables, and then confess in another track. You just get quite close to a line when you are producing a report for a funder.

JS: Two of the examples you have given (Pirrie and Macleod 2010, Pirrie 2003) are 'after' writings. You've said that you will do something, and then the really interesting thing is what you write afterwards. Is that both a problem with the contracts, because they don't allow you to do that, and a particular characteristic of your approach to research, that you will always let that second paper, that second thought, come through?

AP: I do think things take time. There is a settling of contents that has to occur: you need time to think about them, with hindsight. It's not that you don't think when you're doing it, but there's another form of reflection that happens later, or subsequent things you become involved with trigger. I've done a lot of work on inclusion, and that has gone on and on, because I had a lot of unfinished business – other things that I encountered made me think about things again. The thinking never stops.

JS: Do you recognise that some people don't think in that way, so it's a personal thing for you, that you're an inveterate traveller?

AP: Yes. And I think I think I'm quite good at seeing connections between things. I wrote a paper about ethics (Pirrie et al. 2012), and I remember having a discussion with a colleague who was bragging about a publication. I was curious and I read it, and I was horrified. I wrote to him and I said 'I've just read this paper and it is the most unethical piece of research that I have ever seen reported, and rather than boast about it I think you really ought to bury it'. And his response was 'Well, it got ethical approval'. And, and I just thought 'I don't know how to go on with you, something happened that you couldn't have predicted when you went into this, and you just didn't respond, you didn't think'. It's the failure to think that led to this shocking de facto endorsement of a practice over which this person had no control, but endorsing something that I thought was unethical – legitimating it. But the idea that you get ethical approval and then that's it, you've 'done' the ethics. I have examples of interactions with students where the research they do is narrowly circumscribed: there's this fear that it would be too difficult to get ethical approval for talking to children – which is barely comprehensible, considering that this is part of their day-to-day interactions in the schools in which they're practising. Anyway, they fill out this long ethics form. I remember a colleague who said 'Yes, the students are getting a bit stressed out by the ethics form'. And I said 'Do you not think that is a bit of an ethical issue?' She didn't know what I was talking about. Her attempts to get them through this process was to adopt a mechanistic approach, to give the students text with which they might populate particular cells – to take the thinking out of it. So they have a lot of stress, and no thinking – and a greatly impoverished understanding of ethics.

JS: I have two worries. The first is that research ethics has become procedural. But the second is that that's then what people think ethics really *is*. Virtues are more personal, although one of my fears is that there will in the future be a *virtues* form that will stress students out. Talking of such a form, I have given you a list of character strengths or virtues and their opposites or their absences. You talked about kindness, about isolation, about stress or worry, and you talked about persistence, about keeping going. Are there words in there that you find important that you haven't already mentioned?

AP: Bear in mind that image of the bird in flight, the pigeon in the poem we were talking about earlier – Robert Lowell's *Pigeons*

– *For Hannah Arendt* (Lowell 2003, p. 316), that fluttering, I think often there is this oscillation between these words. Some of the words jump out at me. Conformity, boredom, helplessness, obsessiveness, righteousness, hyperactivity, restraint, isolation, loneliness – I'm not sure that obtuseness and cluelessness are the same thing, but I'm somewhat attracted to those two. Unable to be in solitude – that's what I mean by oscillation – there is the avoidance of loneliness and there's sometimes a need to be alone as well –

JS: Comfortable solitude.

AP: Yes. Disruptiveness, compliance, self-deprecation, impulsivity, inhibition – this oscillation is a constant, which might be self-indulgent.

JS: One of the things I've found interesting is some people have seen things that are described here as the opposite of a strength or a virtue, as themselves a strength. One of the interesting ones was the word 'orthodoxy', which Mario D'Souza discusses (earlier in this chapter). Similarly, disruptiveness you might see as *not* a disorder of justice.

AP: I realise I've been dwelling in the absences, the opposites and the exaggerations. Creativity: I have a problem with that word. You can't make it an end of research, otherwise you just get something that's possibly meretricious and showy but 'innovative'. Down this left hand column, vitality is important, truthfulness, sincerity. I'm not sure about the clumping together of authenticity, honesty and sincerity – of these three, I think sincerity would be the one. Persistence, definitely. I think courage is different from bravery and I would use the word courage. Kindness.

JS: I think you're the first person in these conversations to highlight vitality. What does that bring to mind for you?

AP: By 'vitality' I don't mean bubbly and enthusiastic. I simply mean being alive. There's a theatre educator who says 'I want my students to be alive'. While we're struggling with something, it's a sign that we're alive. To me, everything else goes through that. I suspect risk might feature as an exaggeration, but I think risk is the thing about live performance.

JS: Are there things that you were thinking, in advance of this conversation, that you thought we would be talking about that we haven't talked about?

AP: No, but can I ask you is there is anything that you hoped that I would say, or an issue that I would touch upon that I haven't?

JS: I'm interested that trying to hear back through the conversation, I can't work out what research you've done. I've got one or two titles, which are interesting as your titles are poetic and carry a lot of meaning. But if I were to be asked just on the basis of this conversation, I don't know –

AP: what is her field?

JS: Have you intentionally hidden your field, or is it something that actually doesn't matter to you? For example, you didn't even describe the *Trips and Slips* article as writing on research methodology. I can't, from this conversation, work out what you've researched. That's interesting – not a criticism – and it fits with some of what you've said about not feeling you have a centre of gravity.

AP: I think I'm not very good at telling my own story, because none of it ever really goes away, none of it ever is finished. If I were to sum up what I'm interested in, I would say, through different areas of enquiry like exclusion from school, inclusion in school (Pirrie 2010, Pirrie and Head 2007), epistemology of social research, a critique of the fetishisation of method in research (Pirrie and Macleod 2009) – oh I *do* have something, I *have* done something – all that is about being a good person and living a good life through one's activities. That is the animating thing, the vital part of it, and it's not finished, it just carries on – I hope.

JS: So it's the 'livingness' –

AP: it's the livingness of it.

JS: So it's living well, or living good –

AP: and it's also showing that to others. Showing that you can't talk about lifelong learning (Pirrie and Thoutenhoofd 2013) if you don't embody what it is, you can't talk about ethical practice in research if you don't embody what it is, you can't talk about power as so many people do, and abuse it – flagrantly, as so many people do. Particularly those who talk about power. So I like there to be at some level a consonance between the way I live my life, and the way I do my work.

JS: And that's the 'livingness'.

AP: When I use the word consonant, that implies a kind of serenity, which is at odds with what I have said about oscillating between the presence and absence, and exaggeration. You know I am interested in lightness. There is something about lightness that deeply fascinates me. It's not something insubstantial, but it is worth exploring as the antithesis of gravitas, which is a thing that is prized. I suppose that I fear if I were to say my work is in *this* area, I would be open to the charge of some kind of false gravitas – because I actually think it's all dust really. It's all dust. None of it matters. The only thing that matters is that one carries on.

JS: Presumably gravitas, like gravity, pulls you down to a particular place, and you're a traveller. It's easy to live in one place heavily, but harder to *travel* heavily. And you described yourself as someone who is a nomad, who wishes to travel. Or have I mixed the metaphors?

AP: Yes. No.

JS: The book is to be called *Virtuous Educational Research*, which suggests that educational research can be looked at as personal, as a way of demonstrating the personal virtues of people.

AP: Yes, It's about how you do it, and how you engage with the other people with whom you come into contact while you're doing it. And it isn't a solitary thing, even when done in solitude. It's always remembering people past, engaging and interacting with people who are not there, that are in the pages of books.

JS: Thank you, Anne.

Conclusion: Thinking Inside and Outside the Box

Peterson contrasts the virtue of the 'love of learning', with its opposite: 'orthodoxy' (Peterson, in Csikszentmihalyi and Csikszentmihalyi 2006, p. 39). Can those who love learning *also* be 'orthodox' – whether in the specific religious sense, or in the more general sense? Mario D'Souza can be described as 'orthodox' within a Catholic tradition. He is also a passionate advocate of religious education and research in religious education. Peterson recognises such learning-centred orthodoxy: 'I can easily imagine someone within an orthodox congregation who displays a great love of learning about religion and other aspects of the world', but orthodoxy in Peterson's sense is 'not only a disinclination to acquire new information but an active stand against so doing' (Peterson, in Csikszentmihalyi and Csikszentmihalyi 2006, p. 45). Somewhat in contrast to Mario D'Souza, Anne Pirrie sees herself 'as a bit of a nomad', and exhibits 'lightness' (also described in Pirrie 2015). Researchers can untie themselves, they can float across boundaries and be travellers: 'troubadour' intellectuals (Serres 1997). Researchers of this kind are 'outsiders', people who reject the sense of 'heavyweight' research – research that is rather grand and portentous, completed by researchers who are important and powerful figures exhibiting gravitas. However, this defiance of gravitas has its downsides: it may underplay the value of consistent, focused, research, and, as an approach, it 'engenders enormous insecurity'. Mario and Anne, together, suggest that it is possible and valuable to think both inside and outside the box. The philosopher Senechal writes of being asked by friends 'do you think inside the box or outside the box?'

> I had to give it some thought. I wasn't familiar with the expression. Was it possible to think outside the box, whatever the box might be? It seemed to me that there would be another box outside it, and then another, somewhat like Matryoshka dolls. Also, it seemed it would be a lot more interesting to think inside the box; I would get to know its contents. I took a deep breath, leapt over the mental puddle, and replied, 'Inside the box.' They clapped; I had passed the test. We discussed it and agreed that thinking 'outside the box' was an improbable and silly proposition. Ironically, we

were thinking outside the box about the very subject of thinking outside the box, which, I suppose, put us 'inside the box.' (Senechal 2012, p. 95)

It is all too easy to think of the 'right' way to do things, as though there are simple (and correct) universal answers to all questions. It is just as tempting, though, to be so specific and context-dependent, that nothing ends up being said beyond 'here I am'. In research, we are forever haunted by the twin temptations – ideals, for many – of generalisability (what I have found out applies to everyone, everywhere) and validity (what I have found out is right for these people, here). What I think is said, here, is that there is a positive value, for research, in orthodoxy – not a value for everyone in every context, but a value nevertheless – and a positive value in lightness, of intellectuals working 'at the intersection or the interference of many other disciplines and, sometimes, of almost all of them' (Serres 1997, p. xvii).

> Depart. Go out. Allow yourself to be seduced one day. Become many, brave the outside world, split off somewhere else. These are the first three foreign things, the three varieties of alterity, the three initial means of being exposed. For there is no learning without exposure, often dangerous, to the other. I will never again know what I am, where I am, from where I'm from, where I'm going, through where to pass. I am exposed to others, to foreign things. (Serres 1997, p. 8)

All kinds of virtue words and their opposites play in the account, from courage to helplessness, impulsivity to inhibition, with a knowing oscillation between ways of being.

The six conversationalists reported in Chapters 2, 3 and 4 include material that illuminates some of my own early challenges and opportunities as a researcher. They do far more than this, of course. I suspect that many researchers will share my own concerns over positioning oneself theoretically, over whether research respondents are being truthful, and over issues of disciplinary and institutional positioning. Moving on from these matters, the next group of conversations address a range of relationship issues. How might the practice of research help build or perhaps strain relationships?

PART III

Building Relationships

The definition of research I am using in this book ('a process of investigation leading to new insights, effectively shared', Hefce 2011, p. 48) is focused – interestingly – on insights, rather than knowledge. (Here is an alternative: research is work 'to acquire new knowledge' or 'for the advancement of knowledge', OECD 2007, p. 61 and p. 634 respectively.) 'Insight' is a 'penetrating understanding': 'understanding into the inner character or hidden nature of things', and in earlier times also meant 'wisdom' (OED 2005). 'Knowledge', wonderful as it is, is often used in the sense of having acquired a fact. It is a somewhat less *engaging* term. I like the idea of research leading us into the inner character of things – the inner character of things and of people, including ourselves. Research is engaging, even though it can also be lonely – as Lander Calvelhe, Sr Agnes Wilkins and Lāsma Latsone (in Chapters 5, 7 and 8, respectively) all mention. The theme that links the conversations in this part of the book is how research involves building relationships. These may be relationships between the researcher and research participants, with other researchers and professional practitioners, or with oneself.

CHAPTER 5

It's Not Therapy, But ...

Introduction

When I first interviewed people, as part of a research process, I would conclude the interview thanking the interviewee for having taken part. It surprised me how many people responded by thanking me, in turn, saying how much they enjoyed the interview or found it good to have an opportunity to talk about these issues. Such a reaction no longer surprises me, and most researchers have had similar experiences. It happened in the making of this book. When I say to Ron Best 'Thank you so much', he replies 'Well, I've enjoyed it' (in Chapter 3), and Shanaaz Hoosain finishes with 'Thank you: it's been helpful for me to find the words' (in Chapter 7). Taking part in research can be valuable for the 'researched' as well as for the researcher. A focused conversation in order to gain some insight into an issue, can provide insight to both people. In such circumstances, the 'interview' might better be described as a 'conversation', and the talk can be described as 'real dialogue' (Buber 2002, p. 22). For Buber, real dialogue requires a 'leap' to another person. It is as an imaginative leap to the reality of the other person – *Realphantasie* – 'not a looking at the other, but a bold swinging – demanding the most intensive stirring of one's being – into the life of the other' (Buber 1998, p. 71). Nel Noddings (in Chapter 2) described the need for dialogue in education and in all of life, including research. And the mutual thanks, at the end of an interview, may be a simple illustration of the dialogic possibilities of research. It may even be more: it may come close to therapy.

In many ways, Mike Bottery and Lander Calvelhe are contrasting researchers. Mike is a very experienced, established researcher, best known for researching school leadership; Lander is just completing his doctorate, and is best known for researching teenagers in and out of school. Yet both compare research to therapeutic processes, and both talk passionately about feelings and being kind to yourself as a researcher. Both also talk of the creative interplay of theory and practice, and of researcher and researched. Research may not itself be therapy, but ... well, the two researchers provide different descriptions of what it is.

The Evidence Should Provoke Some Kind of Feelings in People: A Conversation with Mike Bottery, University of Hull, England

JS: Do you want to tell me a little about your own research and how or why you came to be doing it?

MB: I have been described as a philosopher, as a theorist, as a historian, even as a geographer, of education. They seldom say I am an empirical researcher. This surprises me because about 40 per cent of the stuff that I do is based upon empirical research. My research is divided into two areas. One is reflecting on the values underpinning policies and practices, and people's actions (Bottery 1990, 1992, 1998, 2000, 2004, 2016). The other is finding those ideas through working in schools, or going into schools to develop ideas that have been thought about philosophically or logically beforehand, and seeing how they match the reality of practice (Bottery 1994, 2007, Bottery et al. 2008a, 2008b). One of the things that I find, from my experience of philosophy, is that philosophical ideas look brilliant on paper, but when you go into schools, they don't often match up with what is happening. It tends to be a lot more complex and messy than philosophers would have. So my academic life has been moving from empirical research to philosophical analysis and then back again. It's grown from being a

career founded on values education in the classroom, to values
education in the school, to values education coming down into
the school, to global forces and how they impinge on what's happening at the national level (Bottery 1997, 2004), and then at
the school level, and then at the individual level. It's an iterative
process that has grown to being a much larger-picture thing than
I would have expected when I started – as my reading and my
talking to people suggests that a lot of the ideas come from levels
above that of the individual the school and the local, and increasingly above the level of the national. I think that's something to
do with faster communication, the use of the free market, and the
breaking down of cultural barriers by economic forces. So there's
a lot that is mediated at the national level, but started beyond the
nation state.

JS: I'm not sure what you mean by values in your research.

MB: They are values as expressed through particular policies, cultures,
and practices. Academics are trying to provide some kind of order,
and some sort of rationality, trying to explain the world. I'm not
entirely sure that the models that they create actually reflect the
complexity and the messiness of reality. We're trying to provide
order, and that necessarily is less complex than reality. I don't
simply present a picture, I usually present an argument as well,
based on a couple of personal values. One of those values is fairness,
equity. There's something in me that says 'The world is wrong if it's
not a fair world, because we have the ability to make it fair – we
don't have to accept inequality and suffering and pain and all the
rest of it'. The other one is wellbeing – other people's wellbeing.

JS: Some will say research shouldn't be about promoting your values,
it should be about exploring others'.

MB: It's impossible to avoid promoting values. If you take a neutral
position, you in effect allow the status quo to exist. I'm upfront
with these values: they are part of an argument that's out there
for people to debate with.

JS: Is one of the characteristics you would want in your research a
sense of fairly representing views that are not yours?

MB: Yes. You have to listen to the opposing point of view, even if you
        fundamentally disagree with it: they come from a place that you
        don't come from, so you may well miss it, and it could be very valu-
        able. That's a real challenge sometimes, because it's easy to go to the
        books that agree with you. I tend to hold fairly strong opinions,
        but they change. The underpinning values are always there, but
        what makes for a fairer world and a world where there is greater
        wellbeing, may well change with my greater understanding of the
        situation. Twenty-five, thirty, years ago, I had absolutely no doubt
        that markets in any sort of description were horrendous things. I've
        got much more nuanced understanding of markets now, largely
        from reading people whom I still fundamentally disagree with,
        but there is something there that you can't dismiss. If you start
        to think you've 'got the answer', then you're deeply in trouble –
        because you have only a very limited view of the world.

JS: When you are dealing with living people, headteachers or kids,
        you are doing the sort of thing that you do with philosophers. You
        talk about their values, their underpinning principles, you try to
        create a picture of their philosophy or their way of living. That's
        why people don't think it's empirical, perhaps, because it looks
        so much like what you do with philosophers.

MB: I hadn't thought of it in that way. There's considerable overlap
        between the two.

JS: I tend to avoid methods which involve me interpreting what other
        people think as a result of a tool, and tend to go more towards me
        trying to find out what they think, how they interpret situations,
        and I will join in dialogue with that. Your portrait methodology,
        written descriptions of people using their words as well as yours
        (Bottery et al. 2008b, 2012, 2013, Bottery 2014), seems to me to
        be representative of that sense of trying to give people a participa-
        tion in creating an understanding of themselves. Your empirical
        research in recent years has been a good example of something
        that cannot be done through a set of traditional survey questions
        that can be analysed and sorted.

MB: You may have put too strong a structure on it. A lot of the time, both philosophically and empirically, I'll be happy to follow my nose. So the portrait methodology started off as a fairly standard piece of work – initially as far back as the early 1990s, when a headteacher I used to work for committed suicide. The pressures on headteachers that came from the introduction of the National Curriculum and Ofsted, I saw at first hand. Some people managed it and some people didn't. It was this wellbeing issue, it was this lack of fairness, where people were blamed for failure of implementation when a lot of the time the legislation was just awful. I wanted to know how the average teacher, or the ones who were actually finding it difficult, were doing. It changed as I realised the research had an effect on them: it directly affected their wellbeing, because it gave them the privacy and the time to talk about these things in an atmosphere where nobody was going to take down what they said and use it against them. They felt constantly under surveillance – Bentham or Foucault's panopticon all over again (Bottery 2000, p. 141). That led me into picking up the idea from the REF of research 'impact' (Hefce 2011, p. 28), and developing this to see how it affected people. I should have known that one of the best ways of supporting people is giving them the time, saying 'I'm here, I'm listening'. That's what counselling does a lot of the time. But there are particular situations that headteachers and principals and senior people in schools have where you need to do more than that: you need to guarantee anonymity and confidentiality even more than standard counselling would. It was immensely supportive for them. Some headteachers said 'I never saw myself in that way before'. There's little doubt: engaging in the portrait methodology can increase their wellbeing. That's a remarkable thing in itself: it isn't just making an argument to say 'Policies are diminishing their wellbeing, therefore policies need to change'. Something originally designed as a research instrument can have a really good effect on them.

JS: You said earlier you didn't have many research challenges, are there any others that you would want to describe?

MB: I do want to persuade people of my arguments, but I'm aware that
        if you spell out a position immediately, half your audience will not
        read you. So one of the challenges I have – it's a technical chal-
        lenge as much as an ethical challenge – is to write in such a way
        that they don't realise that they're contemplating arguments that
        might challenge their fundamental beliefs. What I'm trying to do
        is to get people to read stuff at least to halfway through, and then
        think 'Oh, right, I'm not sure I like this' – but you've got them
        to think about it. There are a lot of people who start off putting
        upfront a Foucault or a Marx, and that seem to me to be saying
        'danger'. I think you have to find ways of introducing those ideas,
        and then only at the end say 'and of course this is what Foucault
        was saying, this is what Marx said'. It seems to be a much better
        way of doing it than ramming it in their face at the start. The issue
        of the human condition is wide enough for anybody to be writ-
        ing about fairness and wellbeing to have a pretty broad canvas to
        write upon, and not be pushing down the throat the notions of
        fairness and wellbeing as the only things that matter. There's a
        much wider canvas to paint on than just two specific issues.

JS: When I read one of your books, I would be confident that you
        would represent different views in a fair way, because that is also
        how you live and you work as a colleague. I would be more con-
        fident in your conclusions precisely because you are not editing
        it in such a way as to lead people through to those conclusions.
        You're allowing people to find their position, and even if you state
        what your position is at the end, you're not requiring people to
        agree, you're allowing people to learn and disagree. That's what
        I think Keats' negative capability is (Keats 1947, p. 72).

MB: Well you're much more generous to me than I am to myself. I am
        trying to convince people. But when it comes to the portraits, it's
        really important that you don't push a view down their throats.
        There are plenty of portraits where I have disagreed with those
        people, but you should never be able to read that in the portrait.
        What I am trying to do in there is show the variety of approaches
        to leadership that people have. The portrait methodology is about

trying to describe different contexts and different personalities. You have a specific objective with the portrait methodology, and it isn't about comparing your ideas with their ideas. If you were writing portrait methodology as other people have used it, mixing your views with theirs, then you would say where you think they are wrong. That's not my purpose. My purpose in the portrait methodology is to present as fair a picture as I can, of what they are doing.

JS: I've got a list of virtues and their opposites. You've already mentioned fairness and honesty.

MB: One of the joys of working in this job, is the ability to be creative. That is a huge buzz, and it fits so well with curiosity and interest. Anyone who is interested in other people, cannot fail but love this job. Judgement, critical thinking, because that's what we do. Love of learning is obviously there. Perspective is as well. Bravery: I've never thought of myself as brave, I've never thought of myself as cowardly. They just aren't a part of my vocabulary.

JS: I think you describe some other researchers and research groups you've been a member of, where people are avoiding disagreeing with policies, are trying to go along with the crowd. Would you say that's research cowardice?

MB: Yes. But you choose your battles. Part of an academic's job is not to make other people look foolish or to destroy them in argument: it's to convince them. It's an intellectual activity and an emotional activity. The evidence should provoke some kind of feelings in people, where they want to change because it's the right thing to do, not because you've beaten them into a pulp.

JS: I remember when I first knew you, you were a professor and I was a lecturer. You taught me that a professor should be someone who professes, who should voice their position as a professor. You can call it courage.

MB: That's right. It comes back to the first thing you were talking about, about values: how could somebody write a book where they didn't profess? You're partly professing it through the way in which you deal with the data and the arguments: the manner is as important as what you're actually saying. Going through the virtues sheet, persistence, yes, you've just got to keep going. Authenticity: I've never fully understood that term. Honesty and sincerity, yes, I think you have to be honest with yourself, that's a really important virtue. An awful lot of academic life is looking yourself in the mirror, and knowing that you've been honest with yourself. That can be hard at times. Truthfulness, well, how could you not. I don't understand vitality, apart from the fact that it's such a good job, how could you not be vital? Intimacy: well that depends. You have to keep a professional distance: there are times when you have to not ask a question, because it's too hurtful and you know that you're pushing at the edges of where they want to go. You're in a position of power, because you are the professor asking the questions, and they've agreed to it. It's up to you to say to yourself 'no, I'm not going there – it would make some lovely juicy quotes in an article, but I'm not prepared to do that because I'm hurting the other person'. It's this thing about wellbeing again. Care: it goes all the way through. Social intelligence: I'm not seeing it as a virtue, I see it as skill. Enstasy, comfortableness with self: some of the best times I've had have been arguing with the computer. That comes back to the professorship and professing. If you're professing other people's views you're hardly professing your own views. It's part of being comfortable with working on your own, and being comfortable with acknowledging when you're wrong. Citizenship, yes: that can include Derek Heater's notions of nested citizenship (Heater 1999) – that there are different levels of citizenship, and you can call for fairness at global, at national, at local, and at an interpersonal level.

JS: At a personal level, that includes being fair to yourself.

MB: I have been known to neglect myself in the process: I don't think I'm alone in that. Forgiveness, mercy. If somebody does you wrong, you're a fool if you simply accept that; if somebody apologises, you're a fool if you don't accept the apology. (Of course, if they keep doing it and apologising, there comes a point where you have to say 'Well I'm a fool if I'm going to accept it'.) That ability to forgive and to be merciful is important. Humility and modesty: yes, but it's not the 'I am worse than other people' kind (Bottery 2016, p. 50).

JS: That's self-deprecation – it's the exaggerated version on this list.

MB: Prudence: you can be too prudent, there are times when you just need to jump off that cliff. Prudence so easily becomes conservatism, where you're not creative, you don't take risks. In sixty years, you'll have spent one year sixty times over, which would be a terrible condemnation of anybody. Self-regulation: again, it's like prudence, if it's overplayed or underplayed it's terribly bad. I'm getting very Aristotelian in my old age.

JS: I think you are the first person to look at that list and go through every single one and recognise elements of it for people's research.

MB: I'll finish them off. Appreciation of beauty: it's not a thing I would normally talk about, but there are some times where you see people's behaviours or people's thinking, and it is beautiful. Academics can become cynical. You want to be sceptical, but you don't want to be cynical. It's like a theatre critic: it's too easy to criticise for the sake of criticism. Gratitude: well, how could you not be grateful for doing a job like this? Hope and trust: I'm not sure that's a virtue so much as a predisposition. People who start off by distrusting, I just can't do that. Five per cent of the time you'll get kicked in the teeth: that's not a bad ratio. Humour: that's a good one. Just as there is tragedy, there is enormous humour as well.

JS: Is humourlessness a vice?

MB: Yes: it's a vice because you're not listening to the other person. Humourlessness suggests a lack of empathy, and humour is looking for the connections. Humour is one part of a set of dispositions along with sadness and regret. They are part of trying to understand where the other person is coming from, and that comes down to empathy.

JS: So empathy is in research, both theoretical and philosophical and empirical?

MB: Yes. Spirituality: I'm not sure how to answer that. All I would say is that I think that the academic pursuit can lead to a deeper understanding of the human condition, and therefore rather than it being something that you do because it provides you with a grant, you do it because it in some way contributes to the betterment of humanity. So if that's what spirituality means, then yes.

JS: Thank you so much, Mike.

I Wanted to Keep on Learning: A Conversation with Lander Calvelhe, The Public University of Navarre, Spain

JS: Would you like to tell me a little bit about your own research in this area, and particularly how and why you came to be doing it?

LC: As a degree student, I found theory and reflection something that made sense to me. The theory and the books I read, and the lectures, were a way of coping and dealing with some of my struggles. So I decided that I wanted to try to find out more, to understand how things were so complex and why things were happening, and why my feelings were that way. I studied fine arts, in the University of Barcelona, but what I described happened in anthropology, sociology, and pedagogy of art, and they were much influenced by social constructivism, feminist studies, and queer studies. There was a bunch of interesting professors and lecturers, many of them members of a prestigious research group (<http://esbrina.eu/en/home/>), so we were reading Judith Butler, Stuart Hall and Kenneth Gergen, among others. In that context I decided I wanted to get into *it* in order to deal with my problems, to understand the problems in Western societies. There is a book written by bell hooks, *Teaching to Transgress* (hooks 1994). I felt we could identify with what she wrote. She said that she came to theory because she needed to heal all the injuries she had:

I came to theory because I was hurting – the pain within me was so intense that I could not go on living. I came to theory desperate, wanting to comprehend – to grasp what was happening around and within me. Most importantly, I wanted to make the hurt go away. I saw in theory then a location for healing. (hooks 1994, p. 59)

I can say now I got into research because of that. However, a few years later I found out that research is not therapy. Theory didn't resolve my problems, although it helped me to think about my problems in another way, in a wider way. If theory had changed my life completely and I had found peace and wellbeing through it – that would've been very surprising. But I didn't.

JS: When you say theory, what do you mean?

LC: Reflection: to read and think about what is knowledge, who is the subject, what is reality, and all the critical and post-modern ways of questioning.

JS: If you put theory in a box, what is outside the box?

LC: Research I guess. When you are dealing with people, when you are asking somebody, when you are taking some action or you are listening, you are confronting, that is more about practice than theory.

JS: When I read Judith Butler or bell hooks or Stuart Hall, I regard myself as in conversation with them, and when I am talking to you, I am in conversation. So I am getting confused about what you would call the theory end of scholarly work, and the empirical and research end. Both, for me, involve conversation.

LC: I do agree. The border, or the difference between one and the other, is problematic.

JS: You said you came to see research as maybe having some therapeutic value, but not the same as therapy. How did you come into doing what you would call research as an academic?

LC: I wanted to keep on learning, so the way to do that as a professional was to get into research. I did my teacher training for secondary school, but I had this aim for more complexity, for understanding more how things work and could be improved. So I applied for a scholarship, I got it, and then research became my job. I went through a bad period at the beginning of my scholarship, and that is when I realised that research is not therapy. One of my supervisors is Imanol Aguirre, and there is a quotation from him that I really like: 'analysis ... is not comprehension' (Aguirre 2004, p. 265). He's talking about education and teaching. For me it has another meaning too: analysis is not healing. From that point on I decided to search for help in other areas of my life. That decision allowed me to face research without the anger or anxiety I used to have because of my fears and aspirations. Many of the worries I used to have were about what other people would say, or, because my research is on gay teenagers, about its activist implications. I was scared of what the activists and what the academy would say about it and I had to put all that aside, and just do the task in hand. That was the biggest challenge: to quiet my mind, to get rid of all those worries and anxieties and aspirations, and be able simply to do the research.

JS: I like to think of senior researchers, all researchers, as professional learners. So I like your description of wanting a life of learning, and seeing that as an academic career path. You must have met academics who, when they have finished their doctorate and have got a job, they now see themselves not as learners but as tellers of other people.

LC: Yes, I've met that kind of person.

JS: Would you describe some of the research that you've done? Research, for this project, is any form of investigation or scholarship or empirical research leading to new insights that are shared.

LC: I've been the intern on two research projects focusing on teenagers and their lives outside the school, the first one in relation to their knowledge and the second to their visual culture production. The groups were very different. One was the group I mentioned before from the University of Barcelona (<http://esbrina.eu/en/home/>). It was quite dynamic, with lots of meetings, a busy schedule, and deadlines. The other one was a small group in a smaller university, the Public University of Navarre (<http://edarte.org/>), and it had one principal researcher and just three more members and myself. Somehow in both experiences I felt lonely. In the first project, 'Rethinking school success and failure

in secondary education from young people's relations with knowledge' (EDU2008–03287), with all those members and deadlines,
it was my first time in research and it was overwhelming. But
some colleagues were nice with me and my friend, really taking
care of us. It had an atmosphere of sharing, generosity. One of the
researchers – his name is Fernando Hernández – was a teacher
of mine when I was a graduate student: I'm meeting him here at
ECER, in Budapest (<http://www.eera-ecer.de/ecer-2015-buda
pest/>), so it's nice to have this kind of relation with him all along
those years. In the second project, 'Young people as visual culture
producers: artistic skills and knowledge in secondary education'
(EDU 2009–13712), Imanol Aguirre is the main researcher and
everybody in the group tried our best, but I believe the project
was too big for such a small group of people in such a small university. Imanol is a good person and very generous too: he has a lot
of patience, but it was quite difficult to put the project together.

JS: You described the experience as lonely. What do you mean when
      you say that?

LC: With the first research group it wasn't really loneliness. I guess
      I was stressed out because I was also working part time at a depart-
      ment store and wished my circumstances were other. But in the
      second, yes, I felt lonely because I was expecting a community
      before moving there – I was expecting seminars, and reading
      groups, and I had got the idea of building my social life through
      that. There were so many expectations. Then I realised I was asking
      for too much and for that reason I was frustrated.

JS: Many people think of research as a solitary activity. That can be
      a good thing, they can withdraw and think, but withdrawal also
      has the difficulty that it can be lonely, as you say.

LC: In my case the contrast between the projects shocked me. I am a
      PhD candidate (Calvelhe 2015, and see Calvelhe 2013) and I was
      a PhD student at that time, so I was willing to have a little com-
      munity of learners being able to discuss things as a group. But the
      idea that nobody was expecting me at university meant it was an
      effort to wake up sometimes, and get into the faculty. This sounds

silly, but for me it was a big deal that nobody was waiting for me there.

JS: It is hard to carry on doing something that nobody shows an interest in. Could you tell me something about the projects? What was your work?

LC: Mostly in the first project we were reflecting about results before interviewing – how our lives in and outside school related to each other when we were teenagers – and from that some pilot interviews were made. That was exciting. When they started the proper interviews my period with them ended. On the other project, we didn't have that self-reflection period. When I arrived they were designing a questionnaire, and then we got a pilot questionnaire and went to some schools to evaluate it. Afterwards the final questionnaire was sent to different schools all around Spain. I liked that kind of work too. The next step was to develop some in-depth semi-structured interviews with teenagers in order to compare with the results of the questionnaires. The most difficult part was to get the participation of teenagers, so one of my main tasks was to find them. That was fun but difficult in the situation I've already described.

JS: Was part of the idea that young people outside school were productive, but inside school they were passive and uncreative, and the idea was to try to tap into their creativity outside school to change how schools work?

LC: Yes. It was a way of acknowledging teenagers as active subjects, not just as passive viewers of the media for instance. In fact in both projects the theoretical framework and background research pointed out that schools needed to change their way of teaching and welcoming students as a whole, holistically. But sometimes teenagers can be very private about what they do after school, and that is their right. For example, we cannot ask them to bring to school their creativity out of school if they don't want to – and what is more, is the school safe for teenagers to do that? In my opinion most schools are not prepared for this kind of sharing because they are not perceived as safe.

JS: So, what were the main challenges and how you dealt with those? I think you were talking about some of those from the start – the problems or advantages of team work or lack of team work, and the difficulties of access. Were there other challenges in those projects?

LC: I think my main personal challenge during the last ten to twelve years is to quiet my mind. As I explained before the expectations and aspirations I had as a PhD candidate were fears, and negative thoughts, that didn't allow me to just enjoy it: they were ways of not being 'present'. Most of the time I was thinking, worrying about the future or evaluating the past. I wasn't *being*, doing the research while enjoying editing or analysing or re-reading transcriptions.

JS: Have you got those virtue words? I think you've talked about courage or bravery, loneliness, being passive or compliant. Are there other words you think are relevant?

LC: We've just been talking about worrying, so I would underline care – care about yourself and caring about other people, I think that is key. In this list, 'worry' is an exaggeration of 'care', but I get the feeling it is the *opposite*. When you care, you don't worry. In other words, because I care about my wellbeing I don't allow myself to worry too much, and the same about other people. Courage is important as well. Courage is for me is not just about bravery. It comes from the Latin 'cor': heart, to take heart, to have heart, to feel the strength of your heart. When you feel the strength of your heart, you are able to put all worries aside, and you are more present. One more is kindness, which is quite related with care. Kindness with oneself. Researchers have a lot of pressure on their shoulders: why can't we be kind with ourselves? We often want to help somebody else, but we cannot care about anybody if we don't take care of ourselves. The wellbeing of the teacher itself teaches a lot to the students. 'We teach who we are' wrote Palmer (2007, p. 1), and I would dare to add, 'we teach how we feel' – and this is probably the same in research matters.

JS: I have used a quotation from Newton and Tarrant: 'Unhappy,
        stressed workaholics are not good role models for young people'
        (Newton and Tarrant 1992, p. 194).
LC: That's a great quotation.
JS: Are there any things you have not had a chance to say?
LC: My PhD is on gay teenagers, and how to introduce sexual and
        gender diversity in a school. I believe that if sexual and gender
        diversity is going to get into schools, teachers need to feel good
        about that, and they need to be at peace with themselves and
        with everybody else to some extent. Indeed this path would lead
        to better schools at every level. I don't want teachers to stress out,
        and feel like 'Oh, and now we have to take care of sexual diversity
        – what's going to be next?'. I've got the feeling that if they have
        developed good self-esteem, and have found the strength and
        courage we've just talked about, they could take care of sexual
        diversity in their own schools in their own unique way. It's a way
        of compassion and trust. For teachers and researchers in educa-
        tion, some personal growth, spiritual growth, is a key element in
        our everyday lives and careers.
JS: That's a positive point on which perhaps we can finish.

Conclusion

A number of conversationalists discuss the personal nature of research.
These two focus on the personal influence of research – influence on others
(the subjects of research, and wider social and political influence), and the
influence on themselves as researchers. Is that a kind of therapy? There are
plenty of counsellors and therapists (including Lynne Gabriel in Chapter 8)
who talk of their professions as close to research, so it is only reasonable to
look at the process of research as – at times – having some of the characteristics of therapy. But in the case of Mike Bottery, the therapeutic value
is primarily for the participants in the research, whilst Lander Calvelhe

says that the therapeutic influence of research on the *researcher* is just as significant – an influence on the whole career, not simply a short-term interest.

The process of research is described as being an opportunity for demonstrating a wide range of virtues, amongst which kindness and fairness seem to be leading the way. This is not a picture of research often painted in the literature on methodology, or at least not so eloquently. It speaks to the relational nature of much research. That theme is continued in the following conversations, which also look to wider professional relationships.

CHAPTER 6

Just Work: Professing as Professor and as Professional

Introduction

To profess is to make a public declaration, and this is linked to being a 'professor', a title for a senior, well-established, academic in higher education (Best 1996, p. 2). There is a further link, to being a 'professional' – a member of a practice-based community requiring an explicit work-related ethical code. Professors and professionals are also linked through the need for advanced learning. In English, the earliest use of 'profess' was as a religious profession, joining a religious community. That is an interesting web of meanings. The central definition of research I am using in this book is 'a process of investigation leading to new insights, effectively shared' (Hefce 2011, p. 48). The 'effectively shared' phrase is not an additional – optional – requirement, once the research is completed. Sharing insights, through publishing and teaching, is *part of* the research. What is the significance of this? Research is not – not only – a private matter, the accumulation in the researcher's head of insights acquired through investigation. Many researchers see research, either positively or negatively, as precisely private, even self-indulgent or solipsistic. I saw it like that myself. Completing a postgraduate degree (Stern 1982), I had funding to continue to complete a doctorate, and chose instead to become a schoolteacher, frustrated – after twenty years of full-time education – with the idea of continuing to accumulate knowledge and generate ideas, without passing them on. It took another 10 years of school teaching before I gained confidence that it was worth researching, not as a selfish accumulation but as a *communal* activity, involving sharing and influencing, rather like the teaching profession itself.

All professions – not just teaching – are 'professing' communities. You are publicly accountable for your own activities, and you are communally responsible for the professionalism of the activities of others. Being a silent witness to another's unprofessional conduct is like being a silent witness to another's crime, and it is unprofessional. The same is true of research. Failure to follow appropriate research ethics codes (such as breaches of confidentiality, failure to gain appropriate consent) is clearly problematic. But there is a second wave of unprofessional conduct: failure to do anything about the unethical conduct of others. This is made explicit in a recent code of practice on research integrity, which says that '[r]esearchers will ... handle potential instances of research misconduct in an appropriate manner; this includes reporting misconduct to employers, funders and professional, statutory and regulatory bodies as circumstances require' (UUK 2012, p. 18).

Professing, whether as a professor or as a professional, therefore brings with it virtues and challenges. Professing is also – I suggest – the 'effective sharing' element required of any activity that is to be described as research. The following two conversations are with people who are professors, professionals, and researchers. They describe some of the interesting challenges, the potential virtues and vices, related to this work. Both Jean McNiff and Jacqui Akhurst describe much of their work as practitioner research or action research. Jean McNiff is, indeed, one of the leading writers on action research methodology (McNiff 1993, 2013a, McDonnell and McNiff 2014). This approach wears its relational character on its sleeve: action research is close to action learning (which is not in itself a form of research), and practitioner research is close to practice (which is not in itself a form of research). That is why some people find the approach attractive, and why others find it puzzling or misleading. As someone who self-identifies as a practitioner (mostly as 'teacher'), exploring the relationships between research and practice is important to me, too.

I Call it Work: A Conversation with Jean McNiff, York St John University, England

JS: Can you tell me about your research, and how and why you came to be doing what you do in this area?

JM: I suppose you could call me an accidental researcher. I don't necessarily call the work that I do research, I call it work. When I'm speaking with a higher education audience, I would tend to call it research, but when I'm speaking with people who are called practitioners, I would always call it work. My view of research is that it is about creating knowledge and generating theory. However, I see all of the work that I do as about finding things out. I see life as a process of research: you have to find out about what you're doing, interpret what you're doing, make sense of it, come up for reasons and explanations – and that's the process of theorising. Politically, I'm aware that sometimes we need to talk about research as a concept and talk about the research that we're doing, but there is just no distinction – there is nothing between research and living. The kind of research that I like doing is research in action, on action, for action – what people tend to call action research (McNiff 2014). I see that as a dynamic, emergent, transformational process. It's liberating for people to see that the work that they're doing in their everyday lives is a form of research. I also don't see any distinction between people who work in universities and are officially called 'researchers', and people who, say, work in the home or work in factories who are working and finding out and making sense of what they're doing, and call that research. I don't refer to mundane repetitive work as research, because that's more reproduction of the existing situation, but anything that requires thinking about it, and making sense of things, I would see as research. When you talk about my own research, everything I do is research, because it's always involved in helping myself, helping other people, to make sense of what we're doing. I do see myself as in a privileged position, because I get to choose what I do and think, and not many people are in that position, therefore a lot of the work I do is trying to help people to emancipate themselves, to influence the kinds of social and political organisational structures that they are in, to help them to explore their own potential for creative and critical thinking.

JS: Has your own life moved to be more of a research life?

JM: I have found myself in situations where other people would like me to work in a more repetitive reproductive way of living, and those have been the episodes where I've worked quite hard to get out of those personal, organisational, political relationships. Those kinds of relationships close down people's capacity for creative thinking, and act as prisons. Some people like to create their own prisons: it's more comfortable to live within boundaries that other people give you, it's much easier and less challenging. But creativity is who we are and what we are. It's the nature of living.

JS: Is there something distinctive about what you would mean by the word 'work'?

JM: I like the work of Hannah Arendt, and her distinctions between labour and practice (Arendt 2004, pp. 611–612). I see work as productive: what I do with my life productively, that's my 'work'. I don't see my work as having a specific form in the sense that it's a job or teaching. It's not just professional activities, it is what I choose to do, what inspires my life and my thinking.

JS: Talking about work, can you describe one or two research projects that help demonstrate how you go about what it is that you do?

JM: Pieces of work that have really had a lasting influence on me were the work in Khayelitsha, in South Africa (McNiff 2013a), and the work in the Gulf States (McNiff 2013b). The work in Khayelitsha helped me to confront my own racism. Before I went to Khayelitsha, I actually had quite a ding-dong email discussion with a colleague who said that I was racist, and I vehemently denied that I was racist – I was quite offended. But when I got to South Africa and started working with the teachers, about fifty teachers in Khayelitsha, all the teachers were black. And it was at that point that I appreciated that I actually was racist, I'd learned to be racist. I can go back to my childhood and think about listening to stories of people who spoke a racist language. Even as I was thinking 'no, this is not right, I don't agree with it', that has always stayed with me. But going to South Africa and working with the teachers really made me face up to my racism. So I've had to combat that intellectually, emotionally. I think I still do: once we learn something that's so deeply ingrained in us, it's quite hard to shift it. Even though you come to an epiphany, where you do change your mind, you've still got the residual stuff to deal with. So that was an important project, and it also made me understand how groups of people position other groups of people, and how they justify that and how they hide behind rhetorics and policies and their own prejudices and put those forward as the truth. So that was a deeply influential project for me.

JS: What about that project do you feel were the things that created that change of mind?

JM: The internal things were that I was responsible for getting people through a master's project. For them it was a huge undertaking, because they hadn't studied formally at a research level. By working with them as a teacher – by that I mean as a supporter helping them to learn about things, acting for their wellbeing, for their flourishing – I found a different way of being with them and understanding them. It was also their attitudes towards me, because they were initially hostile, and saw me as a means to an end. I think it was only my pride that made me continue – it was a three-year project and I didn't have to do this. This is where the external factor comes in: people wanted to close it down, they wanted me to go away. I was actively discouraged in higher education institutions and in board rooms, in political situations. The more they tried the more I dug my heels in and refused to go. And this is when I found the unity with the teachers I was working with. I was experiencing from people in higher education the same responses to me that the teachers had experienced right through their lives – the prejudice, the unwillingness to recognise what they were doing as legitimate work, to recognise them as legitimate people, and the effort to make them invisible and just disappear. The whole project was an inconvenience to people who wanted to maintain the purity of the research that was then the norm in South Africa. By the end of those three years, the teachers were teaching me: they were saying, 'Jean, you do not understand', I said 'Yes, I do not understand, help me to understand'.

JS: You mentioned a second project, in the Gulf.

JM: I'd never worked in the Gulf, and with people in a different religious and cultural context. What I got out of that project was a deeper understanding of concepts of multiculturalism and cosmopolitanism (McNiff 2013b). That was a particularly rich project in terms of understanding what it means to open your mind to other ways of being and other people who espouse those other ways of being. And to appreciate that your own way is not necessarily the right way, and the need to respect other people's cultures.

JS: The people you were working with in the Gulf, were they teachers?

JM: The women were teachers and the men were managers and directors in schools and in other organisations. That reflects the gendered allocation of labour in the Gulf. I was linking with the government and with higher education people. There is a wonderful rhetoric in Qatar, the main place that I worked, about enabling teachers to think for themselves. The words 'critical thinking' are prominent in the discourses. But when you look at the reality of it, they don't exist. That was a big learning experience for me: how people use language to disguise their own imperialist impulses. It is the division between the discourse and the practice, and combatting the strategies that people in power use to disguise their own motivations and to communicate them as 'emancipatory practices', when they are anything but that. It is a constant threat: the language of power is always there as the back story. You just have to recognise that and learn how to work with it to achieve your own values. In my case, those are of emancipation and bringing people together on a free and equal footing. It reflects Sen's ideas (Sen 1992) that we've got the capacity, but we don't necessarily have the capability. In my work as an educator, it's always around offering and providing, where possible, those spaces where people can be creative, can explore their capacity for creative thinking, creative living, without the idea of being closed down. Another main research challenge, along with the external restrictive discourses, is how people internalise those discourses, and come to believe that they're not very good at things, or not able or less than worthy to do those things. I try to encourage people to see themselves as unique talented people, and not believe what they are told and not close down their own opportunities for creative thinking. Some people actively seek out being controlled, because systems are great places to hide, so I think over time I've learned to respect it. I don't accept it, but I can understand it better. It still infuriates me.

JS: And you would see that as true of the people with formal power who are doing the rhetoric as you describe it, as well as people who don't have the formal power?

JM: Yes, except the people with the formal power tend to know what they're doing, and they do it quite deliberately.

JS: Perhaps what you're saying is power allows people to create un-self-awareness or 'false consciousness' amongst less powerful people?

JM: There are different kinds of power. One of the frustrations is that – let me put the word ordinary in inverted commas – 'ordinary' people don't appreciate how powerful they are, and they don't see the power that they've got by the very fact that they are alive. They can use that power in shrewd and canny ways. Part of the work is to encourage people to become aware that they have the power of their own creativity, their own living. By definition they are powerful. This also applies to people in positions of power: I do encourage them to appreciate what they are doing and to make explicit for themselves their implicit values.

JS: Are there other personal challenges in doing the work that you do?

JM: I have just done some writing on action research as a way of living, but these days the idea of action research has been hijacked and turned into a 'thing' – they've reified it. That is one of the greatest

challenges in all the work that we do: how people position other
people as objects to be studied, rather than as people who are
walking the same path or moving through the same life together.
But I choose not to fight battles so much as create open spaces,
and engage in interesting and life-affirming conversations with
like-minded people. That's where I position myself these days.

JS: I'm looking at the list I sent of virtues and their absences. Clearly
        there were things about fairness, prejudice, self-deception, authen-
        ticity, and honesty.

JM: My vocabulary is openness and criticality and emergence and joy
        and ethics. I got to know Spinoza (1955) when I was fifteen and
        have been influenced by that thinking ever since. The idea that
        open forms are ethical forms. Ethicality to me is to do with being
        open to new possibilities and seeing emergence in everything.
        When it comes to human interactions, there is the Bakhtin idea of
        voices in everything (Bakhtin 1981). If we want to turn the values
        into virtues, these are my virtue words.

JS: Are any of the personal or research challenges captured by the
        structures or the formulae implicit in what's labelled as 'research
        ethics'?

JM: Yes, but at a low level. The documents that are put out by research
        ethics boards and organisations like BERA (2011), they're confined
        and they're low level. They simply don't deal with ideas around
        how do you create opportunities for people to explore new ideas
        and so on. They come from a kind of defective stance. I start from
        a *salutogenic* position, that healthy is normal. So ethical guide-
        lines are useful and valuable, but a lot of them are mistaken in
        terms of where we are with new forms of research. For example,
        in practice-based research you value people, you celebrate them,
        and you mention their names: if you go for anonymity you take
        that away.

JS: Is there anything that you're thinking that you wanted to say but
        didn't?

JM: I find it difficult to talk about myself in these terms. I don't see
        myself as a researcher, I don't see myself as a higher education

person. I constantly feel a bit of a fraud, a bit of an imposter. Somebody said they had heard another colleague saying 'Oh, Jean is easy, she doesn't make judgements'. They were saying you don't have to be very clever to get into books. I take that as a huge compliment.

JS: But your own self-positioning is, as you say, part of what liberates other people with whom you work, because you are not positioning yourself as floating on high above them, happily. It won't stop myself or others, as it were, 'floating' you.

JM: Yes: sometimes you are positioned as you wouldn't chose to be. Other people like to do that and, in a sense, you owe them a responsibility. Like the South African teachers: they insisted on calling me 'Prof', which I didn't like, but that serves a purpose for them, and it honours them. So if they choose to have me as their Prof, and I serve a useful function there, well, that's alright – but I wouldn't choose to do it.

To Build Relationships: A Conversation with Jacqui Akhurst, Rhodes University, Grahamstown, South Africa

JS: Would you like to tell me a little about your own research and how and why you came to be doing it?

JA: I'd like to refer to two different strands of research. One project that went relatively well, and another project that's been more tricky. The first project was with allied health professionals and their continuing professional development as occupational therapists, physiotherapists, social workers, dietitians, and psychologists in the UK. The second project was with psychology students who do community-based work placements in South Africa. My motivation for getting involved in both is an interest in the way in which research can underpin practice, and how research and practice intersect. It's also about communities, groups of people doing some sort of work together, in order to enhance the way in which they work or the way in which they think and learn. Underpinning both is the idea of action research and research itself. My preference is for research that's open-ended, that follows the process of whomever I'm working with – so I never know what the end point is going to be, or how it's going to evolve.

JS: Do you want to say what 'research' in that context means to you, and what 'practice' means?

JA: It's a really challenging question, because I think we often use words quite loosely. I guess both terms imply deeper reflection on what one does day-to-day. From a research perspective, that means gathering evidence, gathering data, and making more explicit what might be implicit in day-to-day practice. My sense is that research gathers the evidence, or gathers accounts if you like, of day-to-day practices. Research and practice aren't easily separable, and I'm sure that's the action research coming through.

JS: There is a genre called 'action learning'. People reflect on their practice and learn from and develop as a result of their broadly reflective practitioner models of action learning. What more is there for action learning to be action *research*, for you?

JA: In action learning there's cyclic processes, but I don't think that evidence of what changes, or how it changes, is necessarily captured in those processes. There's a virtue in doing that sort of learning, but it doesn't capture what it is that makes the difference, or how it makes the difference, or accounts of that.

JS: You've said the 'how?' and the evidence. You haven't mentioned that it must be critical, it must be theorised, it must answer 'why?'

JA: There will always be a 'why?' before the 'how?', which would be formulated as a research question. Because I'm a grounded theory type of researcher, I go for the 'how?' first of all, and then go back to the 'why?' later. The theorising comes later, and the theorising might be fresh theorising from what's emerged, influenced by former exposure to theory. It's a sort of a bottom-up grounded theory approach.

JS: You've described the practice of occupational therapists, physi-otherapists, community psychologists, and students of community psychology. You've described their practice as your research, but you've not described *your* practice.

JA: That's true. My research and my practice is to build relationships and to work with people, and the degree to which they become involved as co-researchers will vary. One of the things I've become more aware of latterly is who owns the research? That is a thorny question, because I feel as if it's my research in that I might write and prompt it, I might gather the data and do the leg work, but it's also *our* research, and it needs to have various degrees of own-ership, and that will vary from project to project.

JS: For many of the people you're describing, you are also an authority figure – you are their tutor or their assessor or their supervisor. Research is something that you are implicated in, which brings joys and opportunities, but also risks and –

JA: challenges, in relation to the power dynamics. I guess some of it is my own evolution from a traditional psychology training, which was about this illusion of objectivity. I've become more aware that there is no such thing. I influence whatever the interaction is: there are hidden power dynamics that need to be made clearer and talked about. Thinking about the first project, I was contracted to be a research evaluator of a mentoring project in the UK. It was an edu-cational project on continuing professional development through mentoring, and I was contracted to be the evaluator of the pro-ject. There was a concern about myself as an outsider coming in to observe or evaluate what was going on. What I needed to do initially was to talk about how the action research would work – and that I wasn't coming in as an 'objective' outsider. A lot of these people were familiar with that form of research, and having that conversation right at the outset, and then working with the group, was incredibly beneficial. It fed in to the sense that I wasn't sitting as some sort of a spectator. We were going to work together – reducing the power dynamics in that way. We negotiated – as you have done – the way in which the data would appear, what would be included. Everybody was involved, although the work was done by me in terms of the writing (Akhurst and Lawson 2013). The second project is in a rural setting in South Africa (Akhurst and Mitchell 2012). The people that we're working with in this setting are that much less empowered. The power dynamics are so much greater because of the differences in our levels of education, the language differences, and the resource differences. Going into that community as a researcher is so more fraught that going into a community of empowered professionals. In a much less resourced environment, people are wanting to be involved in the research because they're hoping that it will earn them some money, or contribute to their day-to-day life. So the idea of beneficence, who benefits from the research, becomes much clearer in such a contrasting setting. At the broader systemic level, there's no doubt that in parts of South Africa, people have been exposed to researchers who come swanning in, we do the research and then we disappear. My colleague has been involved in this community for twenty years, so she's built up a sense that her work has benefitted the community, because in parallel to the research she was doing, they raised money for a pre-school which then got built. In this project, we've used what are called 'change laboratories' or developmental work research. It involves running focus groups, in this case about HIV/AIDS and people's awareness of that, and how one can do HIV/AIDS education better. We use cyclical processes of going in, getting people to talk in particular ways, going back with the data and challenging it – and trying to go to a deeper level. There's been this big HIV/AIDS education campaign in South Africa around the ABCs – A is abstinence from sex, B is be faithful to your partner, and C is if you can't do A or B use a condom. Initially in the research, people will spout out the sort of party line about the ABCs, and it's around how one can move from what they think we want to hear, to why is it that in this valley there is still a high incidence of HIV/AIDS – getting to a more honest and open conversation. And to do that in ways that they trust that, as researchers, this is going to be of benefit to them, so the research process itself is educative.

JS: Harry Daniels writes about the difference in schools between children who paint what they see, and children who paint what the teacher sees (Daniels 2001, p. 170). It's the issue about trying to work out what the powerful person wants to hear, and overcoming that. Presumably that's true also where you are researching with your students: they are thinking 'She is the person who will mark my dissertation: what should I be saying?'

JA: It's a challenging question. Interesting you mention Harry Daniels, because Harry's been with us into this particular community, and that was some of the stuff we were grappling with, with Harry and the students. How do I know that what we're generating in the developmental work research is authentically helpful for the people? It's about what are the effects of the research on people's behaviour, and I guess that that's where this research has moved to as we've had a look at what people report on as behaviour changes as a result of having been involved in the developmental work research. We've seen some sort of developmental progress in the nature of the discussions, and the nature of the conversations, but it's a tricky question to answer.

JS: The temptation of power, including intellectual power in an academic context, is that things look cleaner, neater, tidier, and you therefore have increasing confidence that you are right. For me the test is surprise. If I find things out that I'm not expecting to find out, that's a sign that people are not saying what they think I want to hear. In all educational contexts, surprise for me is the sign that real learning is happening (Stern 2013c).

JA: It's like action research: you can never judge what will emerge in the interactions, as you go forward, and those are often unintended. That's certainly been my experience of accompanying my students on these community-based placements. What the students report is often different from what I expected, and from what they expected. The learning is often through the tough stuff – the toughness of being in a group together in a tricky situation – that's when the learning can be most powerful, but it's not comfortable.

JS: The pictures of research in textbooks make the researcher, as it were, a figment, floating around, just getting permissions and asking neutral questions, with no personality. What are the personal issues in the sort of research that you've been talking about?

JA: In a very impoverished context, one of the real challenges is are you living in the community, or do you go and live up the hill in a more expensive place? If you stay in the community, this is really valued because it's saying 'I want to live alongside you, I'm willing to live in the privations of the lack of electricity and running water'. It indicates a sense of solidarity. But it is difficult being able to have privacy. If you live out of the community, then there're these enormous ethical challenges: 'I have so much and these people have so little'. What do I do about the person who says 'No, we can't do this research today because you need to take this 4x4 and take us to hospital'? And then the challenges of conflicts within the group, how one copes with other members of the group who are struggling with the privations. We can't be researchers separate from the research, and there is a need for us to write about these tricky things rather than to write the sanitised version of the research. I believe that taking my students into those settings, I want to be with them so that we can talk about the difficulties, so that those interpersonal discussions and articulations of the difficulties become the meat if you like, the data that I'm interested in. It's how we develop that in ways that are different from any sanitised version of research.

JS: I've got the list of possible virtues or character strengths but also their absences or their opposites, or their exaggeration. We've talked about some of these already – about trust, and about persistence, and issues of intimacy. Are there any of these words that you feel are important for research, or temptations, or risks?

JA: I think I've implied quite a number of the strengths. The one that's standing out for me right now is this thing of bravery and the absence of fright or chicken-littleism. I think that whole thing about courage is inherent in some of this research that we've been talking about. But being frightened and being able to talk about that, and being able to confront one's fears, that's really important.

So I don't necessarily see that as a disorder of courage. I see that as an important measuring stick, being able to talk about what's provoking anxiety.

JS: Perhaps a limit on foolhardiness – the exaggeration of courage.

JA: Other things that stand out to me include creativity, curiosity and interest. Critical thinking is such a tricky concept – I prefer the reflective, because reflexivity will bring in criticality and it's also a very layered thing.

JS: You're nervous of what's called critical thinking. Is that also related to your grounded theory and other aspects of your work – that you don't wish yourself or don't wish other people to rush judgement? Yet as a researcher you are still making judgements, and as an academic you are assessing students – you are making judgements. But you have almost put brackets round it.

JA: I have, yes, but I am aware that one has to make judgements at times in various different ways, but I'm not seeing it necessarily as always a strength. The other strength that pops out is this thing of 'perspective', because it links to one's professional training around trying to suspend judgement at least for a while. Being aware that we're drawn always towards judgement, but trying to suspend that – trying to find ways of being able to take different perspectives – is one of the strengths one can bring to open-endedness, rather than closing down. I'm interested in truthfulness and care, care for self and care for others so that they stay intact.

JS: The ethics of care, some people say this works well in hierarchical relationships: parents caring for children, teachers caring for their students, doctors caring for their patients. There is almost an in-built hierarchy. It's interesting in the professions you talk about, occupational therapy and psychology, the caring itself is an act of power, isn't it?

JA: Yes, to some extent. The whole power dynamic is a challenge, because I would definitely see care also as an egalitarian thing: I wouldn't see it only as a paternalistic or maternalistic. A student on our community psychology course said 'You speak about the pedagogy of the oppressed: what about the pedagogy of the

oppressor – how are we going to work with the oppressor, how
are we going to care about and influence the oppressor?' That
led to some provocative but interesting conversations. I guess the
other word that I wanted to question, the one that worries me, is
magnanimity. I wondered what you were meaning by that?

JS: Magnanimity came from Aristotle. Aristotle described an ethic of
leadership, and he says that if you have other leadership qualities,
good leaders are those who support the led; bad leaders – tyrants
– are those who act for themselves, and get other people to act for
them. The crown of the leadership virtues is therefore magnanimity (Aristotle 1976, pp. 153–158): it means 'great souled' in Greek,
or 'big hearted'. It means you are above the fray, you are relaxed
in the face of things.

JA: How is that different to generosity?

JS: You can be generous in all sorts of situations: I think you can only
be magnanimous –

JA: if you're in a position of power. The last virtue that pops out to me
is 'spirituality'. You asked early on what underpins or motivates my
research, and I guess there is an element of my own spirituality,
which is something about the bigger purpose of why we're here
and why we're doing what we're doing. I don't really want to say
more about it other than that it is an important element for me.

Conclusion

The examples of research given here are concerned with justice, so it seems
fair to say that this research is not only 'just' a form of work, but also a form
of *just* work'. Professing, as a researching professor and as a professional, is
central to these accounts. The challenges are huge, and yet they are faced with
remarkable energy, enthusiasm and spirit, and the work of research is a way
of building relationships. Research as a way of living, of working, in order
to influence people and social and political structures: this is promoted by

both researchers talking here. Whether in the UK, Qatar or South Africa, the research involves professionals who are researching, a kind of 'activist' research (Stern 2015a), influencing society in and through professional practice. For Jean McNiff, research blends into the rest of life, should that life be creative and not mundane and repetitive. Changing oneself and changing relationships, this way of living as a researcher puts an emphasis on 'effectively sharing' the insights or knowledge gained through research. In the examples given, the sharing is with professionals, teachers and managers. That is perhaps one of the reasons that the work does not look so obviously like 'research'. The genre of writing that is done for an academic audience is that which is taken to be research. But writing for professionals, even if it is insightful writing based on a process of investigation, is more rarely recognised as research. Yet the work to help people understand that they have power is certainly an educative task and – incidentally – Jean McNiff does have publications that are recognised as 'research' by the UK's national research audit (<http://www.ref.ac.uk>). The relationships described in this conversation are primarily with professionals who are completing degrees. This is also true of some of the relationships described by Jacqui Akhurst. But later in the conversation, the relationships described are all the more complex, as they involve a set of researchers and professionals at different stages of their careers, but also members of a community without any of the professional qualifications or comparative wealth of the researchers. The influence of the research on the community becomes all the more significant in those circumstances.

For both conversationalists, research and professional practice intermingle – even more than research intermingles with 'life' (including life beyond professional practice). What research adds, for Jacqui, is a process of reflection and – later in the process – of theorising. Letting theories emerge towards the end of a process of research is characteristic of much of practitioner research and action research, and is formalised in the methodology known as *grounded theory* (Glaser and Strauss 1965, 1967, Strauss and Corbin 1990). The delay in theorising is linked to the determination to suspend judgement as a researcher. This self-restraint is also recognisable in the determination to direct the research work as much to professionals and other community members as to academic colleagues. Restraint and engagement characterise the conversations in the following chapter, too.

Taking Time: Prudence and Pacing

Introduction

We live our lives in time. As the poet Larkin says, 'Where can we live but days?' (Larkin 1988, p. 67). My relationship with myself is spread out in time – I reflect on myself in the past and think of how I will be in the future. The thoughtful, reflective, aspects of research therefore seem to be of immense personal value. This may be an almost therapeutic value, and it may be of value in our lives and the lives of other people, as described in Chapters 5 and 6 (and throughout this book). It is the sense of time and timing that is the theme brought out in the following two conversations (as also in Chapter 10). Mention research to any group of academics, and the most common response will be 'we don't have enough time for it' (Stern 2014b, pp. 12–13). But it is not that kind of time that is being discussed here. Instead, it is finding the right time to research, the right time to think, the right time to address problems or move on – whether these timings are short-term (when to talk, when to be quiet in a conversation) or longer-term (when should traumas in previous generations be addressed in this generation).

We Intervene Too Soon: A Conversation with Shanaaz
Hoosain, North-West University, Wellington, South Africa

JS: Would you like to tell me about your research, and how and why
        you came to be doing it?
SH: I'm a social worker, and I think that my research has always been
        practice-driven (Hoosain 2007). I developed an interest in my
        undergraduate days, but it was a while before I did my postgradu-
        ate studies. The research project that I'll be talking about is my
        recently completed PhD on intergenerational trauma (Hoosain
        2013). There was a personal interest in the topic, as well as edu-
        cational. Growing up in South Africa under apartheid, my par-
        ents were born just before apartheid and I have much younger
        siblings who are the post-apartheid generation. Being a social
        worker I was interested in hearing my mum and dad's stories,
        comparing them with my own and my sisters' stories – the 'born
        free' generation. I spent seven years in the UK and did my master's
        in play therapy there, but returned to South Africa and took up
        an academic position. With an academic position you have to do
        your PhD. So I ended up in my current position, as a lecturer for
        North-West University (<http://www.nwu.ac.za>). Values around
        social justice have been such a part of my life, so that's why I went
        down the social work route, and then very practice-driven. Social
        work research is practice-driven, but it also has to influence your
        practice.
JS: I can see the route to social work, being politically engaged. What
        was the thing that tipped you into being interested in research?
SH: What took me into research was the idea that in social work, we
        intervene too soon, without really enquiring. And the way research
        has been done, particularly in South Africa: research hasn't really
        included the voices of people. There is a growing body of indig-
        enous knowledge and voices and marginalised groups, but that's
        only growing. Traditionally our research has been Eurocentric:
        we haven't had the input of local voices, hearing things from their

side. That is what led me into the research, wanting to work and research *with* people rather than *on* people. Because I'd spent years working with communities as a social worker, I also realised that there were some gaps in the way we were working with communities. Some of the social problems that were being experienced were not really understood. If we researched some of these things, we could have a better understanding, and include the voices of the people that our research is intended for.

JS: Fascinating: both the idea that research stops you intervening too soon, or is a pause before intervening, a reflective pause – a thinking before you intervene – and the sense of research voicing people. If you intervene too quickly and too definitely, you haven't thought about what the issues might be, you are not listening to the person. So research re-casts the social worker as someone who thinks first and who listens. Is that a fair?

SH: Yes.

JS: You were not going away from social work, but thinking about the social work process in becoming a researcher.

SH: Yes. When we try to understand, and include those voices that have previously not been heard, we need to sometimes take a step back. We've used models based on research from abroad, and not research undertaken with people in South Africa.

JS: The type of research that you feel is needed, is less unequal in its power relations?

SH: Yes. That is why I was orientated towards a more participatory type of research which involves people. To be sensitive: 'This is a group of vulnerable people that I will be working with'. Research offered me an opportunity to pause, before I intervened. It gives social work that opportunity to really listen, and then intervene, rather than just intervene without thinking. I had to present to the social work department my proposal. There seems to be this idea in social work research that you have to do intervention research. My research was more exploratory: I wanted that pause before we intervened, I wanted to understand what people were saying. I had to justify why I was doing exploratory research and not intervention research. That was one of the first obstacles I encountered.

JS: Could you describe a project that illustrates how you go about research?

SH: I found myself doing research with my PhD, leaning towards participatory research. We've received funding from our national research fund here in South Africa, looking at families and services and service deliveries towards families, looking at strengthening families. The families will decide on what their needs are, and we will look at what the government says in comparison to what families say. We're looking at rural families, whose needs often are marginalised. Research at the university, the group that we fall under, is called 'community psycho-social research'. Some are saying, 'That's not the kind of research we do'. Participatory research sometimes doesn't fit within traditional academic ideas of research. It's been challenging.

JS: Is that because it's not the norm, because it's participatory, or because it's more democratic or communal?

SH: The culture of the university is conservative. On the one hand, in South Africa universities are obligated to do research which is relevant, which involves communities. Yet you have the institutional traditional ways of thinking: 'We do research *on* communities, we don't do it *with* them'. It's starting to cause heated debates. This is where the values of the researcher come in, even in terms of your choice of research topic and the way in which you go about your research. I can focus on individual elements within a family, but for me, I try to equal the power imbalance. When I'm really listening to them, then I'm always looking at the collective as well as the individual. We are interviewing whole families. How do we know whose voice represents the family? Are we going to listen to a male voice, are we going to listen to a female voice, or will the child's view of what's going on mean just as much? We decided we're going to let the families decide who is a part of that family. We're going to go with the family's definition of who is part of the family and who needs to have a say. We are going to try to include the children and have a way in which we can hear what they say. The other research that I'm involved in is a national research project looking at participation in higher education, and how students and educators can equally participate in university. I think the conservative university that I work at, we don't really do research on our own practice, so I'm having to pull out all the stops in terms of evidence to justify why I'm doing the research. To get through the ethics board, I can't do research with my own students. I can reflect on my own teaching but my students will not be participants. So I'm having to make alternative plans.

JS: Those are all research challenges. Are there other challenges? I know we corresponded about the writing challenge.

SH: Yes, my own challenges in writing and publishing and thinking about whether my findings are significant. With my students, what I see highlights my own experiences of struggling to write. I see the inequality in our education system in South Africa even in my own writing, and with my students. My students come from different backgrounds and I can see the differences as they write. I find that a particular challenge as an academic because I want to help and I don't know how much I'm helping. Writing can be cathartic and that was the PhD journey for me. I know it's going to sound strange but I questioned: did I use my participants for my own purposes? I felt uncomfortable, but I felt that it had been my way of working through some of the really difficult issues that I struggled with as the social worker, as an academic and as a black South African woman. I found my way through the research process was a rewarding experience for me, despite the challenges.

JS: You talked about your own research within the institution. What's the relationship between the research you do and the teaching you do?

SH: As I've been writing this proposal as part of this national project where we look at research and our teaching, I've started to realise the really close link between the two. The fact that I've started to think about these things, has started to change the way I think about teaching. I have this book by bell hooks, *Teaching*

to Transgress (hooks 1994), and it's caused me to go and look at
those things again. I didn't make the connection before. I'm starting to realise the real importance of doing educational research,
researching my own teaching and my own practice.

JS: You talked about social workers typically intervening too quickly
          and not listening. Is that also true of teachers: they give stuff out
          rather than pausing and listening and hearing the voices? Is it
          making your teaching more like your research, and perhaps even
          like your social work, that it is more paused and many voiced –
          you listen for the voices?

SH: Yes. I've just taught a module. It was a diverse group of social work
          students doing their master's degrees and I was looking at anti-
          oppressive practice. We had students from all backgrounds, and
          I think I was expecting them to happily engage in the topic, and
          they were really reluctant to address issues around race. They were
          happy to talk about gender and class, but the issues around race
          were avoided. I stopped and thought 'But Shanaaz, you are ready
          and you are happily engaging, but they are not there'. I realised
          that my expectations of the students were not realistic. They were
          on a journey and they needed to trust each other first. I needed to
          create an environment within the class that made it okay to talk
          about sensitive issues. By taking a step back and pausing, I was
          able to do that, and not just rush ahead. I had thrown them in
          the deep end, but then I used a more gentle approach with them.
          That is what happened within the class: once there were points
          of connection, the students were willing to engage and talk about
          some difficult issues for them.

JS: When we were corresponding we talked about vulnerability as a
          researcher. I was interested because of your position in a univer-
          sity – as a newer researcher – and because you are a black South
          African in a predominantly conservative white university, but also
          because of your vulnerability in the research process.

SH: Yes. When I had attended the conference (*Value and Virtue
          in Practice-Based Research*, York St John University, June 2015
          <http://www.yorksj.ac.uk/value&virtue>; and Hoosain 2015), it

started to dawn on me. When you spoke about being courageous, and the strengths and the virtues, it started to echo.

JS: Lynne Gabriel, in these conversations, said that as a counsellor she has a supervisor who cares, but as a researcher, as an academic, she doesn't have that. Is that an issue for you?

SH: Now that you mention it, yes! I decided to have external supervision. He's a psychologist and he's an academic as well. I've been seeing him for a while. I knew how important he was going to be because I knew the nature of my research is very personal and there were some traumatic stories. I could not have done it without him because I had a space in which I could talk about how the research was affecting me. Often, I would want to go down the social activist route, because I'd get so angry or so sad at some of the stories that I'd heard. The support that he gave me, enabled me to experience that but still be the researcher. Maybe that was about still being myself, and not lose part of myself either in over-identifying with the story, or become so involved with the stories that I became stuck.

JS: Have you got that list of virtue words and their opposites that I sent? We've talked about a number of these, including courage. Are there words that you haven't mentioned?

SH: Appreciation of beauty/excellence, and gratitude. That resonates, now, because I was a part of that story: I could give a voice to the story that needed to be heard. I'm reminded of Foucault's work around subjugated knowledge (Foucault 1988, pp. 81–82): bringing stories to life, that had been subjugated. Bringing to life the counter-stories, the stories that don't usually form part of mainstream. I have an appreciation of the beauty of that story – being able to listen and give someone the opportunity to tell their story, as a researcher I have such an immense appreciation of that opportunity. I have a duty to tell some of those stories.

JS: Are there other strengths or virtues, or ones that you try to avoid or see as temptations?

SH: The other ones that are challenging are judgement/critical thinking. Sometimes, I think that I went in with this idea of 'I know this community: this is the community I grew up in, this is the working class community'. Then I discovered how judgemental I can be. I'm a social worker, one of the values is being non-judgemental, but I found myself getting irritated: I made judgements, I made assumptions. For example, a lot of them don't work in that area because of the high unemployment rate, and so I assumed they would naturally be available for me to interview. I made judgements about the families. That highlighted my own privilege. I identify as this black South African woman, but there are points where my education gives me privilege, and I do make judgements and pre-judge people.

JS: Perhaps what you are describing as not jumping to judgement, that pausing, is also an example of humility or modesty, as a strength. It sounds like you have the same issue as a teacher of students, that you try to avoid jumping to judgement, you try to listen to what they are saying and not assume they are the same.

SH: Yes, but then it brings you to this: that you have to be truthful with yourself. I've got to be this researcher: I have to be true to me, and I also have to be truthful about the process. That includes my own shortcomings, my judgements and assumptions, my internal beliefs. The process needed to be truthful for me.

JS: Is that also related to you as social activist and social worker, wishing not to give that up to do research, but to do research in a way that extends and develops that very practised life?

SH: Yes, yes. And that is why the conference unlocked some of the writing in me. I started to look at the values and it somehow started to shift me from that place of feeling stuck: *this* is why I did the research. By the end of my PhD, I think that I'd lost the reasons for and the purpose behind the research.

JS: Are there things that you've thought I would ask about, or you thought you would like to talk about that I haven't given you a chance to talk about?

SH: No, other than saying that by looking at that list, and what you had said about the list of virtues being characteristics of people, I think that definitely started the process for me, it's definitely helped in my process as an emerging researcher. It's started to give me some direction and brings together the different projects that I'm involved in. Thank you: it's been helpful for me to find the words.

Learning to Live With Difference: A Conversation with Sr Agnes Wilkins, Stanbrook Abbey, Wass, England

JS: Do you want to tell me a little about your research and how you came to be doing that?

SA: I'd just done a Catholic theology degree, and I went to a conference on monastic inter-religious dialogue. For the first time, it was on Islam. It was extremely challenging. We had two Muslims there, and most of the people present hadn't a clue what Islam was about. We just sat there, passive, while the Muslims seemed to be telling us how things were, or how things ought to be, in a fairly dogmatic way. We simply were too polite to respond. This was a challenging situation. I felt there was a lot of ignorance among Christians, Catholics, monastics. So I wanted to use my theology degree to address that challenge. It was just before 9/11, and that changed the world as regard to Christianity and Islam. It made this dialogue all the more urgent. My study of Catholic doctrine had given me a certain confidence in my own position, which was challenged by Islam so confidently opposing that position. We don't know what to say: we don't have the vocabulary, and we don't mix with Muslims enough. I'd had Muslims in my family, I knew Muslims also before I entered the monastery – some of them I had good friendships with – so I felt it as a sort of call that I had to respond to.

JS: That's an interesting way to get into research, to want to do the research because of what you described as a failure of effective dialogue. Do you have a sense of what makes you so curious in that sense, so wanting to find out, wanting to do it through research?

SA: When you're living the monastic life, it's more a response to what God is asking, to a sort of inner call. I suppose I could say 'Well, I'll pray about it', and that could be enough. But God's given us minds as well. Despite the disadvantages, I think the monastic life probably gives a depth and a special character to research that you might not get in a more secular institution.

JS: So could you tell us a little about your current research?

SA: I'm at a difficult point at the moment. I started doing the life of two converts. Jean Mohammed Abd-el-Jalil and Hassan Dehqani-Tafti converted from Islam to Christianity. I studied how they looked back on Islam. I've studied their lives and studied what they've written. I'm doing my own dialogue. It's the dialogue that is really the important thing, so it's not about conversion as such, but only conversion as a means of exploring how a Christian who had been a Muslim could explain Islam to a Christian more easily and give you insights that you couldn't get as an outsider. Abd-el-Jalil, for instance, was an intellectual person, and by no means attracted to Christianity – quite the opposite, he studied Christianity in order to refute it. This fascinated me. How he could make that leap.

JS: Is there a sense of the two people you have studied, who have been both Muslims and Christians, being examples of people who are in dialogue with themselves? I was interested what you meant by a dialogue with yourself.

SA: I suppose I was an outsider to Islam before, and when you get a convert you get the outsider and the insider issue. I thought when I began that I couldn't get inside Islam at all. I could only study it from the outside, as a Christian. But then I discovered that I could to a certain point. When I came to studying the crucifixion, I tried to think to myself what it would be like if this had not happened. Supposing the Muslims were right? I tried to think myself into the Muslim position, and had to have a dialogue with myself from there. Some people, if their faith wasn't strong enough, they might go across and think 'Oh, maybe they were right after all, perhaps

I'll be a Muslim'. You can only bracket it for a little while. I think you have to have deep faith. If it's not, it can easily be lost in trying to dialogue.

JS: The ability to be entirely neutral and bracket out everything and treat it as 'over there', and of no significance: you can't do it entirely. You have to be there as a person, if you're going to understand – which does involve some risk to yourself, your feelings, your beliefs. That will need quite a lot of courage. Do you sense that need for courage to do the sort of research you're doing?

SA: Oh absolutely, yes. Your faith is being deepened, but I've got to get even deeper as well. There's something very deep in everybody, often below the level of consciousness. It's been called *le point vierge* in al-Hallaj and Thomas Merton (1966) and Louis Massignon (1994), a something deeper than what we think and believe on the surface. It is God really being there in our inner-most being. We call it conscience, but it can be called other things. Dialogue makes one go down to that deep level and enables you to have compassion for all people.

JS: There are some researchers who think they have all the answers but who think everyone else in the world is wrong.

SA: Yes. I think you've got to have some intellectual humility as well. In the end Truth with a capital 'T' is much bigger than anybody or any particular position that you're coming from. What we *don't* know is so vast. I don't think you can get anywhere without that basic humility.

JS: I'm interested in what you mean by dialogue itself. What makes something a dialogue?

SA: Because of my lifestyle, I can't go out there. So all my dialogue is really churning things round in my head. I did speak to a Muslim in a letter. I mentioned something Kenneth Cragg had said about the incarnation (Cragg 1999, p. 137): surely if God wants to become man he can do? But this was anathema as far as the Muslim I was dialoguing with was concerned. He was not prepared to talk about it. I think perhaps if we'd met on a personal level it might have been quite different. I think people think I'm a bit formidable, this nun living this weird life in a monastery, not meeting people. But meeting me, they find I'm just as human as anybody else. They don't get that chance when it's just what you write.

JS: So what makes a conversation a dialogue rather than just two people at the same, talking alternately?

SA: I suppose it's a deeper listening. You've got to try and listen, or put yourself in their position. What are they saying? Where are they coming from? What does it mean to them? I think it's a basic respect for something you don't understand, a respect for the human person, the innate spirituality of that person, whether they realise they're spiritual or not. It's learning to live with the difference. Try not to impose your own opinion on people. Resist the temptation to try and convert them to your point of view. Until fairly recently there was a strict application of the Catholic doctrine of 'no salvation outside the church', and a Muslim position which believed 'all these infidels are condemned so they must become Muslims'; it's an exclusivist position on both sides. But we don't see things quite like that anymore: it's the individual person's conscience that matters, and they're alone with God. Whether they have any religious beliefs or not, they've still got a conscience and they still know innately what's right and what's wrong. It's more important than ever now. Through the internet and migration there's so much more intermingling. It's a global village. I suppose that is what dialogue is about: how do we live together peacefully?

JS: So the research is partly finding out about the possibility of dialogue across boundaries, and is also itself an example of dialogue.

SA: Yes. For myself it would have to be mainly through writing. I don't have the chance to go round many conferences and talking to people, so it's in writing, and I feed it into my monastic life and into prayer.

JS: I sent you a list of these character strengths. You've talked about courage, humility, and the importance of truth or truthfulness. Are there other words on the list that you think are either strengths or temptations or risks in what you do?

SA: I would say I've got a fair lot of the first two – creativity and curiosity or interest. You spoke about this 'enstasy' in your other paper. Comfortable in solitude, is that what you mean?

JS: Yes: the ability to be within oneself comfortably, as opposed to ecstasy which is to go outside of yourself, to leap beyond yourself.

SA: Solitude and loneliness can be two different things. I am comfortable in solitude, but there's a lot of loneliness as well – in the fact that I am alone doing this research. But I think the solitude of the monastic life makes that bearable because you can combine them.

JS: A number of people find research a lonely business.

SA: I think of its nature it has to be, because only you know what you are doing, and you're forging a pathway, you're not treading where someone else has been.

JS: One of the cures for loneliness, I think, is a structure in which solitude is respected and promoted.

SA: Yes, I suppose some people out there don't have that. This might be in a marriage situation even, and your family's not interested in what you are doing.

JS: Virginia Woolf talked about women lacking a 'room of their own' (Woolf 2014): once women had a room of their own, they could create and write novels the same as men could. That ability to have a protected space.

SA: I suppose like having one's monastic cell. No-one goes in there, I've got my books, and I just have to burrow away. Interesting how you've got forgiveness and mercy, humility and modesty.

JS: A lot of people would see research and think it quite a self-promoting thing, and yet it's humility that allows you to do the research.

SA: Yes. I think that the more you know, the more humble it should make you, the more you know, the more you realise you don't know. This appreciation of beauty, excellence and gratitude, that's interesting. And you've got spirituality down there at the bottom. I thought about prudence. I don't think recklessness is the opposite of prudence, because a martyr can be prudent. You give your life away rather than keep if for yourself, this is a prudent thing

to do in that situation. It doesn't mean holding back, it's a matter
of making a judgement.

JS: Would you say prudence in your sense is something that you need
        in research? What is prudence, then?

SA: I suppose I think of it in terms of moderation, making a right
        judgement. But that right judgement can be a big leap. You might
        think of those people in Syria. Is it prudent to stay at home, or to
        emigrate? It's probably quite a reckless thing to emigrate, taking
        all my family with a lot of risks, but it's probably the prudent thing
        to do. So the virtue of prudence will probably make them take
        the big risk.

JS: Translating that into your own research, I suppose you could say
        you've done that. You could have avoided all the hassle and the
        challenge of these things, as it were staying at home intellectually,
        but you weren't prepared to do that.

SA: Yes. When I was younger in the community, I was not allowed
        to do this research, because of the danger of going overboard. It
        was not the prudent thing to do according to my superiors. But
        now it's judged that I've got enough prudence in myself to be
        able to make right judgements, I suppose. I don't think it is pru-
        dent for a superior to let a very young person in a monastic life,
        before you're deeply rooted in the monastic life and in faith, to
        research as I am doing. Because when you start the monastic life,
        it's like beginning all over again. You go into a learning process
        again. And it's not really prudent to plunge into another religious
        system before you are fully integrated in the life that you're living.
        I think I'm probably beginning rather later in life – in a way I wish
        I were younger and had a better memory. But on the other hand
        there's more spiritual depth. I've lived the monastic life now and
        the spirituality is much deeper than when you first begin. Despite
        the disadvantages, I've got those advantages as well.

JS: Are there any things that you thought I would be asking you
        about?

SA: If you are in research for several years, a lot can happen in your
        life. There are times when you feel like giving up, times when you

feel like you're treading through treacle. What kind of personal characteristics are needed to get through the dark night, as it were?

JS: What is it that you need at those stages?

SA: I think you need encouragement from outside. I have a dialogue with my supervisor. She's Jewish, and that's become a strength. It's really important to have some support from your supervisor, and also from your community. When you begin, you think why on earth do you need all this support and help and all these review meetings, can't you just get on with it? You soon find out that you do need all of those things: you realise that there is a team around you, supporting you. It doesn't take away the struggle, but somehow it can come down to 'Well, I don't want to let these people down, that they've been so good'. They believe I can do it, and when people believe in you, when you don't believe in yourself, it can help enormously and give you an incentive.

JS: Perhaps it is a sign that it's real research if it's troubling and difficult and thorny, a sign that you're probably doing proper research and not just routine tasks.

SA: It just needs sheer grit and determination sometimes. It's like walking a long rough path, a very lonely path sometimes. It tests your inner resources to the utmost, so it's a spiritual journey as well as a research journey, because one gets drawn into one's spiritual life. 'What am I doing this for?'

JS: I suppose it's also the virtue of persistence. Well, thank you so much.

Conclusion

The social-activist justice-driven approach of Shanaaz Hoosain is distinctive, I think, in describing the central role of *research as pause*. Social workers may intervene too soon, and so may teachers and other professionals who work with people for whom they have a caring relationship. To pause, to think, not as a way to avoid people, but precisely in order to be able to listen to people. I have argued elsewhere (Stern 2014b) that universities should not refer to time dedicated to research as 'research leave' or as a 'sabbatical' (like the 'sabbath', a day of rest), as both imply research as a leisure activity – and no-one would refer to time dedicated to teaching as 'teaching leave' or as a 'sabbatical'. Yet what Shanaaz Hoosain says about pausing brings us back into that territory. After all, the original use of 'sabbath' in Jewish and Christian traditions was not simply about resting: it was about *contemplating*. And the original meaning of 'holiday' was a 'holy' day, again, a time for contemplation and prayer. What I find particularly striking about the conversation on this issue is how pausing should be central to professional practice in social work, and to research when that is exploratory rather than interventionist, and to research that is intended to be participatory and 'with' rather than 'on' people. Research, teaching, and social work are all linked, with bell hooks as an important reference point. One of hooks' most shocking accounts is of how 'racial integration' worsened education for her:

> School changed utterly with racial integration. Gone was the messianic zeal to trans- form our minds and beings that had characterized teachers and their pedagogical practices in our all-black schools. Knowledge was suddenly about information only. It had no relation to how one lived, behaved. It was no longer connected to antiracist struggle. Bussed to White schools, we soon learned that obedience, and not a zeal- ous will to learn, was what was expected of us. Too much eagerness to learn could easily be seen as a threat to white authority. ... The classroom was no longer a place of pleasure or ecstasy. ... That shift ... taught me the difference between education as the practice of freedom and education that merely strives to reinforce domination. (Hooks 1994, pp. 3–4)

Open-ended participatory learning – or research – is, for hooks, a form of 'transgression', and the transgressive character of such work is well illus- trated by Shanaaz Hoosain's account of her work in a nominally integrated post-Apartheid university that she describes as predominantly 'white' and 'conservative'. But her account is far from simply being a criticism of structures external to her. She describes her own need to pause as a social worker, her need to pause as a teacher until her students were ready to talk about anti-oppressive practice, and her need to pause as a researcher to allow herself to come to understand situations rather than immediately jumping in to social activism – or jumping to judgement.

Avoiding jumping to judgement and taking care to wait until the time is right: this is also characteristic of Sr Agnes Wilkins' account of her research. Research started from an awareness of failed inter-religious dialogue, and a need to be in dialogue with oneself. Humility and courage are both needed, in the face of dogmatic disagreements. Understanding others requires a risk of being uprooted. So prudence, the ability to make right judgements – including risky judgements – is central. Taking time to think what is the right course of action, and being prepared to forge a pathway along which others have not travelled. A risk of loneliness, miti-gated by opportunities for healthy solitude, also characterises research for Sr Agnes. Both conversationalists talk of the need for support and supervision – to encourage you to take your time, and to give you a sense that there is someone who believes in you – and both talk of the fine line between understanding others and 'going over to the other side'. Ron Best and Mike Bottery (in Chapters 3 and 5, respectively) talk of empathy. It is raised again here. Buber's description of 'real dialogue' is relevant here. For him, dialogue involves 'a bold swinging ... into the life of the other' (Buber 1998, p. 71, quoted above in Chapter 5), but this should be done while 'remaining on one's own side of the relationship' (Friedman in Buber 2002, p. xiv) and not 'wish[ing] to impose himself on the other' (Buber 1998, p. 74). This can be described as a form of *empathy* (Stern 2013b). It is empathy, I would suggest, that characterises the research and professional practice of these conversationalists – listening to others, understanding others, whilst not quite losing oneself to others. Prudence and good timing are interesting and somewhat unexpected research virtues. They are closely related to the long-term sustainability of research and researchers, which is the theme of Part IV of this book.

Sustainable Researchers

It is hoped that this book will show something of the lived reality of research practice. Researchers describe their work and some of the personal qualities they need. It is certainly not easy, doing research, but it can be enormously rewarding – rewarding personally, that is, as well as professionally. Sustaining a career in research takes courage, and needs the support of others – of individuals and of institutions. This is discussed by Lāsma Latsone and Lynne Gabriel. The gritty determination to sustain a research career whether or not support is available is one of the themes of the conversations with Chris Sink and Fedor Kozyrev, whilst Helen Gunter and Ginger MacDonald both talk about how a 'life of research' can be sustained in order to have some sense of completion and influence. 'Sustainability' is currently a fashionable term in higher education, with specialist journals such as the *International Journal of Sustainability in Higher Education* (<http://www.emeraldinsight.com/loi/ijshe>) emerging in recent years. I hope that these six conversations will help illuminate how researchers themselves can be more sustainable.

CHAPTER 8

Courage Enough: The Need to Support and Be Supported

Introduction

Several conversationalists talk eloquently about courage, especially Helen Lees, Anne Pirrie, Lander Calvelhe, Jacqui Akhurst, Shanaaz Hoosain and Helen Gunter (in Chapters 3, 4, 5, 6, 7, and 10, respectively). The reason for having 'courage' in the title of this chapter is that both conversationalists talk with subtlety of the relationship between courage and support. 'Courage enough' suggests having *just enough* courage to research, it is a 'modest' courage rather than a heroic courage, and it is clearly related to and sustained by personal, professional and institutional support. Towards the end of the film *The Wizard of Oz*, the wizard addresses the (apparently) cowardly lion:

> As for you my fine friend, you are a victim of disorganized thinking. You are under the unfortunate delusion that simply because you run away from danger you have no courage. You are confusing courage with wisdom. (Baum et al. 1939)

Lāsma Latsone exhibits the very particular courage of being prepared to hold this conversation in public. At the 2015 *Value and Virtue in Practice-Based Research* conference in York (<http://www.yorksj.ac.uk/value&virtue>), the first keynote, entitled 'The Personal Influence of Educational Research: A Conversation on Ethical Practice', was made up of the conversation between myself and Lāsma. The audience was invited to comment, and members of the audience who are voiced in the transcript below are referred to as M1, M2, and so on. The conversation with Lynne Gabriel describes the courage needed in the face of inappropriate relationships in professional contexts, and the courage needed to research those same issues. Support is needed, and is available for those with professional counselling roles who also research – and is, happily, addressed in the relevant code of research ethics (Bond 2004). Lynne Gabriel herself has had a number of professional responsibilities for supporting counsellors and psychotherapists (including those researching the field), not least as chair, from 2008–2011, of the BACP (the British Association for Counselling & Psychotherapy <http://www.bacp.co.uk>).

Part of my Being: A Conversation with Lāsma Latsone, Liepājas Universitāte, Latvia

JS: Could you tell me something about your research, and how or why you came to be doing it?

LL: I was a music teacher first, and my educational journey was not well planned in advance. Krumboltz has a happenstance learning theory in career guidance (Krumboltz 2009, Krumboltz and Levin 2010). I like his theory because I think my life is a big happenstance: things just happen. The first degree I did because I wanted the degree. I wanted to do some research to fulfil some requirements. Later you get to love this process. That happened to me: I just got involved. Now it's a part of my being, to teach and to also be part of the research.

JS: It's been interesting how different people have talked about research as an *existential* thing, as making meaning of their own lives.

LL: I think it's so related to who I am. Of course we are sometimes not completely free in choosing topics. We choose topics because of a certain conference: we wouldn't be making a presentation with my colleague Linda today on our research outcomes (Pavitola and Latsone 2015) if the conference wouldn't have such a topic. And you teach students and they say something and you want to find out exactly what they are talking about – and the research idea comes from there. Or my own spiritual quest: issues I can't understand how to deal with, so therefore want to find out through research.

JS: Would you like to tell me about any particular research projects that you've been involved in?

LL: First I want to mention my thesis that was more than ten years ago now (Latsone 2004). It was interesting looking back to compare how much the research process and the understanding about research has changed. I did my thesis on religious education: how the Vatican II ideas (the Second Vatican Council, 1962–1965 <http://www.vatican.va/archive/hist_councils/ii_vatican_coun cil/index.htm>) can be implemented in parishes in Latvia. I did surveys and got lots of interesting answers. When I came back from the United States, researching at Fordham University (<http://www.fordham.edu>), I thought that everybody would be interested and some change would happen – because the Latvian Catholic church is very conservative and very pre-Vatican. But actually nobody from church was interested in my thesis. When you talk about virtues, it could be this enthusiasm when you try to do your best and then you get disappointed because nobody reads what you've written. They say 'No, it's not for Latvia, maybe in the United States you can do that way, but not here – we will do everything Latvia used to do'.

JS: How did you manage not to be put off by that?

LL: For me it was a complete switch of research area. I returned to Latvia where there is no such subject as religious education in universities. There are teacher training programmes, so I got involved in teacher training, and the rest of my research was more involved in areas which could be useful for teachers (Latsone 2013a, 2013b). My new job got me going again.

JS: Can you tell us one of your more recent projects?

LL: The other research project I could share would be the most challenging one. Now I live in South Africa, for family reasons, and teach in Latvia. I was invited to be part of a research project called the 'Happiness Project' (<https://sites.google.com/

site/chrissinkwebsite/>), which was generated in Seattle Pacific University by Chris Sink (now at Old Dominion University, <http://www.odu.edu>). He was doing the research in the United States and in Korea, and he said 'Maybe you can join our team and get us some data from South Africa'. That meant going to schools to research children grades three to six (aged eight to eleven), to find out if it is true that if children are happy and satisfied with life and feel good about themselves, are they performing better in educational settings? My task was to go to schools and get the permissions and give questionnaires out to children. It was a long questionnaire for children, and there was also a questionnaire for teachers where they were reflecting on each child in the classroom. I managed to gather about a thousand responses for that research project, but the summary of the results and publication is still in progress. There were quite a few challenges. Permissions were easy, unlike in the UK. The challenge was more about doing research in a country which I am not so familiar with. In Latvia I know how systems work, I know where the schools are, I know how to talk to teachers, but when you are in a different environment you must learn how to approach people. It was interesting for me but also challenging. And there were about forty questions, and they had to circle one to five if they agree or disagree. Sometimes when I was putting the data into the spreadsheet, I saw that some students have circled 'five' for all forty questions. It is a challenge for summarising, if the child didn't put much effort in.

JS: Interestingly, my own doctorate involved people circling numbers, and I wrote about how you get children and adults to be in a position where you are confident that they will want to answer the question meaningfully. I described that in terms of sincerity (Stern 2001, pp. 72–76). Okay, so you've talked about your thesis where the challenge was having any influence – just because it's true, it doesn't mean anyone else will accept it.

LL: Thinking of the personal challenges, the first research, my thesis, that was the support of my mentor. I think how important is the support, not only for early researchers, but the whole research journey: to get encouragement, to get feedback, to get support. If I didn't have that support in the first place, I would never be a researcher now: I would not have the courage. We can also think about being supporters to our students who are doing research. The more we give support, the more safe they feel in their research process, the more likely they will be to continue with research.

JS: How would you describe effective support?

LL: Belief in the students. Belief that you can do it. When I started my research, somebody said 'You can do it'. Also here, this trust virtue: somebody trusts you. Every time I'm in class teaching, I remember my PhD studies and my brilliant mentor who encouraged me, supported me: that makes you do the same to your students.

JS: How do you find the research world? Are belief and trust and confidence, those sorts of things, common?

LL: I don't have horror stories. I have had very detailed feedback on some articles and it has been very encouraging. Sometimes I disagree, but I could see that the other person helped me to make the article better.

JS: Well let's start working on list of virtue words and their opposites and exaggerations. You talked about the need for persistence or courage to keep going, even when the research doesn't work out. Are there other things that you see as either temptations or as strengths in your own research history?

LL: Thinking about the personal challenges, I was interested in solitude and loneliness. Sometimes, especially when I was in South Africa and a bit out of the academic environment, I don't know if I'm in solitude or feel a little lonely. Sometimes the word comfortable solitude is a nice way to put things, and then sometimes I think I'm too alone with my thoughts. I like working with other people, I like when I get feedback. When I was at York here in 2012, I enjoyed your research seminars: you have them regularly and it's an opportunity to come and talk and share and listen. That is something we really miss in Latvia: we don't talk about our research. We go to conferences, we present, because it is a requirement, but we don't share, we don't talk, we are alone, too

much alone with our own thoughts. And we don't know if anybody reads the publication afterwards, unless we ask our students
to read them. There is something we can give to our students: we
can share our research thoughts.

JS: But it's still important to have solitude?

LL: To have *comfortable* solitude, when you don't get that lonely feeling. When you are alone with your research and nobody needs
the research – they just need to check on my report at the end of
the year – then you start feeling lonely and you think, doesn't anybody need what I'm doing? But we need it for ourselves, I believe,
because research becomes part of our *being*. We do it for ourselves,
not only for other people. But anyway, we need feedback – I feel
I need it – and it's always encouraging when you get it.

JS: When I moved here, I was determined that it would be a place
where in the lunch hall you were allowed to talk about research.
People would sometimes say to me 'I'm not coming in today
because I'm researching'. I would always say, 'What is it about a
university that makes it a bad place to do research?' Some people
will say, 'Having an office of my own', or 'Allowing people not to
interrupt me'. And so, most full-time academics have an office
of their own. That sense of a university being a good place for
solitude *and* for talking about research: it's not a taboo subject.
People outside universities think we spend our days talking about
intellectual things. It's only people inside universities that might
ever think it was taboo to talk about research.

LL: That, I would put under 'support'. Our university doesn't talk
about any research hours, we don't have offices, there is no money
allocated for attending conferences. When do we do research?
Night time. That's how we express our love of research. We just
do it.

JS: Research is running through us: this is what we are, and what we
do. But that doesn't mean it can't also be supported.

LL: My personal challenge is also inspiration. Sometimes you know
you want to write something but inspiration – the spirit – doesn't
come. Is that also a virtue, inspiration?

JS: A virtue to persist when you haven't got it?

LL: Yes.

JS: Persistence is there somewhere. Inspiration itself, is that a virtue? Do you think it's a virtue, to be inspired, or is it to allow yourself to be inspired, or to have confidence that you will eventually be inspired? Can I open it up to some other people? Would you like to ask Lāsma about any of these words or about anything that Lāsma has said so far?

M1:   What are the forces that shut down that kind of collaborative collegial reflection on research? You see it in classrooms and staff-rooms in schools quite a lot: the discussion culture is not very rich. In university, what stops that happening?

LL: Something maybe about organisational culture in a university or the classroom? I have two universities to compare and I feel the difference: support, encouragement and providing the space for discussions. That is something to do with leadership: people who are in charge who can open up those things, who call people together, who say 'Now here's a place for talking, and here's a time for talking'.

JS: For me, there are two things. One is fear. Fear is central to *not* learning. Instruction can take place, but not real learning. Fear of taking risks, fear of surprises. Fear stops people being intellectually creative. The other is related to the concept of community. Community is *defined* as something where people work together and act together, without necessarily agreeing (Stern 2009a, pp. 24–28). There's a whole tradition of community theories like that, but there's another tradition of people who think a community is a place where people come together who *agree*: communities are belief groups where everyone agrees. The idea that a community is made in *disagreement* is important to me. A temptation of leadership, whether it's leadership in the classroom as a teacher or in the lecture hall or in any other area, is to believe that because you're the leader you're right and that everyone else is wrong.

LL: And disagreeing doesn't mean fighting: you can disagree in a peaceful way.

JS: So being disagreeable, as it were, is important for a community.

M2:   Coming from South Africa I need to ask, do you work in private schools or in public schools?

LL: Both private and public schools.

M2:   I'm surprised that you did get permission from the schools to do the research: nowadays we find it more than ever difficult to get into schools to do research since we've had to get ethical clearance from the Department of Education, from schools, from teachers, and from parents. That brings to mind 'ethics': I don't see this word here.

JS: That's a good question. In this university as in most, you need to have done ethics training, which is largely a test of procedures. One of the reasons for me doing this project is precisely because I think what's called research ethics has been pushed into a procedural activity that probably misses a lot of the point of substantive ethics. Calling this 'virtuous research' is partly trying to side-step those arguments about ethics. Some ethics policies now have substantive ethics in them, they say the point of research is to do public good, and to improve the situation: '[s]ociological research is a valuable activity and contributes to the well-being of society' (BSA 2004, p. 2), for example. But in the end most of the procedures end up with tests of informed consent by relevant adults. Is that helpful?

M2:   It's helpful, but it's not settling.

M3:   I'd like to ask a process question of you both. You've obviously done several of these conversations before. I'm intrigued at the idea of having a conversation as part of a presentation. I wonder if you have any immediate reflections upon how that has changed – this conversation compared to the previous ones – and how you feel about having the conversation in front of us all.

JS: There is something clearly lost in having an audience, in the sense that when you've got people watching and listening, there's a different sort of performance, a different sort of self that you are with an audience there. However, my inspiration for this style of research was the Bryan Magee books (Magee 1971, 1978). He was conversing in front of TV cameras with TV crew. But over-all I don't know how it changes, and I haven't had a conversation separately with Lāsma – we didn't go through this in advance.

LL: I don't think I would have said anything different if we were just talking two of us for a recording of the interview.

M3:   I thought it was a really interesting idea, to do this as conference pedagogy – a refreshing alternative from listening to someone present. What I was getting from all that has been offered here, was a kind of private versus public research. You talked about how people wanted to be at home doing research, wanted to shut people out. So the idea of open research is interesting. It was also interesting as apprentice researchers, to have a model. And isn't the interviewer as much a source of data as the interviewee?

JS: This is a conversation: I'm using that word precisely because I am not pretending to be an interviewer.

M4:   I would cross off one of the words on the virtues list. On your loneliness and comfortable solitude, the opposite is 'dependence on others'. But that is a fact of life: it is not a negative. We cannot exist if we are not in community with others, and 'in community with others' is a need for dependence and an inter-dependence. I would replace your word with needy.

JS: Yes, I think that word would be better. Thank you.

LL: Thank you.

Research is Messy: A Conversation with Lynne Gabriel, York St John University, England

JS: Could you tell me a little bit about your own research – how and why you came to be doing it?

LG: Two areas come to mind: one is work through my professional body, and the other was through my practice as a counsellor and psychotherapist. The root of my interest is in the ethics of training and the ethics of practice, whether it's educational practice or psychotherapeutic practice (Gabriel and Casemore 2009). As a youngish trainee, I was groomed by one of the trainers, and realised what was happening so pulled back. But he sexually groomed a number of us, and had sex with several others in this learning group. The pedagogy used for the training was highly experiential, with less of the kind of critical reflection or critical reflexivity, and more of the immersion in being and experiencing – without many boundaries or ethical constraints around it. That prompted me to do a piece of research on boundaries in practice, which I did for a master's course. And as my interest in this was growing, I was becoming involved in my professional body (the British Association for Counselling & Psychotherapy, <http://www.bacp.co.uk>), and I ended up chairing their conduct committee. That's the root of it: unethical practice from a trainer, whetting my appetite gradually for research into what happens in unethical training relationships, or unethical practice in psychotherapy and counselling, as well as what's good practice. So looking at all the different kind of values and ethics across the piece: what we do, given the privilege of a trainer or educator position. And you could construe education within a psychotherapeutic context as well, I think. Gerard Egan (2014) would say you're working with the client to educate the therapeutic space, so the client's benefitting from, and learning from, what's happening there.

JS: You could construe teaching as a therapeutic activity as well.

LG: Absolutely. So those early roots were really important: what they gave me was the passion, and my own therapy process gave me the route to resolve some of the issues I might have had about violated boundaries. That passion is still there: it's not a missionary zeal, it's a sense of wanting to explore relationship, whether it's relationship with student, or relationship with client, or relationship with colleague, or citizen. I'm just finishing off a paper on domestic violence, but the nub of it is relationship, and – I use the word inability loosely – the inability of the parent, particularly, to model helpful boundary-setting, and the inability of the youth or the child to manage powerful emotions. Either it's witnessing their mother being beaten, or they're hitting their own mother. There's lots around relational resilience, and learning to be in a relationship, subject to culture and societal constraints.

JS: I'm fascinated because an issue like domestic violence is of course itself an ethical and values and boundary issue. When you use the word 'boundaries', that suggests the distance which seems to counteract the sense of relationship.

LG: Absolutely.

JS: So how you both have a relationship and have a boundary is presumably the same for you as a researcher and as a trainer or educator, and as a human being in a family.

LG: Yes. Those paradoxical positions – being close and distant – or the notion of optimal proximity which will shift according to time and place and context and subject matter. Boundaries are permeable and shifting – they are not fixed, they are fluid, and can be co-constructed.

JS: When you talk about issues, you refer to ethics 'and' values. Is that because they are separate? Or how do you separately describe ethics and values.

LG: I think values are part of ethics for me: values would almost be subsumed within an overarching banner of ethics and practice.

JS: I'm interested in the practice of research, rather than the research methods text book version of it which looks rather neutral and easy, or the version that you and I perhaps write about our research – as we also clean it up.

LG: One of the things that came to mind was the need to be courageous. When I was doing a PhD, I talked to a very well-known person in the field, and turned up at their house and they were dishevelled and quite odd. I found that really difficult because I had read everything that they'd done, loved their work, and was seeing maybe a darker side, a disintegrating side of the person. In subsequent years they killed themselves, so it was quite unsettling. I didn't know what to do with that, as the neophyte researcher, so I just parked it.

JS: What would you say lack of courage does to research? Do you
        read research where you think 'that isn't courageous'?

LG: Some of the ethnographic, action-orientated, in-depth qualitative
        enquiries need some degree of courage to enable the researcher to
        meet other people and facilitate people in some instances baring
        their souls.

JS: Are there some areas of research that can be done without this?

LG: Yes: the more positivist paradigm. That's not a criticism, it's just
        different. There's a need for number-crunching in particular areas.
        But if you're researching people's deeply felt experiences or beliefs,
        then it needs courage to get down and – I nearly said 'dirty' – but
        it's messy. Research is messy, it's not neat and tidy.

JS: Do you want to highlight one or two research projects that illus-
        trate these issues?

LG: One experience was researching dual relationships within the
        profession (Gabriel 2000, 2005) where, let's say you've got a client
        and a therapist, and that relationship moves into other roles – such
        as social acquaintances in the pub on a Saturday night. As part of
        that project, I spoke to people who were disturbed by dual rela-
        tionships, and it left me feeling disturbed about some things that
        therapists did to people. I hadn't gone into the research naïvely, I'd
        gone in wanting to understand more what happened when people
        step outside of professional boundaries. That was unsettling, and
        I got some hate mail: 'You shouldn't be researching this'. I had
        people step forward who were either therapist, or client, in current
        sexual relationships with clients or therapists, but they refused to
        have their information included in the research database: my take
        on that was they needed to talk – like at a confessional – and that
        was quite disturbing. Some of the stories were about power and
        control, some were about appearing to find mutual care – more
        equalisation and sharing of the power-plays. The things that were
        disturbing were when it appeared to be an abusive relationship.

JS: So you mean there can be dual relationships that are both ethical
        and appropriate, and ones that are negative?

LG: Yes. There is also the concept of the wounded healer, the person who goes into helping to heal themselves – described by and of Jung (Dunne 2012). That's fine if it's done in a self-aware way, being cognisant of what one is doing. I think where that wounded healer concept is at its darkest and most dangerous is where the person is driven by their own agenda or their own aims, at the cost of the client or the patient.

JS: Research can work in that way, too, where people do their research in order to find the answers that they already know.

LG: That's interesting. I think one of the outcomes from any research that I've done has always been my learning. It's been a starting place, wanting to know more, wanting to learn, wanting to understand, and this has been the particularly challenging bit I think – a dynamic that's rooted in my history. Whether it's abuse, or violence, or boundaries, or ethics and practice, there's always an element somewhere that's in my personal history. So it's managing what you do with that as researcher, it's how you hold it, how you contain and manage it. In a research text book on phenomenological research, you bracket it off, put it to one side. But my experience is you can't put yourself to one side as a researcher. There's something about how I hold myself as researcher and not become so immersed that I lose the purpose of it. For me the best research is not done in isolation. It's done in a team, or shared with colleagues, so there are different perspectives and people are butting up against you to challenge or question something. Some practitioners and some clients whom I interviewed about sexual or other dual relationships in therapy, for several months afterwards I would get contacted: 'Would you be my supervisor?', or 'Would you be my therapist?', or 'I really enjoyed the interview and I think you really understand me and I'd like to get to know you more'. My own response was a 'No'. A more naïve researcher might be thinking 'Oh that's fabulous, I've clearly I've done a great job'. I spoke about it with my clinical supervisor and with my research supervisor.

JS: As researchers, why, when dealing with sensitive issues, would we set up a project without checking that the researcher has what you would call supervision – personal supervision, or a 'confessor' I suppose?

LG: Yes, that would be good practice, I think essential – for the well-being of the researcher, but also for the reliability, the trustworthiness, the cogency of the research: you're fuelling that through constantly attending to yourself. For me, creative supervision, where you're generating new insights and new ideas – facilitative supervision rather than a normative restorative supervision – can only benefit the research and the researcher. It would allow researchers to have more courage, or appropriate courage –

JS: or appropriate levels of empathy.

LG: In BACP ethical guidelines for research (Bond 2004), supervision is referred to – working with someone to oversee your research. 'In research that requires an extended relationship between researcher and participants and/or the disclosure of personally sensitive issues, it is best practice to ensure that the researcher is supported by regular and ongoing supervision, that is comparable to the ethical requirements for supervision in counselling and psychotherapy' (Bond 2004, p. 6). So I think the notion of some kind of supervisory or mentoring supportive external person is important.

JS: I don't see that in other areas, notwithstanding that they have similarly difficult and upsetting experiences. How much of the challenge you're describing is self-doubt over the value of research to be effectively shared, or the newness of the insights? Or are 'the dark nights of the soul' fuelled by the topic and the memories and the personal relationships involved?

LG: I think they are interlinked. This is something about research: it's an exposing affair, it exposes oneself as researcher to a more public audience. All of those self-doubting internal dialogues: I suspect that might happen with many research students, almost like an existential angst.

JS: There's a connection between being a professor and the respon-
        sibility to profess, which also involves a public statement – the
        duty to disclose, the duty of candour.

LG: Absolutely. Where things often go badly wrong, there's a break-
        down in the relationship, whether it's communication or under-
        standing. And it's not just a breakdown in communication but in
        the ability to manage boundaries. Something about the humanity,
        humility, and courage, to say 'I'm sorry'. Research participants can
        assume that you as researcher know everything about what you're
        researching, but it's not necessarily the case.

JS: For you, what is different about research to being a therapist, and
        being a teacher?

LG: It's interesting because when I'm working with clients, we're con-
        stantly researching, we're enquiring, exploring, inching forwards.
        So I think that there are many similarities between practice work
        and research work. Research needs to be heard or performed or
        written or narrated – so there's more of a community or a public
        sharing – whereas in the therapy room, that's shared between
        myself and the other person, or myself and the group, and then
        that person can choose what they do with that, but I'm not respon-
        sible for sharing it. As a researcher, I have an obligation if new
        knowledge and evidence and information is coming through, to
        do something with it.

JS: The Hefce definition, of the process of investigation leading to
        insights effectively shared (Hefce 2011, p. 48), is a remarkably
        inclusive definition of research, and actually includes a lot that
        children will do, and that, as you say, therapists and clients will
        do.

LG: For researchers who have an academic position, there are the aca-
        demic drivers: I have no issue with those, but it's about getting
        people engaged in *meaningful* research. Mindful, yes, of things
        like citations, but not getting caught up in that as the driver for
        the research.

JS: Yes. We research because we're curious. Being curious is *caring*
        about knowledge and understanding how the world works. Just as

you may care for people, you may care for learning, or for insights, or for understanding.

LG: I do like that. One of the thoughts that it fired off in my head was how when doing research and doing practice – whether it's ministry or psychotherapeutic work, or whatever – you're birthing parts of people's souls. It's soul-spirit work. And research, particularly in-depth research where people become immersed in the dialogue, can be deeply moving for the individual and very soulful. So there's something about midwifery. Midwifery of ideas and souls and spirit and understanding. A sort of birthing of something.

JS: Wenger talks about learning and creativity, and the prime example of that is parent-hood (Wenger 1998, p. 277), bringing something new into the world.

LG: One of the things about the 'virtues' list, maybe this is with my therapist's hat on, there isn't any sexual domain or sexual dimensions of the core strengths and virtues. There's something about intimacy, that could be sexualised, non-sexualised, or spiritual.

JS: There is a whole set of what are called by Peterson disorders of love, and strengths related to that including, as you say, intimacy and kindness, and disorders of temperance, and strengths, both of which you might think would be describable for sexual relations. Are you thinking there are some distinctive character strengths in sexual relations that are not about courage, or care, or kindness, or intimacy?

LG: Absolutely – you could narrate around that. I suppose again it's a therapist hat, seeing how core sex can be to so many people's issues, but you can construe it and narrate it through many of the strengths and virtues.

JS: Are there other words that are not there that you haven't talked about with respect to research?

LG: Yes. Again it's the therapist's hat, but it's the research hat too: the *physicality* of me and the other person, the person that I'm researching. I've never been repulsed by an interviewee, but I have worked with and researched some people that I feel a little intimidated by, and it's what I call their physicality, their actual physical presence. So there is, for me, something about the physicality of the person: that's part of how I might judge someone, or be judged.

Conclusion

The 'happenstance' starting point of the first of these conversations provides a good reminder for us all. There is an illusion that research, in common with the rest of professional life, can be carefully planned. Bids for research funds generally require accounts not only of theoretical foundations of the project, the research questions and the instruments to be used, but also of the results and impact of the proposed research. Research projects, in practice, are rarely that predictable. When writing up research projects, there is a tendency to make the project sound neater and tidier than it was. So, even though each researcher may realise that their own research was unpredictable, every researcher gets the impression that *other people's* projects were neat and tidy. Walford's account of educational research (Walford 1991) was influential for me, as it made visible the messy reality of research projects. (It was one of the books that led me to set up this 'virtuous' project, as I had found the accounts so encouraging to me as a researcher.) Most lives are unpredictable and unplanned. If plans are made then, as the poet Burns says, those plans 'gang aft agley'. The lives of researchers are no different, and education is filled with complex and 'wicked' problems (Bore and Wright 2009). And if it takes courage to face a known and predictable danger, it takes even more courage to face uncertainty. That is why planning, or the illusion of planning, is so popular: it reduces uncertainty and calms us down. However, it can also reduce the quality of what we do: if we are unwilling to take untrodden pathways, we are unlikely to achieve much originality. Research can be completed 'mechanically', as Lāsma says she did at first. To face the uncertainty and risks in 'non-mechanical' existentially significant practice, support is needed. Mentors or supervisors can provide the most useful feedback and support when they express a *belief* in the researcher. Lāsma highlights the need, in turn, for researchers to support their research students in the same way. This will increase courage in the face of the real uncertainty of research, and help sustain people through the difficult times. Research will also be supported if it is talked about. Many people describe the loneliness of research, and this can be exacerbated if colleagues and, collectively, if institutions do not provide support for discussions. Counter-intuitively, loneliness can also be overcome if institutions provide good facilities for solitude: quiet places for reflection on one's own, as research is, for Lāsma, of and for ourselves in the first instance. (Sr Agnes Wilkins talks about this in Chapter 7, and much of Stern 2014a addresses the same issues.) Talking about research should not, however, be entirely agreeable. Researchers need the courage to disagree, and to disagree in a peaceful way, once again complementing Sr Agnes' conversation.

Lynne Gabriel's conversation also links courage and support, and highlights the messy unpredictability of research. An awful illustration of this is her experience, when a new researcher, of meeting a well-known figure in the field who was 'disintegrating' and who later killed herself. Seeing the 'reality' of the lives of published authors – whether happy or sad, integrated or disintegrating – is more surprising than might be expected. Books have such a life of their own, that finding out the author is an ordinary, living, person can be a shock. I presented a research seminar myself, and an undergraduate student who had attended came up to me afterwards, and said 'Oh, I've read your book, I've been using it for my assignments, and' – she paused and then carried on in an animated voice – 'and you're alive!' Given the challenges of 'messy' research, support is essential and Lynne Gabriel describes effective support as being facilitative and not normative: helping rather than judging. The value of support is not just to increase the courage and wellbeing of the researcher. It also helps make the research more reliable, trustworthy and cogent. Researchers need *appropriate* courage – enough courage, that is, to produce good research. They do not need to be perfect, they can be 'wounded'. This sense of researcher virtues as being less than perfect can be compared to the psychoanalyst Winnicott's description of the value of 'good enough' parents – who are better than 'perfect' parents because they do not intimidate their children (Winnicott 1986, p. 179).

The range of references to embodiment is what led to the opening account to Chapter 1. There, I describe the 'embodied' virtues of my relative who has lost most of his cognitive capacities. Virtues are personal, and personhood is embodied: hence, Lynne Gabriel's questioning of the absence of virtue words related to embodiment and sex. Her use of the metaphor of research 'birthing' parts of people's souls is also striking. Researchers are described in so many ways, as less-than-perfect 'performers', as soul-midwives, as wounded people able to develop meaningful research when appropriately supported. Research is messy, but that does not mean it cannot be good. The same may be said of the rest of life. Its messiness, though, makes it somewhat harder to complete than is suggested in most accounts in research methods textbooks or the tidied-up accounts researchers themselves give of their research. How hard this work is, is the theme of the next chapter, therefore.

CHAPTER 9

99 Per Cent Perspiration: The Virtues of Hard Work

Introduction

Research is hard work: there's no disguising it. This is the impression of research held by those who have not yet researched – the students just about to start a final year dissertation, the mid-career educator deciding to get a doctorate, the newly appointed academic realising that teaching and administration takes up a lot of time and energy and research has to be completed as well. A theme running through this chapter is that experienced and senior researchers also find research hard. Some things become easier (perhaps knowing which journals and book publishers to approach), and some things are less off-putting (perhaps negative feedback from peer-reviewers, or failing to get a grant). On the whole, however, the research is just as hard (as in Fitzgerald and White 2012). This chapter, based on conversations with two successful researchers, attempts to explore the reasons why research is – and should continue to be – hard work. There are good, positive, reasons, and there are some that are simply unavoidable frustrations. As Edison said, genius is 99 per cent perspiration, 1 per cent inspiration. But don't even think about it without the 1 per cent. There are many more themes in these conversations, of course, from being caring to being impolite, and much in between.

Re-Imagining the Way we See Children: A Conversation with Chris Sink, Old Dominion University, USA

JS: Could you tell me a little about what sort of research you're doing, and how and why you came to be doing it?

CS: The variety of research projects that are going on span the area of making meaning, and social and emotional learning. These studies harken back to my strong desire and passion to make a difference, not only in schools but in the broader community as well. Certainly my life orientation and worldview provides impetus for the directions of my research, whether it be in spirituality, positive psychology, developmental psychology, social-emotional learning, and so forth. On meaning-making, I'm more focused on children and adolescence (Sink et al. 2007, 2010, 2013, Sink and Bultsma 2014), rather than a broader spectrum of lifespan development, because I think making meaning really starts at an early age.

JS: You said one of the stimuli for it is wanting to make a difference. Could you describe some of the mechanics of that?

CS: It's a big question. I think it is relatively two-fold. One is by modelling quality research for new generations of educators and counsellor-educators (Sink 2005, 2011). You can still maintain integrity and discipline, rather than submitting to 'publish or perish', but to do things that actually mean something to a broader population. Secondly, it's helping to re-envision school culture, and re-envision or re-imagine the way we see children and our interaction with children. So if we can continue to do quality research, these things that we research are important to children's development and they influence school outcomes: I think that provides a meaningful endeavour.

JS: It's an oddity that academic research tends not to be widely read, and many academics think they are not writing for readers, they're writing for themselves or for the sake of the research, and not to be read.

CS: I think that would be solipsism. The exercise of thinking and writing and communicating, whether it be to a narrow audience or to an extensive audience, is part of the good life if you will. You're actually reflecting on higher-order events, experiences that can influence yourself in the direction of your own life, as well as potentially your small circle of friends. And ultimately the ripple can transcend the oceans.

JS: Can you describe one or two research projects and consequent publications that demonstrate the way that you go about research?

CS: I am interested in youth's perspective on life, and there are very few instruments that have been 'normed' for adolescence that assess life orientations. They do exist, but most of them have been tested or explored within clinical settings where they can't really be used in state education because of the red flags that are surrounding words like 'transcendence' or 'purpose in life'. I'm interested in trying to assess in some more formal way, how do kids orient their lives? I took an instrument that existed called the 'spiritual wellbeing instrument'. It was designed for adults, and had something like twelve to fourteen different dimensions. I knew that wouldn't fly in a state school because it takes about forty minutes to administer. And it hadn't been psychometrically analysed for validity and reliability. The kind of work that I do tends to centre on research that has validity and reliability in a broader context, not just in a local context. I created an instrument called 'life perspectives inventory', and we piloted it in American schools as well as in Korean schools (Sink et al. 2010, 2013, Sink and Bultsma 2014). We looked at adolescents' perspectives on their own life, and after distilling the original instrument, we came down to four discernible dimensions. These dimensions hold across cultures. In my work we do what we call cross-validation studies, using sophisticated structural equation modelling, which allows you to then test the validity of the items, and their meaning in multiple settings.

JS: You could imagine a school, say, being interested in whether a particular programme or a particular process of counselling, or a particular curriculum, might help change people.

CS: I try to stay away from using it as an outcome variable for fear that
        we are misusing the whole intent of the instrument which is just
        a snapshot of how kids are. Then you, as an administrator, or an
        educator/teacher can say, 'Okay, in my classroom I've got a number
        of kids who are highly social, that's what they find meaning in'.
        So to do a lot of lectures might not be as effective in connecting
        with them at the purpose level.

JS: You're not trying to have a say over how they will then respond
        to that information?

CS: I'm not dictating. If I'm doing talks in the school I will say this
        research can be used in these ways, but it's not to be used in any
        way to judge, or evaluate, or categorise children. And that's my
        fear of any of these kinds of studies: you begin to pigeonhole
        kids, and of course that's not the goal. The goal is to inform. And
        also to use in a counselling setting as a tool to build rapport and
        further conversation within the therapeutic context.

JS: Can you give examples of the main research challenges you faced?

CS: The constructs themselves are challenging to measure, so construct
        validity is hugely challenging. To understand the construct of
        optimism, you have to rely on a vast literature base, and then distil
        it into questions which may or may not really reflect the variety
        of opinions or research on what is an optimistic outlook – like
        children who have more of an optimistic outlook tend to have
        fewer drug issues or mental health issues. So getting your research
        questions and your items correct, it's not as simple as just sitting
        down and saying what is your outlook on life, and then trying to
        code that in a projective sense. I prefer to just let the kids say what
        they're going to say, but, unfortunately, you're data-gathering, and
        quantitative data-gathering is biased toward the way you define
        it. So, that's a challenge, and it's difficult.

JS: I'm trying to think of a relationship to the literature that you said
        you started from, which is presumably not just psychological lit-
        erature, but philosophical literature on the nature of optimism?

CS: No, I wouldn't go into philosophical literature because it's unsub-
        stantiated, it's just someone's opinion. I don't just base my view

on an opinion, because there are billions of opinions on what is optimism. So what I read is empirical studies, qualitative and quantitative, that actually have collected data and looked at real kids, and checked their ideas, not just said 'I think optimism is this'. It may or may not have merit, but it's never been checked. Philosophical literature informs my own worldview and it informs my perspective, but I tend to value, to appreciate, validated ideas first over speculative.

JS: And tackling another question, are there particular *personal* challenges you face in this branch of research?

CS: I'm not quick on the uptake. I mean I have to learn very sophisticated mathematical, statistical programmes and processes. For example, calculus was never my strength, but many of the statistical programmes and statistical ideas are based on calculus and higher-order mathematics. It's challenging to master those or not even master, but at least understand them enough to use them effectively. So, I really am sort of a plodder versus a brilliant person. I've met scholars who just know this stuff, and they somehow understand the inner workings of these statistical procedures much quicker than I do. So it's a long process and it's taken a lifetime to even master a good portion of them, or even have enough skill to be dangerous. Other personal challenges are finding the time to do this research, because it's very time consuming and requires enormous patience. You can put in seven research applications to state schools systems, and six of them over two years will have rejected the idea for whatever reasons. So you have to be patient, keep plodding, but I get tired of it. I really dislike interacting with bureaucrats who don't really care about research and are only wanting to know what's in it for them, in other words, 'Are you going to fund a new programme or are you going to bring grant money into our district?' Research for the sake of research and knowing kids and knowing teachers and knowing things is often times not of value to them, and so we have a clash. They're pragmatic and they are 'instant gratification'. If you can't do anything for them immediately, if there are not enough 'deliverables' – and I didn't even know what that meant, to be honest with you. It's disappointing and a discouragement to see schools shutting their doors and not recognising the value of quality research. I understand that, because they're so overburdened by the state mandates, that it's just another thing for them to do. On the other hand it's 'Aren't you supposed to be lifelong learners?' You always tell kids you're going be a lifelong learner, so there's a lot of cognitive dissonance in my mind. On one hand they're getting their master's degrees, they all say 'Oh we want to do the right thing for kids' – there's a rhetoric – and then when it comes right down to practice like 'What would be a good idea for kids?', based on our research: 'We don't have time for that'. So there's a sense of 'Don't you see that you're being, in a way, two-faced?'

JS: The examples you have given of a personal frustration are all about gatekeeping and access, whether it's states or schools or individuals blocking access. So you don't find personal frustration when the research is going on?

CS: Well I do in the sense that it's time-consuming. Have you ever worked on a massive data set, poring over mistakes? There's a sense of 'Oh, do I really want to do this, I could just read a book right now, prepare a lecture: am I wasting my time, is this really going to come to anything?'

JS: The stereotype of large scale quantitative projects is that what you get in terms of quantities is lost in terms of the abilities to explore the important issues about world views and meaning-making and life-chances. I suspect that that's just a stereotype.

CS: Well that's not true because the idea is that once you've got trends, then you explore, you drill – I like this word – drill down deeper into those trends, by doing mixed-methods designs, having your students working with kids, to see 'How do we influence their optimism?' PISA data and TIMSS data (<http://www.oecd.org/pisa/> and <http://timssandpirls.bc.edu/>), there's nothing you can do about that. You just get the data, plot it, and call it, but with my data sets, you are able to extend it to another design, like qualitative or ethnographic or cultural analyses.

JS: Do any of the list of various strengths, virtues, and their absence jump out at you, for the research that you've been describing?

CS: Curiosity and interest, critical thinking, perspective, authenticity, honesty, sincerity, truthfulness, intimacy, social intelligence. To some degree forgiveness, humility, self-regulation, appreciation – that's a challenging one – hope, and of course spirituality.

JS: Counselling is typically an intimate area, it explores intimate aspects of a person's life. How does the issue of intimacy come up?

CS: I think the intimacy comes with the work they have to do with the teachers, the administrators, to build the rapport. I spend a lot of preparatory time in the schools. Once the school district has given me the okay, or even if before then I may meet with heads and administrators to talk about their studies. So there is a sense of social intimacy that you have to establish – and trust, which is an intimate quality, and honesty, and transparency, which I think are all parts of intimacy – to allow you to ask the kinds of questions I'm asking. It's really not a problem if I was going in and looking at a new reading programme that they've started: intimacy is probably not that big a deal. But when you're talking about motivational, or what we call non-cognitive variables, that can be controversial with parents and families, you have to create the sort of trust on how the data is going to be used, what it means, for the children, the parents and the school. There's a lot of counselling that you do, and you develop close relationships with people that are in charge. Also there's intimacy between myself and my graduate students. I'm a relational person by nature, and so you have to create a level of trusting intimacy with those graduate students to be willing to do this work and to be vulnerable, to take the hits they're going to get. They go to the school and the teacher's not there, or the kids, half the kids are on a field trip, and so then they have to go back and you know then there's a lot of frustrations that they experience that you have to counsel them through.

JS: Is the issue of gaining the trust of teachers or principals also about them feeling confident with the materials that they're going to work with the young people?

CS: Yes, and you have to convince them that this is safe.

JS: Is there anything else you wanted to say that you think I've not asked about this?

CS: I failed to mention that I care about what I do – just really caring, deeply caring for the kids you're working with, the community you're working with, the outcomes, the data, and the processes. I really care to do it right, rather than sloppily putting something together. Caring for what you do, caring for yourself, caring for the inanimate nature of research. Those are all indescribable, but they do generate a lot of motivation for me. Because care drives the work I do.

JS: And is care always about filling the blank? Do you care *for*?

CS: No, I can just care. It's inside me. I care what you think. But I think people care about what they do. Now there are researchers I know who only care about the product, and using the product to advance their career, which is more of an instrumental care, not what I call a virtuous care. I'd be interested if you could find more diverse kinds of researcher that actually have different, instrumental, goals, versus people like myself. I think this is where it gets to this notion of what is a professor. The virtuous professor, in my opinion, does research because they care. But there are many people who just say 'I have to tick off that research box, I don't really like it, I don't like writing, I don't like researching, but I know I have to get three publications to advance, so I'm going to find a way to do it'. It drives me crazy, and that to me is not virtuous research, but it exists in the 'publish or perish' world.

JS: It's the performativity of that, that you're doing it for another audience –

CS: you're doing it for selfish reasons.

JS: I always say we research because we are curious. If we get good scores, that's great, but we research because we're curious.

CS: We care.

JS: 'Curiosity' has 'care' at its root – from 'cure', meaning 'full of care or pains, careful, assiduous, inquisitive' (OED 2005). That's why we research. And there will be people, of course, pulled in that direction, who started off in the other. And it's related to what you said early on about time, that time isn't the same problem if you have a real passion and motivation. If you don't have any passion but you only have an external motivation, then time becomes a bigger problem. There's a connection with care. I've heard other people compare research to having children. In other words, you care for them, and of course you don't have time to do all the things that you do for your children –

CS: but you do it.

JS: Research in that format will find its time. Whereas if it's conceived as just another task, it will not find it's time, just as we won't have time to babysit for people once we are working.

You Should Not be Too Practical or Nice: A Conversation with Fedor Kozyrev, Russian Christian Academy for Humanities, St Petersburg, Russia

JS: I have read your research for a number of years, but perhaps you could tell me a bit about it, and how you came to be doing research in the areas that you are researching.

FK: I came to be a scholar dealing with issues of religious education, but before that, I was researching in biochemistry. I was always interested in the implementation of quantitative methods, so my first research in religious education started in 2001, on different religious attitudes of school students in St Petersburg (Kozyrev 2003). Then we had a big project 2006–2009, the REDCo project (<http://www.redco.uni-hamburg.de/>). I was co-ordinator of the Russian group, and we made different types of surveys, qualitative and quantitative, recording and interpreting classroom experiences through videotaping and so-called 'incident analysis' (Kozyrev in Avest et al. 2009, Kozyrev 2011). And later, there was a dramatic change of situation with religious education in Russia. Since 2010, religious education was included in the national curriculum and so it became obligatory. There was also a shift of the whole policy of school education in Russia toward more, let's say, educational, not informational, tasks – tasks connected with the moral development of the value education. And there was a demand from the educational system to measure the results of this work. Another factor was a new generation of standards which were competence-oriented, and attainment was divided into the subject attainment, meta-subject attainment, and personal attainment. That's why when we applied for the development of our approach to religious education, we also put one of the tasks to develop methods of studying and of monitoring the process of religious and value education. How to study personal, moral, development for instance, or the process of assimilating values by students? That was the group of problems we became involved in after 2010. So for three years we made thousands of tests of different kinds, and developed our own methods of quantitative measuring of personal development of students.

JS: That's a huge change in Russia. Was your work influential on why the national curriculum developed in the way it did?

FK: No. We founded an Institute for Religious Pedagogy at the Russian Christian Academy for Humanities (<http://www.rhga.ru/>), but we are not influential. What we achieved is that we received a school as an experimental ground, a school laboratory, and it was approved by the school committee of St Petersburg. We have personal support in one of the districts of St Petersburg, but already presenting our results on the city level, we meet some resistance on the part of those politicians who are standing on their exclusivist vision of what a secular school means and what a secular society means. So they are suspicious about our enthusiasm in dealing with religion, even now.

JS: In the earlier REDCo project, I was fascinated by your use of 'dialogue'. It wasn't 'Let's use dialogue because it's friendly', it was 'There are fundamental differences in beliefs between people, that is why we must be having dialogue, in order to engage'. It wasn't a dialogue to solve everything, it was a dialogue to engage, as a fundamental educational activity. Have I understood you right?

FK: You are right. We understand dialogue as one of the essential tools for developing basic competences (Kozyrev, in Bates et al. 2006). This is linked to what we call humanitarian culture (Kozyrev 2010), or hermeneutic culture of interpreting facts or interpreting experiences of your life, and of the life of your neighbours and friends. So it is a great task for children in school to understand that there are different frames of references, or different language games, and then you are in really sincere and deep dialogue. You should first understand that you are not standing in the same position and you don't see facts the same way from the same point of view. If you get this goal, it entails some important consequences for the promotion of tolerance, for the development of cognitive skills, for the ethical and moral development of children, for changing the climate in schools, and for a more open and inclusive way of dealing with others.

JS: There are researchers who would describe themselves as hermeneutic. Would you see this as related to the dialogic approach to the process of researching, and talking about research?

FK: Yes. In the *British Journal of Religious Education* issue devoted to the REDCo project, my article there is about a hermeneutical approach to processing and interpreting data, in support of dialogue and hermeneutics (Kozyrev 2011). The idea was that we should use the hermeneutic culture whatever our methods are, not only qualitative, but also quantitative. And to understand that qualitative methods which are focused on developing a vocabulary – for instance for framing questions – is an inseparable part of serious research. And on the other hand, if you do it only qualitatively, for instance case studies using one or two examples of biographies and we do it intuitively and think that our data are representative, we sometimes are still too subjective. So quantitative studies are still essential in getting a more or less realistic picture of what we are studying. That's why we should look forward to the synthesis of quantitative and qualitative study on the basis of hermeneutic culture, the culture of interpreting results situationally, contextually –understanding that these facts can be interpreted in this way only in this situation.

JS: I'm interested in you, as a former biochemistry researcher, in how you could imagine a scientist coming to educational research and trying to do it scientifically. Clearly you have a different approach, a hermeneutic approach. Was it a personal reason for deciding to be a researcher of a different kind?

FK: The story was not simple. After perestroika, when we could be engaged in church activity, I just dropped being a scientist and I became a missionary in the church. And then I began to study theology, and through theology and inter-church dialogue I became acquainted with John Hull (1996, 1998) and other scholars. There was an impulse for me to begin to study the experience of religious education abroad. That was my way in to pedagogy. So it was research, but historical research of the waves of development of the theory of religious education during the twentieth century. Afterwards, the natural scientist in me overcame, so I began to be more and more interested in empirical research, not historical. And using my expertise in this field, of course I was interested in quantitative methods using statistics. But I saw profound differences and problems connected with using statistics in pedagogy. For instance, when we do research in agriculture, we have a field which is divided into several sections which are levelled on all factors except one, which is under the study. And it is impossible to do that in school. That's the huge problem which I sometimes describe it in terms of Heraclitus' expression that you can't come into the same river for the second time. That's the specific problem of dealing with statistical methods in the humanities.

JS: I know you have written about the heteroglossia of Bakhtin (Kozyrev, in Avest et al. 2009, p. 201) – that within a single group, there are many voices, so within a small family or a single classroom there will be such variety.

FK: Yes. I think we find interesting ways at the moment to deal with
       this issue. We work now mostly with two big groups of methods.
       One is the Q-sort technique, developed by the English mathema-
       tician, Stephenson, but put into practice because of the direct
       influence of Carl Rogers. And the second method is Kohlberg's
       dilemma method. By using the first one, the Q-sort technique,
       we have now developed a way of easily finding persons inside a
       group which are different and can be called 'outsiders'. Our test
       can identify these people very effectively. Usually it's one, two or
       three persons in a group of thirty. You can immediately find out
       these persons, using a series of statements. We use mostly forty
       statements, but there can be sixty or one hundred items. The point
       is that we have a characteristic integral of all these forty items, and
       by this statistical technology, you could present a person as a dot
       on the graphic field, and compare with the others.

JS: One of the difficulties with that approach, is that it depends on the
       respondent trusting you, and not trying to please the researcher.
       The other is the issue of self-knowledge: it assumes that people
       know what their values are. Many of us, when we have testing
       situations, realise our values aren't what we thought they were.
       I'm interested in both of those challenges. First, the challenge of
       sincerity, of how sincere children are being – especially children,
       because they are used to pretending for grown-ups. And secondly,
       what assumption is there of self-awareness?

FK: Regarding the first one, it's important that you mention this. It
       should be a part of the design of the research, for instance the
       anonymity or the confidentiality of the responses. Sometimes
       confidentiality shouldn't be granted and sometimes it should
       be very strictly granted. We believe that our students trusted us
       when we said 'I do my research only myself', and I tried to assure
       them that I would take all the results and the administration and
       the school would never see them. When the teacher who helped
       me looked behind the shoulder what the children were doing,
       I stopped them and ask them not to do it. You will never have
       ideal results, but I think it is possible, quite easy, to check up if

the children trusted you or not. When you have good statistics, you know how usually they respond. If you have a rich set of statements, one of them more challenging, another more neutral: one of them, students are afraid of showing (for instance, when we had research on tolerance, there were statements like 'There are ethnicities which I hate'), you can compare if you have one sincere group, you can compare this group with the others. If they are the same in many other respects but in this respect, you can make conclusions about their sincerity.

JS: It's interesting. In Russia, on the topic of religion over thirty years, the same people had said very different things publically. As a researcher, do you think it's a problem of trust, of sincerity, or of actual changes in beliefs on those issues?

FK: Yes: both. There is a number of students who are not identifying themselves with religion because it is not in their interest. In one piece of research of REDCo, there was a question 'What religious group do you belong to?' and children raised their hands, not children, these were guys of fifteen or sixteen years old, and they asked the lecturer, 'Marie-Anton, who are we, we are Orthodox or we are – ?' They understand that everyone should put the 'right' answer: the person never thought about who is he personally. So of course there is a sort of change in their identification, caused by the introduction of religion into public sphere. But also there is less and less of those who are afraid of showing themselves Orthodox.

JS: Are there other types of research challenges that you have come across in your own research?

FK: For me, the main difficulty is to present our results for persons to understand it, and to find support for the continuation of our research which is difficult to get permission for. And there are real obstacles because freedom of conscience is more and more protected by law. That's why I would be interested in continuing research on moral development, which I believe can be transferred into the sphere of religious development. We have big difficulties getting permission: I can't imagine that a big number of schools will allow us to do this sort of research. People are sensitive to religious issues in Russia, so it makes a huge difference if you are talking about moral issues. Actually, it is not according to the law, but in public opinion, you can talk about everything but not about religion.

JS: In the US, it is similar. Do any of the list of virtues or strengths, and their absences, describe characteristics of your research?

FK: Before I had this list, I sometimes said that to be a good researcher and a good scientist you need only two things. One is to be independent, that is a sort of bravery, and you shouldn't be afraid of public opinion, which is close to truthfulness maybe, or honesty. Bravery, honesty, truthfulness, I think these three words describe what I what I call independence. And the second is not on the list, but it is maybe specific for Russia. You shouldn't be too practical, you should be ready to do the work which will not bring money. What do you call this? I think there is not such a virtue here, it is a more monastic virtue. Interesting that there is a monastic virtue here, there is comfortable solitude. This is a monastic virtue, and so I think that scientists of today, they are close in fact to monks in medieval time – where many monks were researchers and scientists, and very good scientists. Remember Pascal or Mendel? And another part of the monk's life is poverty.

JS: I have to persuade my colleagues, and myself, that we don't research for the sake of research assessment exercises (such as <http://www.ref.ac.uk/>). We must research because we are *curious*. It's interesting how you describe it as a distinctively Russian thing, to do things not for reward.

FK: Of course it is not only Russian, there is always temptation of that kind. I would say it is the possible Fall of the scientist, like the biblical Fall, when he [*sic*] becomes oriented toward the result which could pay. It is a corruption, it is the main moral corruption for the scientist. He can be a good family man, have other virtues, but in science he is finished. I had one research partner for more than two years, a psychologist from the state university, and another person was interested in our study and wanted to be a part of our group and help us in disseminating results. But she saw a result which she didn't like, and she came to me, and began to persuade me that it should be interpreted in a different way. My partner, a friend of hers, said we should work three of us together. I said to her 'no, I will never work with this person, because she doesn't respect facts'. That is for me the image of this other type of scientist, who doesn't need facts. The facts they need only to support, and if they get results, they pull out of them what supports the idea and throw out the other stuff. That's the Fall, that's the original sin of the scientist. These things discredit science and science is strongly discredited in our time. Answering your previous question, you asked about what is the most challenging for me. For me, most challenging, personally, is not only these types of people, but also let's say postmodernists. I am positive about postmodernism and these neo-Marxist ideas that scientific knowledge is always charged with issues of power. That's really so. But it doesn't mean that it is discredited completely, that we don't trust anymore any facts – yet I see it all around in people. Many of them sincerely think nobody should believe statistics, because they may be interpreted in any way we wish. One of the factors contributing to the development of case studies or individual studies, is the distrust of quantitative methods. But we shouldn't discredit these facts. Instead of denying quantitative methods, we should go forward and develop hermeneutic culture to deal with these results. What we need for scholars to deal with technologies like we do, like Q-sort, is high qualifications in the techniques to deal with it. But before qualifications, we need trust and faith in science.

JS: I wonder how you feel we help newer researchers be independent and yet respectful and part of teams, and to trust to truth and not be tempted?

FK: Well, I am a bad consultant in this sense, because I have a very simple answer that you cannot compromise. If you are a scientist you should be trustful and you should be impolite. You should be not a nice person. If you are a member of a team, you always have a choice. If it is a good team, if it is like it was in REDCo, there will be a lot of discussions. There were contradictions between us over which to include and which not to include, especially as there were eight countries, and if in one country there was one result a little bit different from the other seven, do we not talk about it? There were tough discussions, and it was moderated by our coordinator, by Wolfram Weisse, in a very wise way. That's why we had agreed recommendations and nobody split from the group. But there are situations when people split.

JS: I wrote down before you said those things, from this list, I wrote down humility. Not a quietness, but a humility in the face of facts, or in the face of evidence. But you're saying – you're not demonstrating it – but you're saying you have to be impolite, which also suggests that you need some arrogance, you need the ability to say what you feel, even in the face of other people disagreeing.

FK: I think it is it is a basic condition for any type of activity, it is let's say the Hamlet question. To be active or not. Let's try to do something in this world, or not to try. So of course in research, it is as important as in arts, in war, in building your home, in making a marriage, you always should have hope.

Conclusion

Two researchers, each with personal commitments leading to research on topics that, in various ways, face huge social and political, as well as research, challenges. Both use complex quantitative methods, and both see the need for in-depth qualitative work. They face difficulties in gaining access to, as well as influencing, schools and policy-makers. Facing these difficulties, both researchers seem driven by curiosity – at times what might be called a 'bloody-minded' curiosity, what is referred to by Fedor Kozyrev as being 'impolite'. It is hard work, however skilled and experienced these researchers are, and yet it seems to both to be *necessary*. The love of learning provides energy enough to persist. And the hard work, if it involves re-imagining the way we see children or making a contribution to knowledge of the world, is worthwhile and gives us hope.

It is interesting to see how both researchers, looking into the personal or spiritual experiences of children and young people, are determined to develop statistically significant data sets. Most of the researchers in this volume use qualitative or philosophical approaches. Both Chris Sink and Fedor Kozyrev recognise those approaches but emphasise their limitations – if not complemented by the more quantitative approaches described here. And, contrary to the stereotypes of more quantitatively oriented researchers, intimacy and care are important themes: the intimacy of relations with those being researched and the 'gatekeepers' of research, care for oneself and for participants in the research and for the data themselves. As in a number of conversations, especially that with Nel Noddings (in Chapter 2), care and curiosity overlap – and performativity therefore risks undermining virtuous research. It is curiosity that is the theme of the following conversations, too.

A Curious Life: Research as Legacy

Introduction

Academic research can sometimes seem like 'just another job'. For some, it is precisely that. What is referred to in the UK as 'contract research' often involves short-term and insecure employment contracts for researchers who contribute to reports or evaluations for which a fixed amount of external funding has been found. But the majority of research carried out in universities is carried out by people who have research as part of a broader job as an academic – typically involving teaching and administration as well as research. Inevitably, those for whom research forms only part of a job will be challenged to balance the various pressures on them. This chapter is not specifically about those balances, although such issues are raised. It is, instead, about the role research plays in the lives of two experienced and successful academics. What these conversationalists have in common is a sense of research being central to their identities – as also discussed in earlier conversations, especially those with Nel Noddings, Ron Best, Helen Lees, Anne Pirrie, and Lāsma Latsone (in Chapters 2, 3, 4, and 8). Research may be a 'life project', a project that gives meaning to one's life, a meaning that might – or might not – last beyond one's career. Research could in that sense become a legacy, perhaps a 'gift' to the world – just as writers on education may talk of 'the gift to the child' (Hull 1996, Grimmitt et al. 1991). Seeing research as a long-term project, the virtues needed and tested by research are all the more important. The life of a researcher is a curious life.

Time is my Worst Enemy: A Conversation with Ginger MacDonald, University of Washington, USA

JS: Could you tell me something about your research, particularly how and why you came to be doing it?

GM: I think that my research has always been motivated by both my curiosity, my desire to make meaning for myself, and then also opportunities. Even though my research has meandered a bit, it always has the combination of those. When I started, my doctoral studies focused on cognitive processing and developmental psychology – how people think as they learn and they grow – and a whole strand was around how counsellors understand themselves, how they make meaning at different stages of their careers (MacDonald and MacDonald 2004, MacDonald and Sink 1999). Then, when I became involved in teaching, in counselling, and then quickly moved into university administration/leadership, it took a different form. While it was still around how people think about themselves and how they learn, this idea of identity formation became much stronger for me, because I was always helping faculty – academic staff. In my work I was helping faculty learn who they are, how do you become, how do you think of yourself as a faculty member, as a scholar? I began doing research around that, because of the opportunity. And then most recently my work in higher education has taken the form of how universities or colleges form their sense of identity. I work at a branch campus, at Tacoma, which is a twenty-five year-old branch of the University of Washington, and a lot of the recent work has been spurred by what it means to work in a place connected to something else, and how does your identity form there. So that's the short version of how curiosity and meaning-making plus opportunity made for my research. And then the final theme is the area of retention of students. I started thinking about why are some students retained and others not. And then I got into the world of first generation students, and then I put my cognitive processing developmental hat on again, and thought how do they identify with the institution enough to feel a sense of belonging so they want to stay? It's the same thread but it has taken different forms. You have to take a good look at the culture that you create (MacDonald 2014). Is it authentically inclusive, and not for show?

JS: And are you included just on our terms? The *Whistling Vivaldi* issues – the account by Steele (2010) describing how a young African American was perceived as less threatening in a predominantly white neighbourhood in Chicago when he whistled Vivaldi.

GM: I love that book.

JS: He's a good writer, elegant. US writers tend to be much better rhetorically, I think – and I mean that as a positive thing – than a lot of British writers.

GM: There's something about this point that you're making that I think I strive for. I came on as second author to a book called *The Helping Relationship* (Brammer and MacDonald 2003). I came on in the fifth edition, and it's just now going out of print in the eighth edition. This book is to provide counselling theory, knowledge and skill to people that will not be counsellors. It was written intentionally for pastors, or business people, or nurses, or physicians, so the book is as close as we can make it free of jargon. In doing that, I really learned the value of writing in plain language. Not that it's dumbed down or anything. And I've tried to do that subsequently, even in my more academic or theoretical work – to say it as plainly as possible, so people can understand what I mean. That's a value that I hold, trying to be very, very clear.

JS: I'm interested you mentioned several times that you are curiosity-driven.

GM: I think for me, it's partly my personality: my parents say I was always saying 'Well why, why does that work that way, how does that work?' I used to get into trouble questioning authority, because I didn't like the answer of 'Because', or 'Because I said so', or 'It just is that way'. So as a scholar, that motivates my work.

JS: I think learning is not 'you versus the world', it's 'you living curi-
        ously'. Would that be fair?

GM: I think that is quite fair. One of the values that I hold in my
        research, but also in my practice (as a theory-to-practice person
        or a scholar-to-practice person), is that it's the *process* that is really
        important. I don't even think there ever is a 'product' of higher
        education, or of research or of practice: we have a sense of who
        we are that grows and changes all the time. What's interesting is
        to look at that process. That is my theory-building. I know it's
        true for people; I think it's also true for institutions. If institu-
        tions decide 'We are this and it will never change', then they will
        probably die. One of the things that spurred this work for me was
        coming here to this branch campus fifteen years ago, when it was
        ten years old. We were trying to do strategic planning. Academic
        staff were saying 'How can we possibly create a strategic plan, we
        don't know who we are?' I said 'Well, maybe we could talk about
        who we are today, who we were, who we want to be: let's not try
        to make it into concrete right now, because that would be foolish'.

JS: What would you say the main research challenges are for you, in
        this?

GM: Time is my worst enemy. I had an interesting challenge with this
        article. I had suggested three 'lenses' to look at the situation, and
        the editor, who wrote from a different theoretical perspective,
        was adamant that I must address that person's theoretical orienta-
        tion as part of the article. I wasn't an expert in that theory, and it
        had not influenced me. I was a little offended, to be honest. But
        because I wanted to get the article published, and I respect that
        journal, I chose to go ahead and revise the article. It probably took
        me three more months to get where I felt comfortable enough
        to write about that particular 'lens' with that paper. I do think it
        improved the paper in the end. But that's the kind of challenge
        of someone else's orientation, brought in in a way that I really
        didn't think was necessary. It did take me into a deeper knowledge
        around a different orientation, so that was fine. But I didn't get
        the idea that it was done for the betterment of academia, I think

it was because that person liked it. One time, a long time ago now, I had done a mixed-methods work with three other people, and we'd tried a new qualitative methodology and submitted it. The editor of that journal was probably the leading expert in the United States on qualitative research, and this editor would not publish this paper because we did not use her methodology. It was really a good paper, but she had the lock and key on what is 'correct'. That was really unfortunate, because a lot of work went into it, and then we all went separate ways and we just never picked it back up to try again. That piece would have been a good one to have out there for other people to learn from. I guess you just have to let go.

JS: Or persist through different routes, different genres?

GM: Yes, but when I was younger, I took stuff more personally. Now I have more perspective: it's annoying, but I will just send it somewhere else. I have a rule that if I get a rejection it stays on my desk no longer than one week before I re-do it and send it back out.

JS: Also presumably you have a history now as a researcher and administrator, so you have less fear that you won't get tenure.

GM: Exactly. There's no pressure from anybody but myself, and also wanting to get the word out. There's another personal challenge, though, I was thinking about as I looked at your question. Because I do scholarship around identity development, it always makes me think about myself when I'm doing it. Sometimes it brings up really important things and then I have to stop writing, or partition off my emotional side for a bit, so that I can keep writing. I'm going to be retiring probably in five to eight years from now. Thinking about identity myself as a scholar, does anybody care what I think anymore? The new work coming out is really good.

JS: Is that about legacy, or about who you are with all of this?

GM: I don't know. What happens when you stop contributing to the field academically, intellectually? Will anybody notice? That's really egocentric, but we've worked so hard, and feel like we're contributing, we go to conferences, we write, we teach. When I'm finished, what difference will it make? Who will I become as a person with my own identity when I don't have that work to contribute any more?

JS: Friedman comments on Bakhtin and Buber on the nature of the self through others. For Bakhtin, '[a]bsolute death is the state of being unheard, unrecognized, unremembered', whilst 'Buber says in strikingly similar fashion that abandonment is a foretaste of death, and abandonment is not just being left alone but being unheard as the unique person that one is, being "unconfirmed."' (Friedman 2002, pp. 355–356).

GM: The man with whom I've been co-author on *The Helping Relationship* – Brammer – he's still alive, in his mid-nineties, and I go have lunch or coffee with him and his wife about once every three or four months. I know that he still tries to write things, but he doesn't really publish anymore. I know he feels – I don't know if it's sad or wistful, I guess – that he's not the influence on the international stage that he used to be in counselling psychology. It's interesting to listen to him talk, because when I got to know him, he was about the place I am in my career right now. So that's what I'm thinking about right now, personally.

JS: Research is clearly a deeply personal thing for you. It isn't a thing that you happen to do, it's not only of yourself but as you say it's central to your identity.

GM: I would say yes. Except that you don't always see the evidence of that, because I allow the rest of my world, my work, to get in the way of it sometimes. So I'm not as committed to it as some of my colleagues who are strictly faculty members and that's what they do all the time.

JS: Yes, you have other parts to you, you are in high level leadership at your campus, just as I'm a Dean. It is for you a challenge in terms of time. Is it also a research challenge? Particularly as you're doing work on higher education identity, and you are a leader of a campus – a leader in a university – are there things that people will say 'Well she would say that, but how can she know about us or what we do?'

GM: Yes, that happens sometimes.

JS: Are there ways of you overcoming that?

GM: I don't think that has gotten in the way too much for me. I never thought about that as being a barrier. A lot of the recent application of my research, I have put into mentorship of new administrators – not in an official way, but quietly meeting with them once a month over coffee to say 'And how are you doing, and what is your sense of contribution, how would you like to explore influencing this institution?'

JS: Making use of your research in that conversation

GM: Yes, and that's joyful to me. I kind of try to turn it back into the practitioner side, to use what I've learned to help the next generation. That generativity stuff – as in Erik Erikson's notion of generativity in contrast to despair (Erikson 1980, pp. 103–105). I went to the University of Washington on the Seattle Campus, and so my professors for a while were still there. When they found out I was going into administration and giving up my chair of counselling psychology, they were like 'Ginger, how could you do this, you were so good at counselling, you're so good at helping people train counsellors'. I said 'Don't think for a moment that in higher administration you're not doing counselling, 24/7 practically'. So every skill I learned, my master's degree and in my early years running the school counselling department and mental health counselling areas, all of that I use now, every day. I just don't write about it much anymore. I'm not doing therapy, I make that clear, but I'm using the skills, confrontation skills and observation skills, and critical theory.

JS: I sent the list of virtues or character strengths, it comes from positive psychology. Were there either strengths or virtues or their absence or their opposites, that strike you – that you haven't mentioned already? You've talked about curiosity.

GM: Yes, that first group is about wisdom and knowledge. I think pretty much all of those strengths, somewhere along the way, fit in. The next group, disorders of courage: persistence is a quality that I know people talk about that I have. I do not let things get me down, and I just keep working, so I know that's a quality that

I have. It probably does show in my research as well as my work. Authenticity, honesty, sincerity, truthfulness: I would hope those would be about me. That's why I try to write with clarity and not with an elitist attitude. Social intelligence: I think that's probably a strength, although I would probably say 'emotional intelligence', like in Goleman's work (Goleman 1996). This word you have, 'enstasy'? It's a new one to me so I looked it up. I like that word. One definition was standing inside oneself rather than standing outside. I like that, I have to think about that. When I write I have to do that. I go away to retreat centres. 'Self-regulation' I think is really important, and I think I have a pretty strong meta-cognitive sense. I know when I'm getting too tired, or too excited about something to be rational. So I think I have a pretty good self-regulation. And then the last group you have, hope and trust. Most people describe me as extremely optimistic and so I think that would fit with those.

JS: You've gone down the 'strengths' on the list. Are there any of the other ones that you think are particular risks in the process of research?

GM: Under the strength of judgement is critical thinking, the opposite being gullibility. I don't think I'm gullible, but other people sometimes think I am, because I'm open to listening to what people that don't think like I do, what they want to say. I will listen to every point of view that wants to be put on the table, and then try to respond. It's not that it's not critical thinking: it's waiting until I have enough perspective to think. This sometimes looks like gullibility.

JS: So that could be a strength – something like humility?

GM: Certainly tolerant of others' points of view that are different from mine. One strength that's interesting to me is your very last one of spirituality, and alienation could happen as the opposite. Taking spirituality in its broadest form, for me it's willingness to look at the divine in each person.

JS: Is anomie, the sense of not having a place, is that something you were talking about in terms of when you retire?

GM: Maybe. I wouldn't say I dwell there but I think about it – you know, what's my life meant, and things like that.

I've Had to be Very Brave: A Conversation with Helen Gunter, University of Manchester, England

JS: I'm interested in how research actually works. Would you tell me something about your own research – how and why you came to be doing it?

HG: Thank you for giving me the opportunity: it's very rare to be able to talk like this. I would describe my research as being the politics of education policy – the political and sociological power processes underpinning policy development. I've tried to do that in a number of ways. One is conceptually through the work of Bourdieu and then more recently Arendt. And then I've tried to site it in the experience of doing professional work, and the issues around the construction of professional work as leadership (Gunter 2016). It's got a number of origins. My first degree is in modern history and politics, and that tells you everything about the sorts of issues that I engage with. My politics work was extended when I did my master's in education management part-time, in the latter part of the 1980s, focussing on the decentralisation of education from the local authority to the school. The sociology came out when I did my PhD (described in Cole and Gunter 2010, pp. 81–98), which was an intellectual history of educational management from 1960, focused on how educational management, as an area of research and teaching, was brought into the university.

JS: That seems an unusual starting point for a research career, researching the research, as it were.

HG: Yes, and I did my PhD not long after joining HE, after eleven years as a school teacher. My PhD was an intellectual history of educational management, and there is work that focusses on the abstract ideas, but that's not much of a history without the people who created it, so you need to look at the intellectuals. And then I read Raewyn Connell's work (Connell 1983, pp. 231–254, Connell 2007), who argued that it's intellectual *work*, not intellectual ideas that float free of people: it's a labour process. There is an interplay between ideas and practice, and people doing their jobs in school. My engagement with Bourdieu and Arendt is around illuminating and enabling understandings of practice, so neither of them are abstract theories. You don't ever 'apply' Bourdieu or Arendt: they are only of any use as long as you use them with data.

JS: Where do you see education professionals in this? Are they at least in part intellectual workers?

HG: Yes. I see children as intellectuals and teachers as intellectuals: it's not just in the 'ivory tower'. The ivory tower notion is a construction that's designed to keep us out: we are dangerous because we enable children and teachers to think – which is Arendt's view, that thinking is dangerous. Bourdieu has done quite a lot of critical work on the media, where he talks about 'le Fast Talker' (Bourdieu 1998). The idea of complexity, debating, talking through, not necessarily knowing the answer all the time, but certainly problem-posing – people have learnt to become irritated by that, because we're in a kind of fast-food fast-talk situation.

JS: When you talk about research, is that a sub-set of intellectual work, or how would you bound what you mean by research?

HG: I think I do intellectual work, whereby I do conceptual work, which I think is research. I also do field work, which is research. I think research is a process through which intellectual work happens.

JS: Is the teaching you are doing, whether university or school teaching, intellectual work and/or research?

HG: Yes, I think it is. I think that intellectual work in education is under threat in a number of ways. One is the denial that it exists and that it matters – even though to make that denial you actually have to do intellectual work. And I think the location of the social sciences and the humanities as the disciplinary underpinnings of educational research is therefore under threat. Educational researchers draw on disciplines in order to provide ideas that describe and give understandings and explanations – political science, sociology, psychology, history. I don't think that you can understand education without history – both the knowledge of history and of course historical tools. I think I was probably in the last year that had the 'ologies' in the training of teachers, in 1979–1980. Removing that source of knowledge for teachers to draw on, I think has been very damaging. When I get students who come to do master's and doctoral work, they don't have that background knowledge regarding how the world that they're in has been constructed and how there are other possibilities, that the world can be different.

JS: People like Unger write on the myth of no alternative, the idea of false necessity (Unger 2004). For a lot of political decisions, it is easy to persuade people that this is all you can do if you take away from them either the tools to analyse or the knowledge of other systems. Are there other research challenges that you would say that you face?

HG: I think I face a number of them. One is, education is not a discipline, it's a field, therefore we are outward-facing and we interconnect with the broader world. That speaks to current agendas, which is right and proper, but it also means that education within the academy can be seen to be suspect because it's not directly library-based or laboratory-based, shall we say, it's actually happening out there. Tony Becher's book *Academic Tribes and Territories* (Becher and Trowler 2001) shows that research that's concerned with people in real life situations has a lower status than pure research, like pure maths. Linked into that, you've got the changing role of the university, in terms of globalisation and the entrepreneurial agenda regarding the income streams and how we get our research funded – and how we relate research to other responsibilities, admin, teaching, supervision, and so on. You've also got the growth in the performance regime, with various audits of which REF 2014 (the Research

Excellence Framework, Hefce 2011) is just one example of many that happen around the world. All of those change what you're doing, and how you think about reporting what you're doing, and the different audiences. One of our challenges is that one of our audiences has to be the profession, but that might not count in relation to the REF and vice versa. And then I think you've also got the broader culture that we're in. In the UK – certainly in England – intellectual work is not valued in the main. Alan Bennett describes standing on a pavement having a chat to somebody. Somebody tries to push past and says 'Out of the way, you so-called intellectuals': Bennett says 'It is, of course, only in England that 'intellectual' is an insult' (quoted in Gunter 2001, p. 14).

JS: So those are research challenges. What would you say were the personal challenges?

HG: Increasingly it's time. Not getting through the day or whatever, but the sense that I have ahead of me a huge project that I don't think I've got enough time left on this earth to complete. That sense of mortality obviously grows, the older you get, and that you're surrounded by agedness and the sense that it will come to an end at some point. I've got a sense now that I've got about another ten to fifteen years' work. I've got the next ten to fifteen years mapped out, but will I be able to do it? I've got to come to terms with that and make a decision about what I can do, and what my final contributions might mean. I'm still young, I'm healthy, I'm in a good place, I've got good colleagues, and I have a fantastic life. But I'm increasingly concerned that I may just be running out of time. I want to examine what public education means and what it means to be a public professional. And the big thing that I'm going to work towards – probably my final thing – will be to write an intellectual history of the comprehensive school, from which I am a beneficiary. The way that both the Right and the Left have denigrated the comprehensive school, and public education, is shameful. All the stuff about heads as leaders is essentially a means through which to attack the comprehensive ideal. I think schools unfortunately have lacked that thrust towards citizenship and the sense of the democratic polity, because the UK is not a democracy – it's a constitutional monarchy that's been overlain with corporate demands.

JS: Do you see other countries where that's different?

HG: Yes. If you look at the work of Luis Gandin and Michael Apple about the city of Porto Alegre in Brazil (Gandin and Apple 2002), there are aspects there around democracy that are different to what you see in the Northern hemisphere. We've seen it here in this country, historically, but often it's ridiculed and often it's unable to survive because the political culture strangles it.

JS: So therefore the challenges are the same at school level and at nation state level?

HG: Yes. John Smyth did an edited collection a few years ago about student voice (Smyth 2006, Smyth and McInerney 2012), and he made the point that in order for student voice to seriously make an impact, it requires the strong leadership of the school principal to make it happen. It's a bit like how markets require a strong state. Neoliberals criticise the strong state, but they need a strong state to enable markets to enter and also to be sustained. There are all kinds of contradictions.

JS: Can I ask how you see the relationship between research work and other kinds of work, especially teaching?

HG: I think that I see it all integrated, teaching and research. I see teaching as integral to research because there's no point doing research if you're not going to communicate it in some way, and then you learn a lot about your interpretation of your data through sharing that data and other people coming at it from other directions – and then new ideas are developed as well. Research is a social and political activity, which teaching is, too.

JS: Moving on, the 'virtue words' list: I think some of those you've been talking about, curiosity and citizenship. Are there other words in there that you either see as important to you, or as important that you avoid, in your own research?

HG: I think the wisdom and knowledge ones, I think there's lots there in the creativity, critical thinking and the love of learning. The issue of courage I found interesting. I've had at various stages had to be very brave, because I have faced attack, very nasty attacks. Very deceitful and cowardly attacks. I'm not the only one, but I think I might be the only person who went to the police and reported it to the police.

JS: To have that in research is not something that anyone expects. It's not the same as an *intellectual* battle.

HG: Yes: there's never been any attempt to read, think and engage in scholarly argument: it's been a pure personal and sustained attack on my integrity. I've had to be really quite brave because I could have given up. Part of my, shall we say, proliferation of outputs is not just about the fact that I love writing and doing research – I don't want to retire, I don't want to stop, I've got so much more to do – it's also a clear statement that I'm not going anywhere, and that I'm doing this for other women who will come after me.

JS: That persistence fits with your account in Cole and Gunter (2010) of getting to be in a position to do the research in the first place, from a situation that it was not expected of you. You describe there the almost oddity for you, of ending up as a researcher.

HG: Yes, very odd. And the most demanding aspect to doing my job isn't being a woman professor, it's being a professor of working class origins. It seems to me that this has the biggest impact on people in higher education. When I talk about these things, people talk about how they can see it happens every day – the way in which people are seen as 'one of us', or 'not one of us', dependent on things like accent. In the North there are a lot of loud mouthed working class girls, that's who we are. We open our gobs and talk, and therefore we don't fully understand – I certainly don't understand – the ways of talking but not saying anything.

JS: There's a connection between your earlier life and your persistence.

HG: Yes, and I think it also means that temperance is important: there's been a strong sense for me of self-regulation, and also while what's gone on has been deeply hurtful, particularly since I can't answer back except by reporting it to the police, I've also had to forgive as well. Not so much what's been done. Perhaps forgiveness is wrong: I opened a box, put it in, closed the lid, and that's it. I'm not going to allow it to hold me back. On the virtues list, I think the sense of getting spirituality in other than church-based ways, through drama and music, through the countryside, through friends and so on, and hope, also, is important. Hope comes not from giving people solutions, but actually helping people understand that they're not responsible for the situation that they find themselves in. Stephen Ball said, 'I gave a talk about performativity, and afterwards a woman came up to me and said 'I resigned as a teacher last year', and she said 'now I know why I resigned' ... And although ... that's a ... negative example I was very pleased ... because ... she had the tools to make sense of her experience ... she now knew why she had made the right decision from her point of view' (Gunter 2013, p. 219, quoting Ball). So when you are a professional, and you're constantly told that you are failing the children, and the whole weight of the failure of the education system is put upon your shoulders, it's quite crushing. What's important in Ball's work, is that he enabled people to have that sense of liberation – that they are not guilty. It gives a sense of agency and of enabling people to think differently and to get a sense of a grip, and try and understand. That connects with Gerald Grace's work around complex hope (Grace 1994).

JS: Yes, absolutely. Are there things that I haven't asked about, or that you wanted to say?

HG: We need to accept that teaching can't happen without scholarship – in the sense of reading and knowing and understanding your field – but then beyond that, doing primary research and the use of that within your teaching. I can't see what you're teaching in higher education if you're not actively researching, because what makes us distinctive from say, consultants, and other people out there in the knowledge market place, is primary research. Even if you accept a neoliberal understanding of the university in regard to what makes us distinctive, it has to be primary research, otherwise why come to your university, why come to mine?

Conclusion

Research is presented as central to the identities of these two conversational-ists. It is the 'making' of the identities, the 'current' identities, and the future or 'legacy' identities that are variously touched upon. The conversations at various points seemed to move towards framing research as a 'life project' – both a lifelong project, and a project that is central to life's purpose or meaning. Ginger MacDonald and Helen Gunter both lead curious lives, lives of asking 'why?' – and sometimes getting into trouble for that, either as a child (in Ginger's case) or as an adult. The relationships to, and a rootedness in, their professional histories – as counsellor and as schoolteacher – are integral to the current roles as academics and as researchers and, especially in Ginger's case, as a university manager. University-based academic work including research is not 'another life'. It is a continuation of professional identities that encompassed well-established curiosity-driven practices. And the virtues of persistence and courage shine through both accounts.

These two 'life project' conversations complete the eighteen conversations presented in this book. I have put the conversations in the order they appear here (which is not the order of the original conversations), from starting points, through relationship building, and concluding with sustainability. I realise that there is a danger that I might have imposed a structure and a 'neatness' in the conversations that is not there. However, in presenting each of the conversations in the form of a script, and in keeping the order in which things are said, I hope that the voice of each researcher is well represented here.

PART V

Facing the Future of Educational Research

In my conversations with eighteen researchers, presented in Chapters 2 to 10, there are enough themes and issues to make for a whole book's worth of analysis. I am restricting myself to two chapters, both looking to the future of virtuous educational research. The first, Chapter 11, explores the conversational process itself, and its importance for educational research. Each conversation is a kind of portrait of the researcher. Portraiture is a recognised research method, with a leading exponent being Lawrence-Lightfoot (Lawrence-Lightfoot and Davis 1997, Lawrence-Lightfoot 2000, 2009), and another being Mike Bottery (Bottery et al. 2008b), who describes his approach in Chapter 5. It was Mike Bottery himself – in reading drafts of several chapters – who noted that this book was developing into a book of portraits. He sees the value of portraits of school leaders (their value as research and their value for the school leaders themselves), and I would like to explore the value of these portraits of researchers and to add one, briefer, portrait. However, I would like to go further. In Chapter 12, I want to present a bigger picture. How does educational research work within universities? What is the value of such research? And, given the focus throughout on research virtues, what theory of virtuous research emerges from the conversations?

CHAPTER II

Portraits of Researchers

Introduction

Each conversation in this book is a kind of portrait of the researcher, and together they add up to more than a group of portraits. This chapter begins making explicit the portraiture approach and how the set of portraits, together, add value to the sum of the individual portraits.

The word 'portrait' suggests a description of a person at a particular time, in contrast to a 'biography' which describes a whole life. All of the conversationalists talk about their lives in research, how their started and, in many cases, what they are hoping for the future. However, all the accounts have an emphasis on current understandings of the processes involved in research and what virtues may be demonstrated. I am therefore comfortable using the term 'portrait' – and might contrast that with a more immediate and very short-term 'snapshot' of a person. Mike Bottery (Bottery 2007, 2014, Bottery et al. 2008a, 2008b, 2012, 2013) writes of the value of portraits of school leaders, their value as research and their value for the school leaders themselves, and he talks about this in Chapter 5. I would like to do something similar, and explore the value of these portraits of researchers and to add one, briefer, portrait.

Lawrence-Lightfoot says that her portraits seek to 'combine systematic, empirical description with aesthetic expression, blending art and science, humanistic sensibilities and scientific rigor' and are 'designed to capture the richness, complexity, and dimensionality of human experience in social and cultural context, conveying the perspectives of the people who are negotiating those experiences' (Lawrence-Lightfoot and Davis 1997, p. 3). She continues:

> The portraits are shaped through dialogue between the portraitist and the subject, each one participating in the drawing of the image. The encounter between the two is rich with meaning and resonance and is crucial to the success and authenticity of the rendered piece. (Lawrence-Lightfoot and Davis 1997, p. 3)

Making use of her own methodology to describe the methodology, Lawrence-Lightfoot creates a portrait of portrait photographer Dawoud Bey.

> Through his lens, Dawoud sees many sides of a different person, a more complex reality. ... [T]he camera allows you to really take a good, long look at a person in a way that would be 'socially unacceptable' in ordinary interaction. 'I am able to stare at the subject for two or three hours, indulging the full range of my curiosity, finding out all the things that I can't find out in normal social intercourse, and sharing that with the viewer,' says Dawoud. And on the other side of the camera, the 'subject' feels – often for the first time – fully seen and acknowledged, bathed in the light of Dawoud's keen interest and unending curiosity. (Lawrence-Lightfoot 2000, pp. 151–152)

Bottery's portraits are conducted by peers (educational leaders talking with educational leaders), and, like Lawrence-Lightfoot, the portrait is negotiated with the subject of the portrait. In 'technique', my approach is closer to that of Bottery, in being based – typically – on a single taped conversation of an hour or two, transcribed and checked with the conversationalist. However, my approach differs from his, and from that of Lawrence-Lightfoot, in being presented as a conversation rather than as a portrait illustrated with quotations from a conversation. In that way, I am being less of an 'artist' (in Lawrence-Lightfoot's terms), although my editing of the transcripts (from roughly eleven thousand to two-and-a-half thousand words) is a skilled and perhaps artful process. And, unlike Bottery, the text presented in each chapter has not, in this form, been shared with or checked by the conversationalist. As I say in Chapter 1, the long transcript and a medium-sized transcript were shared with and could be re-written by each conversationalist, but the shortest edit was not shared. The decision to keep control of the final version was taken in part for reasons of timing (as the conversations were taking place up to four months before the manuscript of the book was submitted), but I did a check of the validity of the final versions by sharing with Anne Pirrie a draft of the chapter in which she appeared, and with Mike Bottery drafts of four of the conversational chapters, including the one in which he appeared. All the medium-sized transcripts are to be made available on the Peter Lang website (<http://www.peterlang.com>), so readers can gain more details there, including details on the decisions I have made in the final editing process.

This chapter starts with one, final, portrait, and goes on to consider the significance for researchers and for research management of what has been said in all the portraits.

One More Portrait

As this project progressed, several people asked if I would be 'conversed with' myself. For the sake of completeness, I think it is helpful for me to respond, at least briefly, to the questions I asked each of the conversationalists. Although I have written these responses towards the end of compiling the book, I have written them as 'innocently' as I can, as – I hope – I would have written them prior to holding the other eighteen conversations presented in this book.

• Could you tell me a little about your research, and how and why you came to be doing it? Can you describe one or two research projects, that demonstrate the way you go about research?

My first systematic research was for a philosophy degree. Philosophy can make you question everything, the meaning of every little (and big) word. My first suggestion to my prospective supervisor (the moral philosopher J. L. Mackie, 1977), was to research what I saw as the challenge for social science of the ambiguity of questionnaire questions and responses. He didn't think this a good idea, and suggested I might look at the philosophy of sociobiology. I got enormously involved in this, and following the death of J. L. Mackie, was supervised by the economist Paul Seabright (2004). I explored models of human behaviour of political philosophers such as Aristotle (1976), Hobbes (1968) or Marx (1976), and choice theorists such as Elster (1979) and how they compared to – and might even be similarly modelled within – Darwinian sociobiological theories of biologists such as Wilson (1975), Maynard Smith (1972), Dawkins (1976) and Cavalli-Sforza and Feldman (1981) in Stern 1982. The topic is not one I've worked on since then, but the interest in philosophy that stretched across disciplinary boundaries, and the concern to understand human behaviour in groups, has continued.

After ten years working as a schoolteacher, I started researching again – for, and alongside, a doctorate (Stern 2001). Again, it was a philosophical doctorate, what I would eventually refer to as a 'philosophy of schooling', and, again, it stretched across disciplines. It started from the word 'support', intending to explore the relationship between how school leaders supported teachers and how teachers supported pupils. Supervised by a sociologist (Jean Jones, 1994) and later a psychologist (Phillida Salmon, 1988, 1992), it made use of philosophical theories of community (Macmurray 1946) and leadership (Aristotle 1976), the learning theories of Lave and Wenger (1991), and the school development approaches of Dalin (Dalin and Rust 1983). The thesis title was *Developing Schools as Learning Communities* (Stern 2001) and, notwithstanding the 'obviousness' of the topic, I found few other works that tried to explain *schooling* (in contrast to the many works that tried to explain *education*), and that looked at the distinctive, school-based, relationships between the learning or development of the organisation and that of the individuals in the organisation. That research topic has been central to all my research since, looking at the character of schools (their 'spirit'), at the forms of school learning in particular subjects (history, religious education), at the 'boundaries' of schools (marked for example by homework, parental involvement, or computing), and at the relationship between schooling and broader social issues (such as religion) (Stern 1997, 1999, 2006, 2007, 2009a, 2009c, 2012, 2014a, 2015b). I have stretched the topic to include universities (Stern 2009b, 2014b) and other professions (Stern and James 2006), but I have kept to the communal, dialogic, learning-centred approaches – to schooling and to research. Looking back, I realise that my first, rejected, proposal for research – on the ambiguity of questions and of answers in social scientific research – came back into my doctorate, in the form of 'sincerity' as a research virtue.

• Can you give some examples of what you might call the main *research* challenges you faced, and how you dealt with those? Can you give some examples of what you might call the main *personal* challenges you faced in this research, and how you dealt with them?

There have been two big sets of research challenges. One set is related to access. The kind of access I want, to work with schools, has tended to mean working within normal lesson time with teachers and pupils, and the time taken to build up those relationships with teachers and also with headteachers and other gatekeepers is considerable. As much of my work is philosophically driven, the time spent on scholarly research of the literature, along with time spent in schools, along with time spent gaining appropriate access and consent, makes for a complex and frustrating network of pressures and limitations. I can give two examples. One is the *Spirit of the School* research (Stern 2009a). The research was carried out in the UK and in Hong Kong. I had originally intended to carry out the research in the USA too, and had at least one school and teacher, and an academic colleague, agreeing to take part. But the permissions from the district and the state were so difficult to gain, that time ran out and I completed the work without any US input. And for the *Loneliness and Solitude* research (Stern 2014a), I only managed to get two UK schools to agree to take part, notwithstanding considerable interest from around the world, and those schools only became involved late in the project – with the data coming to me within six weeks of the deadline for submitting the book manuscript. Although I don't like the distinction between 'empirical' and 'scholarly' research, much of my 'empirical' research has been completed for books rather than articles. And I only start the empirical research once I have a contract with a publisher – which is typically twelve to eighteen months from contract to submission of manuscript. This makes the time-scales inevitably quite tight.

The other set of challenges is related to disciplinarity. I am by nature somewhat undisciplined, in the sense that I want to be able to cross over disciplines, drawing on philosophy, sociology, economics, psychology, religious studies, literary theory, and more. In theory – as it were – this might give my research a wider readership. However, it also means that I do not have a single, solid, discipline into which my work fits. This is a challenge for me, as there are few limits to the literatures on which to draw, making research a bigger task than it would be within a single discipline or sub-discipline, even after more than two decades of researching. It is also a challenge for my peers, including peer reviewers, who will often be able to see the gaps in my understanding of any single discipline – and that becomes a challenge for me. I have no obvious disciplinary 'home', therefore: wherever I lay my library card, that's my home. And both sets of challenges, those related to access and those related to disciplines, are exacerbated by my tendency to research alone, and to do so within a career that is not primarily focused on research. After teaching full-time for ten years, I started my doctorate whilst seconded two days a week to carry out teacher education, but I carried on school-teaching the other three days a week. For nine years, I mixed school and university contracts, or a range of part-time or temporary university contracts, whilst completing my doctorate and publishing a number of books and articles. The most time given to research during that period, and since, was 20–22 days a year. The next fifteen years (taking me to today), I have had established university posts, focused on teaching and, for all but the first two years, on management – as head of a large department and then as dean of three large faculties. My research has complemented my other work, but setting up large, funded, research teams for my own projects has not been viable.

Looking at the list of virtues, the first one that I thought about, in my research, was sincerity, and this was related to my first suggested research topic, as I've described. I explored magnanimity at the same time, as a leadership virtue described by Aristotle (1976, pp. 153–158), and that has, since then, become more important to me as a research virtue: the need to be 'big enough' to allow for other authors and research participants to have their say, without trying to prove them wrong or force them into my own beliefs or theories. Creativity and curiosity are always there, as uncreative research would not be able to keep me interested. I hate being bored, and am lucky enough to have avoided that in all my jobs and all my research.

Hope and trust have always been important to me, and I am relatively unusual, I think, in completing a great deal of educational research that is both critical (I hope) and hopeful and optimistic. I think that professional educators, in schools and in higher education, have more in their power than they sometimes think they have. Finally, I value humour, and see that as an important way of marking and celebrating the breaking of boundaries between fields or concepts. However, I recognise that my use of humour – in writing and even more in speaking – can be interpreted as 'buffoonery', from Peterson's list, or as trivialising lightness. That is one of the risks I am prepared to take.

The Significance of the Portraits

Having presented eighteen portraits, along with a little analysis, in Chapters 2 to 10, and a nineteenth in this chapter, I ask myself, 'So what?' That is a research question, not an existential question: what is the value or significance of what is said in the portraits, or of the processes that created the portraits? I will therefore present, once more, some of the key points made by the conversationalists, and follow them up with some ideas about their significance.

Starting with some general themes, it is important to explain that the portraits are more personal than I had expected, in that they end up exploring personhood – as I mention in Chapter 1. An alternative title for the book might be *Research and Personhood*. Why is this significant? Going in to this project, I had thought of myself as a researcher for whom research was central to personal identity, but I had thought this relatively unusual. What I found, however, is that the conversationalists – at different stages of their careers, and researching in different ways a wide range of topics and disciplines – all seemed to describe how research was of existential significance. Research makes us who we are. A second surprise for me, related to the 'personhood' surprise, was that the themes emerging from the conversations were not those predicted by me – other than the broadly philosophical theme of Chapter 2 and the action/practitioner research theme of Chapter 6. The themes that I had predicted were more descriptive of the research topics, such as intercultural research, politically engaged research, or research into the private lives of research participants. Issues relating to those 'missing' themes were certainly mentioned, and yet the chapters did not divide up according to the predicted themes. The emergent themes were more personal – being an insider/outsider, therapy, professing, time, courage, curiosity – more concerned with personhood. Even though I had wanted to explore the lived experience of research, I was surprised by how the focus remained on the 'livingness' (as Anne Pirrie described it), whilst the topics and methods took a secondary role.

Finance was the third surprise. I expected more concerns to be expressed about research finance. Morwenna Griffiths does say how research finance can be part of the 'structure of violence', and Chris Sink talks of bureaucrats looking for finance, and of having to put seven funding applications to get a chance of one success. Ron Best mentions chasing finance as a researcher and as a research manager, and Anne Pirrie compares financed research projects with the work that followed – the interesting research 'alone with dead people'. Fedor Kozyrev insists on researchers being 'ready to do the work which will not bring money', part of the monastic virtue of poverty, and describes the 'Fall' of the researcher being 'oriented toward the result which could pay'. And Helen Gunter talks about the entrepreneurial agenda in universities with respect to funding. Yet research funding still has a lower profile in the conversations than I had expected, especially as many of the conversationalists work on large, funded, projects.

'Virtue', defined briefly at the start of the book as 'the cultivation of a set of dispositions conducive to good character' (Arthur 2010, p. 3), has a stronger identity now. It seems to me that a person does not 'acquire' or 'exhibit' virtues. A person *is* their virtues, at least in part. People may well – in the Aristotelian tradition – become good as 'the result of habit' (Aristotle 1976, p. 91) or 'by consistently doing good things and avoid-ing bad things' (Arthur 2010, p. 3), but insofar as they are alive, they are always being good, bad or indifferent. Education in virtues, or education for character, is not an additional activity for which teachers or supervi-sors or managers are responsible. It is what characterises all our activities, our everyday lived experiences. Teachers, supervisors or managers – one hopes – will help nudge us in the right direction, but all we do contributes to virtue development. At least, my understanding from reading these conversations, is that all we do as researchers – the engaging, dialogic, solitary, brave, prudent, curious work we do as researchers – contributes to our virtue development.

What about the significance of the individual conversations? I will draw on elements of each conversation, picking out some issues and their significance. The issues are often mentioned in the conclusion of the chapter in which the conversation is reported. Here, the emphasis is on what significance those issues have for educational research. Morwenna Griffiths talked about how 'virtue has an outcome that is virtuous, but it is also how you conduct yourself personally and with others, as a virtuous person', so 'virtuous educational research is something that is both personal, and ... an outcome'. Virtues are dispositions to act, so 'with my values of justice', for example, 'I should be acting justly'. The practice-orientation of virtue discourses is important, and can be helpful in overcoming the tendency in talking about research ethics to say that once something has been approved, that is the end of the matter. Morwenna Griffiths notes here that 'you're forever negotiating'. The significance for educational research of taking more account of virtues is that the work may be harder, but, by taking this on as a *personal* task, researchers will be owning their own hard work. This is in contrast to the performativity pressures on academics – the pressures to perform for an audience that is not interested in your ideas but in the number of publications or the finance raised by research or the 'star quality' of the publication or the journal in which it is published. Nel Noddings is concerned with exactly the same performativity pressures, described as academics trying to get so many papers published, or trying to find something to correlate. Rather than looking outwards to such performance indicators, educational researchers should be contributing to the 'interminable discussion' of what makes a 'better' person, and how education can contribute to that. Schoolteachers need to recognise the importance of the 'continuity of persons'. That personal continuity is important for researchers, too – driven by curiosity and 'initiating conversations across social classes, across ages, engaging conversations with kids'. Educational research is expected to be more personal and more actively engaged with those outside the academy.

Ron Best also describes the work of educational researchers in terms of their careers. He provides a different perspective on how researchers progress: taking opportunities as they come up, aligning their own interests with those of universities and research auditors. His position is one of consistent concern with personal issues in schooling, and with care and empathy for the people being researched: 'it's about persons'. And the emotions of researchers need looking after, too, through supervision. The implications of what he says are as much for the management of research as for researchers themselves: how to support researchers, personally, and how to provide appropriate opportunities for researchers to progress their research in a way that is sustainable institutionally as well as intellectually and personally. This is a valuable reminder that the virtues of researchers do not stand alone (see also Bottery 2016). They are also dependent on social and institutional contexts. Curiosity and the 'responsibility to know' is central to Helen Lees' view of researchers and of all adults. Like Nel Noddings and Morwenna Griffiths, she describes herself as 'a philosopher of education who, to do philosophy, wants to talk to people'. What distinguishes researchers from other 'knowing' adults is the genre of research writing. That genre is not simply a style of writing, but an opportunity to be original – to be courageous enough to face freedom. What both Ron Best and Helen Lees say has implications for the management of academic journals, and their ability to encourage originality and to present research to a variety of audiences – within and beyond the academy.

The role of the educational intellectual exercised Mario D'Souza. He writes on Catholic education and is troubled by the anti-intellectual approach of many practitioners, when they seem to retreat into the 'reality' of immediate, local concerns. As a researcher, he is trying to understand the fundamental purposes of education, and is doing this in the context of Catholic philosophers of education and Catholic church policy documents. Definitely part of the 'interminable discussion', he is concerned that he may not be as original as is sometimes expected of researchers. Should he be more original, more different? 'The only way I could see that paradigm changing is if I changed – if I were no longer Roman Catholic, or possibly no longer a Christian', but of course jumping out of one paradigm means jumping into another. As the environmental writer, Hill, says, 'When you say you're going to throw something away – where's "away"?' She continues, 'There is no away' (Hill 2010). In the same way, an intellectual can leave one tradition, but cannot simply 'go away' from all possible traditions. The virtuous quest for originality is not a quest for 'being different for its own sake'. This needs to be taken account of in how researchers are supported: to have the courage to move, but not the recklessness to think moving is all there is to be done. Anne Pirrie presents another approach to movement and 'place' in a researcher's life. She is something of a traveller, a 'nomad', and just as there are social practices that help or hinder nomads and other travellers, there are academic practices that help or hinder 'nomad' researchers in the style described by Anne Pirrie. How do we manage research in such a way that 'farmers' and 'nomads' can both be productive? Any simple solution is likely to be inappropriate.

Anne Pirrie shares with several conversationalists a concern that the substantive ethics of the research process can be marginalised by research ethics procedures that give the impression that following procedures is all there is to ethics. Researchers have power, as researchers, and they can use this power to do good (including by trying to describe what 'good' is), which is more than simply avoiding harm. It is part of the 'good life' or, in Anne Pirrie's words, the 'livingness' of a researcher's life. Mike Bottery is also conscious of the contribution of research to society – to fairness and wellbeing. In the 'portrait' research, the influence is directly on the research participants. Research should provoke feelings, as part of the process of convincing people. That 'convincing' needs to be open enough to allow people to change, and the researcher must be able to change ideas too. A delicate balance, then, between persuasive writing and an openness to other views. In a world where simple solutions – perhaps in just 140 characters – all too often gain immediate popularity, the nuanced influence of research has to fight for its place. It is good to see the recognition of feelings, too. As Neumann says, based on her own interviews with mid-career researchers:

> Serious scholarly work is rarely discussed in terms of the scholars' emotions. Yet scholarly learning implies the pursuit of thought, with feeling at its center. For some, that

learning is nothing less than the pursuit of beauty. ... I portray professors' scholarly learning as emotionally complex and as punctuated at its high points by an experience that I call 'passionate thought,' at times amid strivings for beauty. (Neumann 2009, p. 43)

Shanaaz Hoosain, Helen Lees, and Mike Bottery all mention beauty, with Mike Bottery noting that this is not the language he would normally use, but 'there are some times where you see people's behaviours or people's thinking, and it is beautiful'. And emotions are central to Lander Calvelhe's account of his own ability to complete research without anger and anxiety, as research is not itself therapy. How research teams work together is one of the ways he finds support, or, when it works less well, finds more loneliness. Personal growth is important to researchers, and – as Lander Calvelhe says – this requires courage and 'heart'. Support that enables researchers to be more courageous is also described by Lāsma Latsone. The support is framed as 'belief in you', a confidence or faith. But it is also practiced in management support for talking about research, discussing ideas, and creating the conditions for disagreeing, peacefully, within a community. The community creates conditions in which a supported researcher is in a better position to pass that on to newly researching students. A different kind of courage is described by Lynne Gabriel, who highlights the courage needed to face the 'messiness' in life. In one sense, a researcher is trying to bring some kind of order to the world, to explain and systematise. But researchers generally recognise the messiness in research as well as in the rest of life, even at the times that they are making it look more tidy. Mess is rarely acknowledged, but, happily, Helen Gunter has described it as a not entirely negative quality:

> The book will inevitably be a 'messy text' because the stories are on-going and changes are still happening in our lives. The stories we tell today may not be the ones we would tell tomorrow as we continually struggle to make sense of our assumptions, experiences and lives. (Cole and Gunter, in Cole and Gunter 2010, p. 12)

The word 'mess' originally referred to food, and is still used as the name for a military canteen (as in 'the officers' mess'). I prefer to think of 'mess' as hospitable and like eating together, rather than as muddle. So the courage to face messiness is also the courage to be with people in their real, messy, lives. Lynne Gabriel's research on dual relationships – relationships that have more than one meaning, more than one value – is a model for all researchers who are working with people: living, breathing, eating, people.

Lynne Gabriel's concern over power, including the misuse of power, suggests that support for researchers should be more 'facilitative' than 'normative/restorative'. This is an interesting principle to apply to all research support, and the idea of research ethics as a 'list of what not to do' would certainly fall in the 'normative/restorative' category. She says that it can be dangerous when you are driven by your own agenda alone. But even that, helpful, advice needs to be balanced by what Fedor Kozyrev says about the need for a researcher to be 'impolite' and 'not a nice person' in order to follow the evidence rather than what is popular. A virtue can be good in one circumstance and bad in another. The poet Larkin writes about virtues and vices, and in a poem about love, describes how selfish you need to be to disturb someone else's life by loving them, and how you also need to *avoid* the selfishness of solitude. He describes someone (probably himself) who is unable to love, avoiding the first selfishness but having the second, as 'Selfish this wrong way round' (Larkin 1988, p. 150). What Fedor Kozyrev recommends, however, is not blind persistence in one's own beliefs. He stresses the need for all researchers, including those involved in large-scale quantitative research, to be using their hermeneutic, interpretive, skills. In such ways, his approach is similar to that of Lynne Gabriel, as also is his stress on dialogue between people from different perspectives. And, as with so many people in these conversations, he is particularly concerned with performativity, describing the bias towards 'the result which could pay' as 'the Fall' of the scientist.

If making public, through research, the 'messiness' of real life is what such work can add to therapy, for Lynne Gabriel, then the conversation with Jean McNiff indicates that all of life, made public in this way, can be a form of research. The slightly disconcerting phrase 'there is nothing between research and living' is clarified by Jean. It is the creativity, the search for truth (or unmasking of untruth), and the ability to make the world a better place, that research and life, at least 'non-routine' life, have in common. She 'accidentally' became a researcher because her work – with teachers, academics, and others – is 'effectively shared' in ways that are recognised as research, through books and articles. The idea that research is a specific form of curious, creative, and shared way of living, rather than an activity that is quite distinct from other forms of work, is a valuable insight. It brings us back to Hanks' description of learning as 'a way of being in the social world, not a way of coming to know about it' (Hanks, in Lave and Wenger 1991, p. 24). Jacqui Akhurst also blurs the distinction between practice and research. Reflective practice becomes research by making the implicit more explicit and by providing *explanations*. The idea is that research includes activities that are similar to other activities, and that for some types of research, researchers will see their work as blending with other kinds of work. Research approaches with these characteristics include a great deal of practitioner research, some forms of action research and grounded theory, and some ethnographic studies. Recognising the personal nature of research – the fears and the pleasures – is important for all research, but what this tells us is how certain forms of research are even more closely related to other forms of practice, especially professional practice.

It is professional practice, as a social worker, that Shanaaz Hoosain describes as being continued in a different form, as a researcher. Introducing 'pause' in social work, and seeing research as a form of reflective pausing, is a significant articulation of the nature of research. Shanaaz Hoosain also relates it to professional practice as a teacher in higher education, the reflective pause to allow students time to consider their own positions, to learn. Educational research tests our sense of time and timing, and this is also addressed by Sr Agnes Wilkins, who recognises the prudence of having been 'paused' herself, before her community thought it an appropriate time in her life to complete the research she is now carrying out. Both researchers want to make a difference to society through their research, and both also have a sense of restraint – of not jumping directly into 'activist' mode, for Shanaaz Hoosain, and of not directly taking part in much of the dialogue that she sees as the key to 'living together peacefully' for Sr Agnes Wilkins. They are relatively new researchers, so it is not surprising that they are conscious of the need for and the value of support. Yet experienced researchers also talk of the same need and value. Chris Sink describes the negative side of the issue, his frustration with education bureaucrats who are narrowly 'pragmatic' and look for 'instant gratification' in research – funding or clearly identifiable outcomes. Amongst the virtues he therefore highlights are intimacy and care, somewhat unexpected choices, given his specialism in large-scale quantitative projects. Yet that ability to build up good, caring, personal relationships with research gatekeepers – bureaucrats, school leaders, teachers and students or others working as research assistants – seems obvious once it has been described in this way. Care for people as well as for the 'product' of the research might be described as an 'intellectual' virtue; care for the people involved in research is most definitely a 'moral' virtue – to use Aristotle's division of virtues (Aristotle 1976, p. 90). (That division is not central to this project, but seems a relevant distinction to make in this case.)

Conclusion

My conclusion to this chapter draws on the conversations with Ginger MacDonald and Helen Gunter, as these combine a number of themes raised by others, and seem to be somewhat synoptic – summarising the role of research in personhood itself. Ginger MacDonald's own research is on identity formation of individual people and of organisations. Driven by a lifelong curiosity, research is by its nature 'generative' rather than 'despairing' (in Erikson's terms), so a life with research in it is in that way a productive, generative, life. Persistence, optimism (to the point almost of gullibility), and the ability to focus, alone, are all mentioned as virtues. However, the final product of such a curious life is a partial, as yet inconclusive, answer to the question 'What is the meaning of my life?' Mortality and the sense of a life-project of research is highlighted by Helen Gunter. She, like Jean McNiff, describes research as intellectual *work*. Pausing to think is the contribution research can make to a culture otherwise dominated by 'le Fast Talker'. A life of research that is persistent, even in the face of personal attack, is also one that is difficult to understand until the project is complete.

A flourishing life or, using Aristotle's term, a eudemonic life – sometimes translated as a 'happy' life – is one of virtue:

> We ... define the happy [eudemonic] man as 'one who is active in accordance with complete virtue, and who is adequately furnished with external goods, and that not for some unspecified period but throughout a complete life'. And probably we should add 'destined both to live in this way and to die accordingly'; because the future is obscure to us, and happiness [eudaimonia] we maintain to be an *end* in every way utterly final and complete. (Aristotle 1976, p. 84)

In this sense, we will not know how fulfilling our lives have been until they have been completed – and beyond, as our work may be judged more or less valuable after our lives have ended. So Ginger MacDonald's optimism, combined with the uncertainty over what her curious life will finally mean, and Helen Gunter's concern to complete a life's-worth of project, within a career, are characteristic of a virtuous researcher's life.

CHAPTER 12

Conclusion: Educational Research in Learning Communities

Introduction

This chapter explores the place and the value of educational research work within universities, and proposes a theory of virtuous educational research, based on all the conversations and analysis already presented. The theory emerges from the conversations: the conversations do not test a theory. This approach has the characteristic of much 'grounded theory'. Grounded theory was developed by Glaser and Strauss initially through a study in hospitals of awareness of dying (Glaser and Strauss 1965). Patients, their families, nurses, and doctors all had different levels of awareness, and only by listening to and observing those people could a good description and explanation be given of the situation. This, they called a 'substantive theory', 'grounded in research on one particular substantive area (dying)', which 'might therefore be taken to apply only to that specific area' (Glaser and Strauss 1965, p. 275). They continue that this 'level' of theory, which at that time was the kind of research that was most common in sociology, might yet have more 'general' significance and might 'contribute to the formulation of new formal theory' (Glaser and Strauss 1965, p. 276). Some social scientists would describe 'substantive' theory work in terms of the validity of the account of a specific situation, whilst 'formal' theory work would be more generalisable. There are all too many binary divisions confronting researchers: empirical and non-empirical, quantitative and qualitative, scientific and interpretive, generalisable and valid. A number have been challenged in the conversations reported here. However, I would still like to draw out some of the broader implications of the work already presented, and would happily refer to them, in Bassey's words, as 'fuzzy generalizations' (Bassey 1999, p. 44).

The three fuzzy generalisations here are related to performativity, voice, and support. Although I have explored aspects of each of these ideas in previous research papers, they have all been significantly developed as a result of the conversations with researchers. They constitute something of a 'non-ideal theory' of virtuous educational research. A contribution, at least, to what may be an interminable conversation about how to flourish as a researcher. The ethical, political and professional roles of researchers come together in this conclusion.

Performing and Performativity

Virtuous educational research should be performed, made public, and this should be sincerely done. Research can be a solitary activity, and yet it necessarily involves something of a performance. The 'effectively shared' element of the definition of research used here is, rightly, 'making public' or, in the broader meaning of the word, 'publishing' the research – whether the publishing is in a journal or book, or an oral presentation at a conference, or a teaching session, or a conversation with a colleague. The act of publishing may itself have a value: it may earn money for the researcher, it may help the researcher's career or status, it may damage the career or status of another researcher. 'Performativity' is a term developed in its current form by the philosopher Austin, for whom performative utterances are those such as making a bet which have a direct effect, without or independent of any truth or falsehood (Austin 1975, p. 8). Austin understood performative utterances as, potentially, positive or negative – placing a bet, saying 'I do' at a wedding, or using an insulting term to refer to a person. Saying 'I congratulate you' may be wholly positive, but if insincere it may have a different effect (Austin 1975, p. 40). It is the negative – harmful and/or insincere – performative utterances that have more recently become central to the sense of performativity. '[S]ome speech not only communicates hate, but constitutes an injurious act', Butler says (Butler 1997, p. 16), and this starts with 'name-calling', which is 'one of the first forms of linguistic injury that one learns' (Butler 1997, p. 2). Lyotard sees performativity (especially 'insincere' forms of performativity) as problematic because it dissociates people from the ethics of their own positions, producing 'universal measure[s] applicable to all entities, regardless of the regime of statements from which they derive' (Lyotard, in Benjamin 1989, p. 356). Derrida, writing about Rousseau, describes the effects of people who 'do not assume ethical responsibility for their word'. They 'become actors' and '[i]mmorality ... attaches, to the very status of the representer (performer)', such that '[v]ice is his natural bent' (Derrida 1976, p. 304).

Within both school-based and university-based education, performativity is seen as or has become 'a technology, a culture and a mode of regulation that employs judgements, comparisons and displays as means of incentive, control, attrition and change – based on rewards and sanctions (both material and symbolic)', such that 'performances ... serve as measures of productivity or output, or displays of 'quality', or 'moments' of promotion or inspection' (Ball 2003, p. 216). Ball says 'a kind of *values schizophrenia* is experienced by individual teachers where commitment, judgement and authenticity within practice are sacrificed for impression and performance', and he sees this as a threat to the teacher's 'soul' (Ball 2003, pp. 215–228). '[W]hile we may not be expected to care about each other we are expected to 'care' *about* performances' (Ball 2003, p. 224). He contrasts 'performance' and 'authenticity', whilst Troman contrasts performativity with creativity, with performativity needing to be mediated or subverted in order to maintain creativity (Troman 2008, Jeffrey and Troman 2011). A common response to performativity is an ironic separation from the pressures, explored by Hoyle and Wallace (2005), characterised by insincere performances 'for show'. An alternative response is an unthinking policy conformance. Both responses are understandable yet unhealthy, personally and professionally.

Amongst the few educational researchers who wish to frame performativity positively is Barnett. Writing of higher education, he notes that '[t]he idea of performance has come in for a battering of late: 'performativity' has become a term of abuse, in its implication that educational activities might be structured by considerations of impact and return (especially in the economic sphere)' (Barnett, in Barnett 2005, p. 106). However, he continues, 'the ideas of 'performance' and even 'performative' and 'performing' can have more positive connotations: such ideas can point to and urge practices that invite involvement, commitment and energy on the part of the student' (Barnett, in Barnett 2005, p. 106). Parker similarly notes how a university 'is currently a place governed by performance', notably the '[pre]scripted, assessed display' exemplified by teaching dominated by learning outcomes when they are 'teleological' and 'determine what should be aimed at', rather than 'commentatory' (Parker, in Barnett 2005, p. 151, brackets in the original). This should be replaced, she says, by the idea of the 'theatrical university', drawing on 'the rich developmental possibilities inherent in a performance culture: a culture in which character is formed, refined and challenged in all kinds of intellectual and other display' (Parker, in Barnett 2005, p. 151). Barnett later develops his position, drawing on Parker's theatrical terminology, to describe '[t]he most powerful performances ... [which] are not just alive; they are life itself in its fullness, at once creative, engaging and significant' (Barnett 2007, p. 79). Performance in this sense can be seen 'as creative and as reaching out to an audience' or, in its linguistic uses, as in 'the idea of language-as-performance, itself being creative, of speech as action' (Barnett 2007, p. 79). Even Derrida contrasts his account of the corrupting power of theatrical performance with the possibility of the 'representer' who 'represents himself [sic]', so that 'the representer and the represented are one' (Derrida 1976, p. 305). He continues, '[t]he identity of the representer and the represented may be accomplished ... by the effacement of the representer and the personal presence of the represented (the orator, the preacher)' (Derrida 1976, p. 305).

Why is this so important for educational research? It suggests that virtue may be forgotten if performance is measured in outcomes, if the performer – the researcher and others represented in the research – do not have 'personal presence' in the research, speaking other people's words or speaking insincerely. Morwenna Griffiths describes the performativity of publication and financial targets as having 'really corrupting effects on how people view themselves, and what they think they need to do', as it makes a person 'pretend that I am doing this, and I will pretend really well'.

Nel Noddings talks about the desire for recognition and the compliance such a desire encourages – stopping young researchers from working on 'what really grabs them' and leading them to 'wander up and down the halls saying "what shall I correlate?"' In a similar way, Chris Sink talks of the 'virtuous professor' who 'does research because they care', unlike those who 'have to tick off that research box, I don't really like it, I don't like writing, I don't like researching, but I know I have to get three publications to advance, so I'm going to find a way to do it'. Such an attitude 'drives me crazy', but is a result of the 'publish or perish' world in which academic research exists. Research is completed for 'selfish reasons'. Fedor Kozyrev goes even further, describing the bias towards 'the result which could pay' as 'the Fall' of the scientist.

Helen Gunter talks of the audit-driven 'performance regime' for researchers, and notes in particular how this distorts which audience the 'performance' is for: 'one of our audiences has to be the profession, but that might not count in relation to the REF and vice versa'. Interesting to note that she uses the term 'audience' to refer to the readership of the research, with an implication that performance itself is not being questioned, but the *audience* targeted by the performance. There is an impact of performativity on researchers, just as there is an impact on schoolteachers. In the latter case, teachers may have learned their performance scripts so well that they believe them, and therefore believe themselves guilty for failings that are created by policy-makers. The job of a researcher is to enable them to realise that 'they are not guilty'. But of course if researchers are distracted by research audits from addressing professional audiences, they will not support teachers in that way.

Although Helen Gunter and Ron Best seem to be saying quite different things about performativity, on closer reading, they have complementary views. Ron Best talks positively about how a researcher might be opportunistic, looking for funding gaps and topics that might score well in research audits. He gives one of his own topics, deliberate self-harm, as an example: 'I can remember becoming aware by chance that there was a problematic bit of children's experience ... that I knew nothing at all about, ... nor did many other people ..., so my reaction was ... I might be able to get some money for it, and I'll be able to publish articles that could go in the RAE'. He says that 'one's motives are not altruistic in this regard'. Yet this description was moderated by him saying that 'it was also worth doing', and by describing a whole career of exploring a specific line of research on linked topics (on children's personal development) that is as curiosity-driven as that of any other 'virtuously curious' researcher. He also finds ways to address a variety of audiences, writing once for the research audit, and a second time for a professional audience. Anne Pirrie describes a similar approach, for example writing commissioned research reports for government agencies, and then writing interesting articles, independent of the commissioned work, analysing some of the issues raised by the earlier reports. She also writes positively about the sense of researcher as performer, and the quality – and risk – of 'live performance', which brings some of the quality of vitality, or livingness, to her research life.

Lynne Gabriel talks of the distinctive nature of research, in contrast to therapeutic work, as something that 'needs to be heard or performed or written or narrated – so there's more of a community or a public sharing – whereas in the therapy room, that's shared between myself and the other person, or myself and the group, and then that person can choose what they do with that, but I'm not responsible for sharing it'. She is not concerned that there are 'academic drivers', such as audit regimes, as long as researchers are 'engaged in meaningful research'. You can be 'mindful ... of things like citations, but not ... as the driver for the research'.

My understanding is that, when it comes to researchers, performativity is not wholly negative. Performance is central to the research process, and being expected to perform for particular audiences is reasonable. It is problematic when the researcher or the audience is not interested in the research itself, but only the 'outcomes' (in Chris Sink's terms). It is problematic when performing for one audience (such as fellow academics or research auditors) prevents one from performing for a more important audience (such as schoolteachers). And it is problematic when the performance is insincere. I am therefore promoting a sense of the value of performance, in research, and the need to avoid misdirected or insincere performativity. When the performance of research becomes an entirely insincere process, researchers will have lost their voices. Voicing is the next element of my fuzzy theory of virtuous educational research.

Voicing Researchers

All research is 'voiced', as it must be 'effectively shared' if it is to count as research. Sincerity indicates that the voice heard is 'positively expressing what you do think and believe' (Macmurray 1995, p. 76), and by 'positively', Macmurray implies the 'performance' is judged by the situation in which it is performed, and whether the performance is to the audience's advantage. Enabling researchers to reach their wished-for audiences has been explored above, in the section on performativity. But there is more to be said about voicing. Research tends to look much tidier than it is, and the world of research can be portrayed – in research methods textbooks and the accounts of researchers themselves – as rather neat, and smooth. There are good reasons for that; there are dangers too. Wittgenstein writes of the danger of the 'smooth' language of logic – his own smoothness, it should be noted, of his own earlier writings:

> The more narrowly we examine actual language, the sharper becomes the conflict between it and our requirement. (For the crystalline purity of logic was, of course, not a *result of investigation*: it was a requirement.) The conflict becomes intolerable; the requirement is now in danger of becoming empty. – We have got on to slippery ice where there is no friction and so in a certain sense the conditions are ideal, but also, just because of that, we are unable to walk. We want to walk: so we need *friction*. Back to the rough ground! (Wittgenstein 1958, p. 46e)

We want clear, neat, tidy language, but such a pure language would be unusable, too slippery. As Buber says, 'it is not the unambiguity of a word but its ambiguity that constitutes living language', as '[t]he ambiguity creates the problematic of speech, and it creates its overcoming in an understanding that is not an assimilation but a fruitfulness' (Buber 1998, p. 104; see also Empson 1961). And if that isn't clear enough, he explains why he – in unexpected common cause with Wittgenstein – finds the 'pure' distasteful.

> I am not concerned with the pure; I am concerned with the turbid, the repressed, the pedestrian, with toil and dull contrariness – and with the break-through. With the break-through and not with perfection. (Buber 2002, p. 41)

From words to voice, Buber continues: '[i]t is the communal nature of the logos as at once 'word' and 'meaning' which makes man man, and it is this which proclaims itself from of old in the communalizing of the spoken word that again and again comes into being' (Buber 1998, p. 105). When educational research attempts to speak with one, pure, unambiguous, voice, it is doomed to become unusable. A musical metaphor is helpful.

> Music is always contrapuntal in the philosophical sense of the word. Even when it is linear, there are always opposing elements coexisting, occasionally even in conflict with each other. Music accepts comments from one voice to the other at all times and tolerates subversive accompaniments as a necessary antipode to leading voices. Conflict, denial and commitment coexist at all times in music. (Barenboim 2008, p. 20)

'Voices', therefore, interest me more than 'voice'. Voices are in relationships, in dialogue, even when – especially when – they are opposed to each other. Each of the researchers represented in this book – those of the conversationalists, and those quoted by and alongside the conversationalists – has a voice. (It is probably fair to say that each person has *at least* one voice; most have *more than* one voice.) The many-voiced approach of this book is not intended as a prelude to a pure and single-voiced conclusion. It is a presentation of dialogue and of complexity. Despite the chorus of denials from postmodern theorists, there may be 'the truth', somewhere. But as Sr Agnes Wilkins says, 'In the end Truth with a capital 'T' is much bigger than anybody or any particular position that you're coming from'. Each of the people in this book are in dialogue, dialogue with me and with other researchers and professionals and poets and all kinds of people. Each voice can be regarded as singular, individual, complete, but the world – even the small world of this book – is plural, many-voiced, and each individual only exists in and through dialogue.

Voices, the count noun, not 'voice', the mass noun; many-voiced research, not a single 'collective voice' of research or of researchers. That is my primary interest in presenting the voices of this book. A researcher who is only concerned with their own voice, or who uses the voices of others – research participants or the authors of books and articles – merely as a means to strengthen their own voice, this is monologic research. Such research may gain success in the world, but it misses out on the opportunity to contribute positively to the lives of others, or even to their own life. 'He who speaks the separated *I*, with emphasis on the capital, lays bare the shame of the world-spirit which has been degraded to spirituality', says Buber:

> 'But how lovely and how fitting the sound of the lively and impressive *I* of Socrates! It is the *I* of endless dialogue, and the air of dialogue is wafted around it in all its journeys, before the judges and in the last hour in prison. (Buber 1958, p. 89)

Research is 'a process of investigation leading to new insights *effectively shared*' (Hefce 2011, p. 48, emphasis added), I repeat once more, and the voices, not voice, in research are part of that sharing – the sharing that can happen before as well as after publication, voicing research participants and other authors.

My intention in this book is that each conversationalist has their own voice. Many of them also talk about the various voices in their own work. Helen Lees talks about how research participants 'are philosophers in their own right' and 'I'm offering them a platform for their voice to be a part of the presentation, and I don't interfere with their voice'. And Jean McNiff talks of Bakhtin's 'voices in everything'. Mario D'Souza talks of the need to present the voices of previous philosophers in a respectful way, and a way that allows them to be part of a contemporary dialogue. Shanaaz Hoosain is concerned with voicing the unvoiced, the voices of marginalised groups, and she is committed to 'includ[ing] the voices of the people that our research is intended for'. This is not simply a general principle for her. The messiness of research involves working out how, within a family, different voices may be heard – children, men, and women. Foucault's work on subjugated knowledge becomes, for Shanaaz Hoosain, work on subjugated *voices*. Simply by identifying as a member of a group does not put her in a position to be the 'voice' of that group. Hence, although she identifies as 'this black South African woman', she can 'make judgements and pre-judge people', including other black South African women. Helen Gunter talks of student voice and the need for people in power to 'make it happen', and this echoes Helen Lees' concern for adults to have the strength to be silent, in order to allow children and young people to have their voices. As a 'loud mouthed working class girl', Helen Gunter also realises her voice carries with it a challenge – an institutional challenge and a challenge to other researchers who can talk 'but not say anything'. In my own research, I have attempted to 'voice' children and young people and adults (notably in Stern 2001, 2009a, 2014a, 2014b), and have attempted to voice other researchers in every publication. And yet it is only when I have come to write this book that I have found myself thinking that I have more gener- ously voiced people – in presenting the conversations in dialogue form, rather than quoting from them in order to illustrate my own argument.

The fuzzy – messy – generalisation I am making, to create this second element of a theory of virtuous educational research, is that virtuous research should 'voice' people. In voicing the researcher (rather than the researcher pretending not to be there), in voicing research participants (rather than simply using what they say to confirm our own prejudices), and in voicing the research to others – effectively sharing the research – in a dialogic way, rather than as an act of 'monologue disguised as dia- logue' (Buber 2002, p. 22), the research can add to the world. The term 'dialogue' is important, and I retain the distinction made by Wegerif between 'dialogic' and 'dialectic' approaches to education. Dialogue continues, even when unresolved; dialectic may involve disagreement but that is eventually resolved into a synthesis (Wegerif 2008). Schools will properly encounter dialectic discussion: there are issues that can be resolved. But when there is an expectation that all will be resolved, dia- logue is suppressed. The dialogue, as Nel Noddings vividly describes it, must be engaged in even if it is interminable.

An educational researcher's life is the life of a 'performer', someone who makes their insights public, and who does so sincerely. The researcher is 'voiced', and in turn voices others, and contributes to on-going dialogue. Returning to the question that I first raised in my earliest educational research (described in Chapter 11), how can that educational work be sup- ported, and what is the relationship between the support offered to, and the support offered by, a researcher? That topic forms the third element in my theory of virtuous educational research.

Researcher Support

Educational work, including educational research, is work that supports other people's learning. Yet research is itself a form of learning – the kind of learning that involves investigation (finding out, rather than just being told), and that leads to new insights (rather than confirming the already-known) which are effectively shared (rather than kept to oneself). So educational research is, by its nature, exemplifying what it promotes: learning. This is not how all researchers concerned with education, or how all researchers in other disciplines, see their work. Some see the generation of new knowledge being completed by its dissemination – its publication, its 'application' to or 'impact' on different contexts, and/or its commercialisation (in the 'knowledge economy'). Such research – including a great deal of what is referred to as 'scientific' research – can be entirely appropriate and virtuous, but it is not an example of what I describe as 'educational' research (with the 'al' carrying a lot of weight), as described in Chapter 1, and discussed with Morwenna Griffiths in Chapter 2 and elsewhere in the book. Educational research, as I see it, *is* interminable, and, as has been described in the sections above on performativity and on voices, it involves mutuality. Jean McNiff continues her educational work as an 'accidental researcher', and this is telling: educators can be supported to become researchers without giving up their prior commitment. They may in fact be becoming 'more of an educator' as they fall into research. This section, building on the 'support' theme in Chapter 8, therefore explores the forms of support needed for, and given by, educational researchers. I will consider support within higher education institutions, and then support beyond those institutions.

Nixon writes of the need for 'authentic dialogue' in the 'deliberative spaces' of what he calls *virtuous* universities (Nixon 2008, p. 37). I completed a research project on supporting research in higher education (Stern 2014b), and it was based on my conversations with researchers over a number of years, including with colleagues for whom I had a management responsibility, and those from whom I was independent. In that research, several forms of support were described. Researchers were concerned with space, Nixon's 'deliberative spaces', and they discussed the access they had to both solitary and sociable spaces. Single-occupancy offices were the most common solitary spaces that researchers described as being needed. The need for 'a room of one's own' has been described for hundreds of years, with Montaigne describing a room being needed for 'establishing ... our true liberty, our principal solitude and asylum' (Montaigne 1991, p. 7), and Woolf describing the impact on women of not having such a room (Woolf 2014). These are solitary places, but they are still dialogic: dialogue with other authors, with distant and long-dead people, and with oneself. Researchers described the need for sociable spaces too, places to eat lunch, common rooms to discuss issues, and, more rarely, they described conference venues as good places in which to 'confer'. It was not just the physical spaces that were needed. Researchers needed those spaces to be recognised as spaces for *research*: offices should be allowed to have 'do not disturb' notices on their doors, and lunch halls needed to be places where the discussion of research was not seen as an unpleasant intrusion, but an accepted part of social discourse. In the conversations for this book, there were more mentions of space. Sr Agnes Wilkins describes the value of her monastic cell for her research activity, a place where others do not interrupt her, and where she can read and write about, and engage in an at-a-distance form of inter-religious dialogue. Lāsma Latsone talks about the contrast between two universities, one of which offers her an office – and the value of that office. She also talks of the value of research discussions in social spaces, including in research seminars and conferences. Shanaaz Hoosain also notes the value of conferences for giving her courage, as well as giving her ideas.

A second theme in my earlier research on researchers was that of time. Researchers and those who support researchers will be familiar with calls for 'more time'. What emerged in the earlier research was a need not simply for a quantity of time, but for particular 'kinds' of time – certain blocks of time, for example, or times during the normal working day in which it was acceptable to complete research. I felt that the labelling of research time as 'research leave' or as a 'sabbatical' was itself damaging to research, because it confused research and leisure, and tended to give academics a sense that research was not as important as teaching or administrative activities. However, I have changed my view, as a result of the conversations held for this book. Shanaaz Hoosain, in particular, noted the value of the 'contemplative pause' for researchers, for university teachers, and for social workers – the need to pause themselves, and the need to offer pauses to others with whom they work. Mike Bottery also provides valuable time to the school leaders in his portrait research, to think about their work. The ability to see research as precisely a 'break from' other activities may be helpful, therefore. Nevertheless, research is still a form of work – it is, as Helen Gunter says, a form of intellectual *work*, not an entirely ethereal act of thinking. Lāsma Latsone complains that research can be identified as primarily a night-time activity, an alternative to sleep, which cannot be helpful. Both Sr Agnes Wilkins and Ginger MacDonald talk of the time issue as being about one's whole life, and not just about evenings and weekends. Sr Agnes Wilkins discusses the right time in her life to start research, and Ginger MacDonald discusses how her research may continue to influence academics or professionals over the years after she retires. And it is Helen Gunter's concern to complete her project before she retires that structures her current work. Since the earlier research (Stern 2014b), I have therefore gained a far richer sense of the significance of time – as something that researchers need themselves, and need to offer their respondents and colleagues and students. Research is also something that may take many years, a lifetime, in fact, and its influence may last much longer. Aristotle writes of a flourishing life being determined, perhaps, after a person has died – and he is, himself, a good example of someone whose research has had influence long since his death.

The practicalities of research were the third theme I found in my earlier research on researchers. By 'practicalities', I include an understanding of what the *practice* of research is like (for newer researchers), and how research fits with other aspects of an academic job (for researchers at every stage of their career). Making research seem 'normal' was important to many: a form of work like any other, a rather ordinary activity. A peer-reviewed research article might be six thousand words long, and in that way – and in being evaluated – it is remarkably similar to an assignment completed by a student. Academics who are happy setting assignments for their students, and evaluating and feeding back on those assignments, often felt that writing an article for a peer-reviewed journal was quite a different – a more 'special' and unusual – type of activity. Yet the similarities are clear. In roughly the same way, presenting at an academic conference was seen as more intimidating, by less experienced researchers, than presenting to a group of students – even though the presentation itself may take a very similar form. In the conversations for the current book, some similar issues were raised, although they were more often raised as positive points. Shanaaz Hoosain linked her research (as 'pause') directly to her teaching, Helen Lees talked of the genre of article-writing as a skill to be learned – in her case – through journal editing, and Lāsma Latsone talked of the support she receives from colleagues being translated, in turn, into the support she provides for her students. Those three are all earlier in their research careers, but a number of the most experienced researchers said similar things. Chris Sink talked of his work with students (who were often acting as research assistants), and Ron Best talked of the specific practicalities of getting published in academic and in more professional journals.

    What appeared more strongly in the conversations for this book than in the earlier research, was the importance of the attitude of the supporter. Lāsma Latsone talks of her mentor's support, and the support that this inspires in her to provide for her own students. It centres on 'belief that you can do it', a sense of being trusted – and therefore being able to trust others. Lander Calvelhe talks of the attitude of his supervisor and the wider research team – and whether anyone cared whether or not he was present in the university. Both Ron Best and Chris Sink talk about care – their own care for students and for research participants, and care for the research itself. For all four of these researchers, an interesting issue is how much support was needed from, and needed to be given to, people beyond the university. Lāsma Latsone felt somewhat unsupported by the Latvian Catholic church, early in her research career; Lander Calvelhe was conscious of the need to gain support from – or avoid criticism from – pressure groups; Ron Best talked in some detail about the relationship between his research and those working in schools, and how – with difficulty – he could maintain a mutually supportive relationship; and Chris Sink talked of the challenge of gaining support from 'bureaucrats' and those in schools, and the value of have good inter-personal skills that would help generate the 'intimacy' needed between researchers and those in schools. Mike Bottery talked, also, about how his 'portrait' research process might provide support for school leaders. 'One of the best ways of supporting people is giving them the time, saying "I'm here, I'm listening"', but you can do more: 'engaging in the portrait methodology can increase their wellbeing'. In this way, 'something originally designed as a research instrument can have a really good effect on them'. Lynne Gabriel talks of the link between therapeutic dialogue and research dialogue. Similarly, the 'pause' that Shanaaz Hoosain uses as a researcher, should also be used in social work practice. Morwenna Griffiths' evaluative work with schools should enable teachers and pupils in schools to be reflective practitioners. These researchers describe forms of support for their own research as stretching not only to colleagues and students in universities, but well beyond – to professional and other communities. This may be a challenge, as Jacqui Akhurst vividly illustrates in her research on HIV/AIDS education, but it is a kind of mutuality that is at the heart of virtuous educational research.

'Support' is a simple word, but a complex process. Supporting researchers is something that is done 'horizontally' and 'vertically'. Horizontal support includes the ways in which researchers support each other, engaging in peer dialogue. Vertical support can be the exercise of care by university managers (as Lāsma Latsone describes, where managers set up opportunities for research to flourish, and as Ginger MacDonald describes of her own work as the head of a university campus), care by researchers of their students (as Shanaaz Hoosain describes), care by researchers of less powerful social groups (as Jacqui Akhurst and Nel Noddings both describe). But support – the care – is not 'one way' support, even if there are hierarchical power relationships involved. As Buber says, '[w]e are moulded by our pupils' (Buber 1958, p. 30), and as Nel Noddings says, even in a professional caring situation 'that doesn't mean that the cared-for doesn't contribute anything to the relation'. She wants to promote a 'kind of openness, reciprocity' so that 'it isn't this powerful group of carers, care-givers, who decide what the other folks need and then they're generously going to give it to them'. Instead, they should be 'meeting together and realising that both contribute to the relationship'. I have argued elsewhere (Stern 2010) that, as research is a form of learning, there is a strict relationship between researchers, schoolteachers, and school pupils: all should see themselves as learners, and all should see themselves as – at times – investigating, generating new insights, and sharing those insights. Hence 'research' can be itself the central element of 'pedagogy' (the understanding of teaching), and 'learning' can be the defining characteristic of both schools and universities. This may sound obvious, but some schools, and a larger number of educational policy-makers, describe schooling as primarily driven by wealth-creation (hence '[e]ducation is the best economic policy there is', Blair 2003), and many universities categorise themselves as 'research-led' or 'teaching-led', rather than the more inclusive phrase 'learning-led'. Support for researchers is therefore support for particular forms of educational institutions, as well as the more intimate, personal, forms of support provided by attitudes of trust and the wish to enter into dialogue.

Conclusion

In this chapter, I have attempted to provide a set of fuzzy generalisations about virtuous educational research, a kind of non-ideal theory of the place of research in its wider social context. What I have avoided is a specific and structured theory of research virtues. Peterson's classification of virtues (the basis of Table 1) is not a single theory, and I have adapted that classification, in any case, in the light of my own earlier research and the views of the conversationalists. Whereas Aristotle talks of a kind of hierarchy of virtues, with 'magnanimity', for example, described as the 'crown of the virtues' (Aristotle 1976, p. 154), I make no such attempt. Some of the conversationalists pick out particular virtues as more central than others – Ron Best describes the combination of care and critical thinking as central, Chris Sink centres on care, Anne Pirrie on vitality, Mario D'Souza on a love of learning. Some, such as Mike Bottery, found a value in each virtue on the list. But it is precisely this variety in response that makes me confident in avoiding a single structure of virtues appropriate to description of virtuous educational research. Each researcher will find a different relationship to virtues and vices. That does not mean 'anything goes'. Rather, it means that dialogue about virtues, and a realisation of both the specificity and the mutuality of each research career can support virtuous educational research. More than this, it can support virtuous educational *researchers*.

These conversations on ethical practice will I hope generate more confidence in the possibility of leading the curious life of a researcher. Supporting the 'performance' of research without getting corrupted by inappropriate performativity, voicing researchers and those who are researched, and seeing researchers as in need of and also able to provide support for a better life, makes for a theory – however fuzzy – a theory of what might be called virtuous educational research. That is, eudemonic research: of and for a flourishing, curious, life.

Bibliography

Aguirre, I. (2004) 'Beyond the Understanding of Visual Culture: A Pragmatist Approach to Aesthetic Education', *IJADE: International Journal of Art and Design Education*, 23:3, pp. 256–270.

Akhurst, J., and Lawson, S. (2013) 'Workforce innovation through mentoring: An action research approach to programme evaluation', *International Journal of Therapy and Rehabilitation*, 20:8, pp. 410–416.

Akhurst, J., and Mitchell, C. (2012) 'International Community-Based Work Placements for UK Psychology Undergraduates: An evaluation of three cohorts' experiences', *Psychology Learning and Teaching*, 11:3, pp. 401–405.

Alexander, H. A. (2015) *Reimagining Liberal Education: Affiliation and Inquiry in Democratic Schooling*; New York: Bloomsbury.

American Political Science Association (APSA) (2008) *A Guide to Professional Ethics in Political Science, Second Edition*; Washington, DC: American Political Science Association.

American Sociological Association (ASA) (1999) *Code of Ethics and Policies and Procedures of the ASA Committee on Professional Ethics*; Washington, DC: American Sociological Association.

Anderson, E. (2010) *The Imperative of Integration*; Princeton, NJ: Princeton University Press.

Arendt, H. (2004 [1951]) *The Origins of Totalitarianism*; New York: Schoken.

Aristotle (1976) *The Ethics of Aristotle: The Nicomachean Ethics*; London: Penguin.

Arthur, J. (2010) *Of Good Character: Exploration of Virtues and Values in 3–25 Year-Olds*; Exeter: Imprint Academic.

Association of Social Anthropologists of the UK and the Commonwealth (ASAUKC) (1999) *Ethical Guidelines for Good Research Practice* <http://www.theasa.org/ethics/Ethical_guidelines.pdf> accessed February 2012.

Austin, J. L. (1975) *How To do Things With Words: Second Edition*; Cambridge, MA: Harvard University Press.

Avest, I. ter, Jozsa, D.-P., Knauth, T., Rosón, J., and Skeie, G. (eds) (2009) *Dialogue and Conflict on Religion: Studies of Classroom Interaction in European Countries*; Münster: Waxmann.

Bakhtin, M. M. (1981) *The Dialogic Imagination*; Austin, TX: University of Texas Press.

Ball, S. J. (2003) 'The Teacher's Soul and the Terrors of Performativity', *Journal of Education Policy*, 18:2, pp. 215–228.

Barenboim, D. (2008) *Everything is Connected: The Power of Music*; London: Phoenix.

Barnett, R. (ed.) (2005) *Reshaping the University: New Relationships Between Research, Scholarship and Teaching*; Maidenhead, Berkshire: Open University Press.

Barnett, R. (2007) *A Will to Learn: Being a Student in an Age of Uncertainty*; Maidenhead, Berkshire: Society for Research into Higher Education & Open University Press.

Bassey, M. (1999) *Case Study Research in Educational Settings*; Buckingham: Open University Press.

Bates, D., Durka, G., and Schweitzer, F. (eds) (2006) *Education, Religion and Society: Essays in Honour of John M. Hull*; Abingdon, Oxfordshire: Routledge.

Baum, L. F. (novel), Langley, N., Ryerson, F., and Woolf, E. A. (screenplay) (1939) *The Wizard of Oz*; Los Angeles, CA: MGM.

Becher, T., and Trowler, P. R. (2001) *Academic Tribes And Territories: Intellectual Enquiry and the Cultures of Disciplines: Second Edition*; Buckingham: Society for Research into Higher Education and the Open University Press.

Beer, D. (2014) *Punk Sociology*; Basingstoke: Palgrave Macmillan.

Bell, P. and Best, R. (1986) *Supportive Education*; Oxford: Blackwell.

Benjamin, A. (ed.) (1989) *The Lyotard Reader*; Oxford: Blackwell.

Best, R. (ed.) (1996) *Education, Spirituality and the Whole Child*; London: Cassell.

Best, R. (ed.) (2000a) *Education for Spiritual, Moral Social and Cultural Development*; London: Continuum.

Best, R. (2000b) 'Empathy, Experience and SMSC', *Pastoral Care in Education*, 18:4, pp. 8–18.

Best, R. (2001) *Pastoral Care and Personal-Social Education: A Review of UK Research*; Southwell, Nottinghamshire: British Educational Research Association.

Best, R. (2005a) 'Spiritual Development and Affective Education: An English Perspective', in S. Karppinen, Y. Katz and S. Neill (eds) *Theory and Practice in Affective Education: Essays in Honour of Arja Purula*; Helsinki: University of Helsinki, pp. 65–84.

Best, R. (2005b) 'Self Harm: A Challenge for Pastoral Care', *Pastoral Care in Education*, 23:3, pp. 3–11.

Best, R. (2005c) 'An Educational Response to Deliberate Self-Harm: Training, Support and School-Agency Links', *Journal of Social Work Practice*, 19:3, pp. 277–289.

Best, R. (2006) 'Deliberate Self-Harm in Adolescence: An Educational Response', *British Journal of Guidance & Counselling*, 34:2, pp. 161–175.

Best, R. (2007a) 'The Whole Child Matters: The Challenge of *Every Child Matters* for Pastoral Care', *Education 3–13*, 35:3, pp. 249–259.

Best, R. (2007b) 'Deliberate Self-Harm: Findings from a Study in an English University', *The Skill Journal*, 89, pp. 19–24.

Best, R. (2008a) 'In Defence of the Concept of "Spiritual Education": A Reply to Roger Marples', *International Journal of Children's Spirituality*, 13:4, pp. 320–327.

Best, R. (2008b) 'Education, Support and the Development of the Whole Person', *British Journal of Guidance and Counselling*, 36:4, pp. 343–351.

Best, R. (2009) 'Students Who Self-Harm: A Case-Study of Prevalence, Awareness and Response in an English University', *Pastoral Care in Education*, 27:3, pp. 165–203.

Best, R. (2011) 'Emotion, Spiritual Experience and Education: A Reflection', *International Journal of Children's Spirituality*, 16:4, pp. 361–368.

Best, R. (2014a) 'Spirituality, Faith and Education: Some Reflections from a UK Perspective', in J. Watson, M. de Souza and A. Trousdale (eds) *Global Perspectives on Spirituality and Education*; New York: Routledge, pp. 5–20.

Best, R. (2014b) 'Forty Years of Pastoral Care: An Appraisal of Michael Marland's Seminal Book and its Significance for Pastoral Care in Schools', *Pastoral Care in Education*, 32:3, pp. 173–185.

Best, R., Heyes, S. A., and Taylor, M. (1988) *Library Provision and Curriculum Planning*; London: British Library LIR Report No. 61.

Best, R., Lang, P., Lodge C., and Watkins, C. (eds) (1995) *Pastoral Care and Personal-Social Education: Entitlement and Provision*; London: Cassell.

Best, R., Maher, P., Baderman, G., Kirby, K., and Rabbett, P. (eds) (1989) *Whole Person: Whole School*; London: Longman/SCDC.

Best, R., Ribbins, P. and, Jarvis, C. (1977) 'Pastoral Care: Concept and Process', *British Journal of Educational Studies*, 25:2, pp. 124–135.

Best, R., Ribbins, P., Jarvis, C., and Oddy, D. (1983) *Education and Care: The Study of a School and its Pastoral Organization*; London: Heinemann.

Blair, T. (2003) *Biography* <http://www.pm.gov.uk/output/page4.asp> accessed August 2003.

Bond, T. (2004) *Ethical Guidelines for Researching Counselling and Psychotherapy*; Rugby: British Association for Counselling and Psychotherapy.

Bore, A., and Wright, N. (2009) 'The Wicked and Complex in Education: Developing a Transdisciplinary Perspective for Policy Formulation, Implementation and Professional Practice', *Journal of Education for Teaching*, 35:3, pp. 241–256.

Borradori, G. (1994) *The American Philosopher: Conversations with Quine, Davidson, Putnam, Nozick, Danto, Rorty, Cavell, MacIntyre, and Kuhn*; Chicago: University of Chicago Press.

Bottery, M. (1990) *The Morality of the School: The Theory and Practice of Values in Education;* London: Cassell.

Bottery, M. (1992) *The Ethics of Educational Management: Personal, Social and Political Perspectives on School Organization*; London: Cassell.

Bottery, M. (1994) *Lessons for Schools?: A Comparison of Business and Educational Management*; London: Cassell.

Bottery, M. (1997) 'Global Forces, National Mediations and the Management of Educational Institutions', *Educational Management Administration Leadership*, 27:3, pp. 299–312.

Bottery, M. (1998) *Professionals and Policy*; London: Cassell.

Bottery, M. (2000) *Education, Policy and Ethics*; London: Continuum.

Bottery, M. (2004) *The Challenges of Educational Leadership*; London: Paul Chapman.

Bottery, M. (2007) 'Reports from the Front Line: English Headteachers' Work in an Era of Practice Centralization', *Educational Management Administration Leadership*, 35:1, pp. 89–110.

Bottery, M. (2014) 'The International Reach and Significance of Portrait Methodology Upon Individuals and Organisations', *Research Excellence Framework 2014 Impact Case Study* <http://impact.ref.ac.uk/casestudies2/refservice.svc/Get CaseStudyPDF/39122> accessed January 2016.

Bottery, M. (2016) *Educational Leadership For a More Sustainable World*; London: Bloomsbury.

Bottery, M., Ngai, G., and Wong, P. H. (2008a) 'Leaders and Contexts: Comparing English and Hong Kong Perceptions of Educational Challenges', *International Studies in Educational Administration (ISEA)*, 36:1, pp. 56–71.

Bottery, M., Ngai, G., Wong, P. M., and Wong, P. H. (2008b) 'Portraits of resilience: headteachers in two different cultures', *Education 3–13*, 36:2, pp. 183–199.

Bottery, M., Ngai, G., Wong, P. M., and Wong, P. H. (2013) 'Values, Priorities and Responses: Comparing English Headteachers' and Hong Kong Principals' Perceptions of Their Work', *School Leadership & Management*, 33:1, pp. 43–60.

Bottery, M., Wright, N., and James, S. (2012) 'Personality, Moral Purpose, and the Leadership of an Education for Sustainable Development', *Education 3–13*, 40:3, pp. 227–241.

Bourdieu, P. (1998) *On Television*; New York: The New Press.

Brammer, L. and MacDonald, G. (2003) *The Helping Relationship: Process and Skills: 8th Edition*; Needham Heights, MA: Allyn and Bacon.

British Educational Research Association (BERA) (2011) *Ethical Guidelines for Educational Research*; London: British Educational Research Association.

British Psychological Society (BPS) (2009) *Code of Ethics and Conduct: Guidance published by the Ethics Committee of the British Psychological Society*; Leicester: The British Psychological Society.

British Society of Criminology (BSC) (2000) *Code of Ethics*; London: British Society of Criminology.

British Sociological Association (BSA) (2004) *Statement of Ethical Practice for the British Sociological Association*; Belmont, Durham: British Sociological Association.

Buber, M. (1958 [1923]) *I and Thou: Translated by Ronald Gregor Smith: Second Edition with a postscript by the author*; Edinburgh: T&T Clark.

Buber, M. (1998 [1965]) *The Knowledge of Man: Selected Essays: Edited by Maurice Friedman*; New York: Humanity Books.

Buber, M. (2002 [1965]) *Between Man and Man*; London: Routledge.

Butler, J. (1997) *Excitable Speech*; New York: Routledge.

Calvelhe, L. (2013) 'Arts-Based Research, Visual Culture and Coming to a Pragmatist Approach While Researching Self-Identified Gay Teenagers' (Aesthetic) Experiences', in F. Hernández-Hernández and R. Fendler (eds) *1st Conference on Arts-Based and Artistic Research: Critical Reflections on the Intersection of Art and Research*; Barcelona: University of Barcelona.

Calvelhe, L. (2015) *Adolescentes Gays Y Cultura Visual: Experiencias, Usos Y Contextos Implicaciones Educativas [Gay Teen Boys & Visual Culture: Experiences, Usages & Contexts Educational Implications]*; PhD Thesis, Pamplona, Spain: Universidad Pública de Navarra/Public University of Navarre.

Canadian Institutes of Health Research, Natural Sciences and Engineering Research Council of Canada, Social Sciences and Humanities Research Council of Canada (CIHR) (2010) *Tri-Council Policy Statement: Ethical Conduct for Research Involving Humans* <http://www.pre.ethics.gc.ca/pdf/eng/tcps2/TCPS_2_FINAL_Web.pdf> accessed January 2016.

Cavalli-Sforza, L. L., and Feldman, M. W. (1981) *Cultural Transmission and Evolution*; Princeton, NJ: Princeton University Press.

Cherry, F. (1995) *The 'Stubborn Particulars' of Social Psychology: Essays on the Research Process*; London: Routledge.

Cole, B. A., and Gunter, H. M. (eds) (2010) *Changing Lives: Women, Inclusion and the PhD*; Stoke-on-Trent: Trentham.

Connell, R. W. (1983) *Which Way is Up?: Essays on Sex, Class and Culture*; Sydney: Allen & Unwin.

Connell, R. W. (2007) *Southern Theory: Social Science and the Global Dynamics of Knowledge*; Cambridge: Polity Press.

Cragg, K. (1999) *Muhammad and the Christian: A Question of Response*; Oxford: Oneworld.

Crossley, M., Arthur, L., and McNess, E. (eds) (2016) *Revisiting Insider-Outsider Research in Comparative and International Education*; Oxford: Symposium.

Csikszentmihalyi, M., and Csikszentmihalyi, I. S. (eds) (2006) *A Life Worth Living: Contributions to Positive Psychology*; Oxford: Oxford University Press.

Dalin, P., and Rust, V. D. (1983) *Can Schools Learn?*; Windsor: NFER-Nelson.

Daniels, H. (2001) *Vygotsky and Pedagogy*; London: Routledge Falmer.

Dawkins, R. (1976) *The Selfish Gene*; Oxford: Oxford University Press.

Derrida, J. (1976) *Of Grammatology*; Baltimore, MD: The Johns Hopkins Press.

Douglas, J. D. (1976) *Investigative Social Research: Individual and Team Field Research*; Beverly Hills, CA: SAGE.

D'Souza, M. O. (2000) 'Religious Particularism and Cultural Pluralism: The Possible Contribution of Religious Education to Canadian Political Identity', *Religious Education*, 95:3, pp. 233–249.

D'Souza, M. O. (forthcoming, 2016) *A Catholic Philosophy of Education: The Church and Two Philosophers*; Montreal, Quebec: McGill-Queen's University Press.

D'Souza, M. O., with Seiling, J. R. (eds) (2014) *Being in the World: A Quotable Maritain Reader*; Notre Dame, IN: University of Notre Dame Press.

Dunne, C. (2012) *Carl Jung: Wounded Healer of the Soul: An Illustrated Biography*; London: Watkins.

Egan, G. (2014) *The Skilled Helper: A Problem-Management and Opportunity Development Approach to Helping: Tenth Edition*; Belmont, CA: Brooks/Cole.

Elliott, J. (1991) *Action Research for Educational Change*; Buckingham: Open University Press.

Elster, J. (1979) *Ulysses and the Sirens: Studies in Rationality and Irrationality*; Cambridge: Cambridge University Press.

Empson, W. (1961) *Seven Types of Ambiguity: Third Edition*; Harmondsworth: Penguin.

Erikson, E. H. (1980 [1959]) *Identity and the Life Cycle*; New York: Norton.

Fines, J., and Nichol, J. (1997) *Teaching Primary History: Nuffield Primary History Project*; Oxford: Heinemann

Fitzgerald, T., and White, J. (2012) *Hard Labour? Academic Work and the Changing Landscape of Higher Education*; Bingley, West Yorkshire: Emerald.

Foucault, M. (1988) *Power/Knowledge: Selected Interviews & Other Writings, 1972–1977: Edited by Colin Gordon*; New York: Pantheon.

Frideres, J. S. (ed.) (1992) *A World of Communities: Participatory Research Perspectives*; North York, Ontario: Captus.

Friedman, M. S. (2002) *Martin Buber: The Life of Dialogue: 4th Edition*; London: Routledge.

Froebel, F. (2009 [1826]) *The Education of Man*; Charleston, SC: BiblioLife LLC.

Gabriel, L. (2000) 'Counselling Challenge: Maintaining Boundaries in Supervision', *Counselling: Journal of the British Association for Counselling and Psychotherapy*, 11:8, pp. 475–476.

Gabriel, L. (2005) *Speaking the Unspeakable: The Ethics of Dual Relationships in Counselling and Psychotherapy*; London: Brunner-Routledge.

Gabriel, L., and Casemore, R. (eds) (2009) *Relational Ethics in Practice: Narratives from Counselling and Psychotherapy*; London: Brunner-Routledge.

Gandin, L. A., and Apple, M. W. (2002) 'Thin Versus Thick Democracy in Education: Porto Alegre and the Creation of Alternatives to Neo-Liberalism', *International Studies in Sociology of Education*, 12:2, pp. 99–116.

Glaser, B. G., and Strauss, A. L. (1965) *Awareness of Dying*; Chicago: Aldine.

Glaser, B. G. and Strauss, A. L. (1967) *The Discovery of Grounded Theory: Strategies for Qualitative Research*; New York: Aldine.

Goleman, D. (1996) *Emotional Intelligence: Why It Can Matter More Than IQ*; London: Bloomsbury.

Grace, G. (1994) 'Urban Education and the Culture of Contentment: The Politics, Culture and Economics of Inner-City Schooling', in N. P. Stromquist (ed.) *Education in Urban Areas*; Westport, CT: Praeger, pp. 45–59.

Graham-Matheson, L. (2012) 'Who Do You Think You Are? Developing Your Identity as a Researcher', *The Guardian Higher Education Network*, 16 August 2012 <http://www.theguardian.com/higher-education-network/blog/2012/aug/16/phd-students-originality-conforming-academia> accessed January 2016.

Griffiths, M. (1995) *Feminisms and the Self: The Web of Identity*; London: Routledge.

Griffiths, M. (1998) *Educational Research for Social Justice: Getting Off the Fence*; Buckingham: Open University Press.

Griffiths, M. (2003) *Action for Social Justice in Education: Fairly Different*; Maidenhead, Berkshire: Open University Press.

Griffiths, M. (2009) 'Action Research For/As/Mindful of Social Justice', in B. Somekh and S. E. Noffke (eds) *The SAGE Handbook of Educational Action Research*; London: SAGE, pp. 85–99.

Griffiths, M. and Troyna, B. (eds) (1995) *Antiracism, Culture and Social Justice in Education*; Stoke-on-Trent: Trentham.

Griffiths, M. and Woolf, F. (2009) 'The Nottingham Apprenticeship Model: Schools in Partnership with Artists and Creative Practitioners', *British Educational Research Journal*, 35:4, pp. 557–574.

Grimmitt, M., Grove, J., Hull, J. M., and Spencer, L. (1991) *A Gift to the Child: Religious Education in the Primary School*; London: Simon & Schuster.

Gunter, H. M. (2001) *Leaders and Leadership in Education*; London: Paul Chapman, 2001.

Gunter, H. M. (2013) 'On Not Researching School Leadership: The Contribution of S. J. Ball', *London Review of Education*, 11:3, pp. 218–228.

Gunter, H. M. (2016) *An Intellectual History of School Leadership Practice and Research*; London: Bloomsbury.

Habermas, J. (1974) 'The Public Sphere: An Encyclopedia Article (1964)', *New German Critique*, 3, pp. 49–55.

Harber, C. (2002) 'Schooling as Violence: An Exploratory Overview', *Educational Review*, 54:1, pp. 7–16.

Harber, C. (2004) *Schooling as Violence: How Schools Harm Pupils and Societies*; Abingdon, Oxfordshire: Routledge.

Heater, D. (1999) *What Is Citizenship?*; Cambridge: Polity.

Higher Education Funding Council for England (Hefce), Scottish Funding Council, Higher Education Funding Council for Wales, Department for Employment and Learning (2011) *REF2014: Research Excellence Framework: Assessment Framework and Guidance on Submissions*; Bristol: Hefce.

Hill, J. B. (2010) 'Julia Butterfly Hill: We Live In An Age Of "Disposability Consciousness" (VIDEO)', *Huffington Post* (9 July 2010, updated 17 November 2011) <http://www.huffingtonpost.com/2010/07/09/understanding-disposabili_n_641070.html> accessed January 2016.

Hobbes, T. (1968 [1651]) *Leviathan: Edited by C. B. Macpherson*; Harmondsworth: Penguin.

Hooks, B. (1994) *Teaching to Transgress: Education as the Practice of Freedom*; New York: Routledge.

Hoosain, S. (2007) *Resilience in Refugee Children: A Gestalt Play Therapy Approach: Dissertation for Magister of Diaconiologiae Degree, University of South Africa*; Pretoria, South Africa: University of South Africa.

Hoosain, S. (2013) *The Transmission of Intergenerational Trauma in Displaced Families*; Cape Town, South Africa: University of the Western Cape: PhD Thesis.

Hoosain, S. (2015) 'Values for Personal, Social and Political Influence', *Value and Virtue in Practice-Based Research Conference*; York St John University, June 2015 <http://www.yorksj.ac.uk/value&virtue>.

Hoyle, E., and Wallace, M. (2005) *Educational Leadership: Ambiguity, Professionals & Managerialism*; London: SAGE.

Hull, J. M. (1996) 'A Gift to the Child: A New Pedagogy For Teaching Religion To Young Children', *Religious Education*, 91:2, pp. 172–188.

Hull, J. M. (1998) *Utopian Whispers: Moral, Religious and Spiritual Values in Schools*; Norwich: RMEP.

Jeffrey, B., and Troman, G. (2011) 'The Construction of Performative Identities', *European Educational Research Journal*, 10:4, pp. 484–501.

Jones, J. (1994) *Teacher as Reflective Professional*; London: Institute of Education, University of London, Occasional Papers in Teacher Education and Training.

Keats, J. (1947 [1848, 1878]) *The Letters of John Keats: Edited by Maurice Buxton Forman*; London: Oxford University Press.

Kesey, K. (2002 [1962]) *One Flew Over The Cuckoo's Nest*; London: Penguin.

Kozyrev, F. N. (2003) 'The Religious and Moral Beliefs of Adolescents in St Petersburg', *Journal of Education and Christian Belief*, 7:1, pp. 69–91.

Kozyrev, F. N. (2010) *Гуманитарное религиозное образование: Книга для учителей и методистов [Humanitarian Religious Education: A Book for Teachers and Trainers]*; St Petersburg: Russian Christian Academy for Humanities.

Kozyrev, F. (2011) 'Russian REDCo Findings in Support of Dialogue and Hermeneutics', *British Journal of Religious Education*, 33:2, pp. 257–270.

Krumboltz, J. D. (2009) 'The Happenstance Learning Theory', *Journal of Career Assessment*, 17:2, pp. 135–154.

Krumboltz, J. D., and Levin, A. S. (2010) *Luck is No Accident: Making the Most of Happenstance in Your Life and Career: 2nd Edition*; Atascadero, CA: Impact Publishers.

Lang, P., Best, R., and Lichtenberg, A. (eds) (1994) *Caring for Children: International Perspectives on Pastoral Care and PSE*; London: Cassell.

Larkin, P. (1988) *Collected Poems: Edited with an Introduction by Anthony Thwaite*; London: The Marvell Press/Faber and Faber.

Latsone, L. (2004) *Renewing Parish Education in the Roman Catholic Church of Latvia: Implementing the Reforms of the Second Vatican Council*; PhD Thesis, Ann Arbor, MI: Fordham University.

Latsone, L. (2013a) 'Socially Intelligent Intercultural Education', *Educational Research Journal*, 28:1&2, pp. 145–162.

Latsone, L. (2013b) 'The Role of Religious Education in Creating Participative and Inclusive Parish Communities: Challenges for Adult Religious Educators of Latvia', *Religious Education Journal of Australia*, 29:1, pp. 22–27.

Lave, J., and Wenger, E. (1991) *Situated Learning: Legitimate Peripheral Participation*; Cambridge: Cambridge University Press.

Lawrence-Lightfoot, S. (2000) *Respect: An Exploration*; Cambridge, MA: Perseus.

Lawrence-Lightfoot, S. (2009) *The Third Chapter: Passion, Risk, and Adventure in the 25 Years After 50*; New York: Sarah Crichton Books.

Lawrence-Lightfoot, S., and Davis, J. H. (1997) *The Art and Science of Portraiture*; San Francisco: Jossey-Bass.

Lees, H. E. (2012) *Silence in Schools*; Stoke-on-Trent: Trentham.

Lees, H. E. (2014) *Education Without Schools: Discovering Alternatives*; Bristol: Policy Press.

Lees, H. E., and Noddings, N. (forthcoming, 2016) *The Palgrave Handbook of Alternative Education*; London: Palgrave Macmillan.

Lonergan, B. J. F. (1974) *A Second Collection*; Philadelphia: Westminster Press.

Lowell, R. (2003) *Collected Poems, edited by Frank Bidart and David Gewanter*; New York: Farrar, Strauss and Giroux.

McCutcheon, R. T. (ed.) (1999) *The Insider/Outsider Problem in the Study of Religion: A Reader*; London: Cassell.

MacDonald, D., and MacDonald G. (2004) 'Adjustment Disorders', in F. Kline and L Silver (eds) *Educators Guide to Mental Health Issues in the Classroom*; Baltimore, MD: Brookes.

MacDonald, G., and Sink, C. A. (1999) 'A Qualitative Developmental Analysis of Comprehensive Guidance Programs in the United States', *The British Journal of Counseling and Guidance*, 27, pp. 415–430.

MacDonald, G. P. (2014) 'Retaining First Generation Students in College: Planning for Student Success', *Social and Moral Fabric of the School, 8th International Conference*, Hull, August 2014.

McDonald, J. P. (1989) 'When Outsiders Try to Change Schools From the Inside', *Phi Delta Kappan*, 71:3, Nov 1989, pp. 206–212.

McDonnell, P., and McNiff, J. (2014) *Action Research for Professional Selling*; Farnham, Surrey: Gower.

Macfarlane, B. (2009) *Researching with Integrity: The Ethics of Academic Enquiry*; New York: Routledge.

MacIntyre, A. (1981) *After Virtue: A Study in Moral Theory*; London: Duckworth.

Mackie, J. L. (1977) *Ethics: Inventing Right and Wrong*; Harmondsworth: Pelican.

McLaughlin, T. H. (2003) 'Teaching as a Practice and a Community of Practice: The Limits of Commonality and the Demands of Diversity', *Journal of Philosophy of Education*, 37:2, pp. 339–352.

Macmurray, J. (1946) 'Freedom in Community', *Joseph Payne Memorial Lectures*, King's College, London, 29 November 1946.

Macmurray, J. (1995 [1935]) *Reason and Emotion*; London: Faber.

McNiff, J. (1993) *Teaching as Learning: An Action Research Approach*; London: Routledge.

McNiff, J. (2013a) *Action Research: Principles and Practice, 3rd Edition*; Abingdon, Oxfordshire: Routledge.

McNiff, J. (2013b) 'Becoming Cosmopolitan and Other Dilemmas of Internationalisation: Reflections from the Gulf States', *Cambridge Journal of Education*, 43:4, pp. 501–515.

McNiff, J. (ed.) (2013c) *Value and Virtue in Practice-Based Research*; Poole, Dorset: September Books.

McNiff, J. (2014) *Writing and Doing Action Research*; London: SAGE.

McNiff, J. (ed.) (forthcoming, 2016) *Values and Virtues in Higher Education Research: Critical Perspectives*; Abingdon, Oxfordshire: Routledge.

Magee, B. (1971) *Modern British Philosophy*; London: Secker and Warburg.

Magee, B. (1978) *Talking Philosophy: Dialogues With Fifteen Leading Philosophers*; Oxford: Oxford University Press.

Maher, P., and Best, R. (1984) *Training and Support for Pastoral Care*; Warwick: NAPCE.

Marenholtz-Bülow, B. von (2015 [1877]) *Reminiscences of Friedrich Froebel*; London: Forgotten Books.

Maritain, J. (1962) *The Education of Man: The Educational Philosophy of Jacques Maritain*; New York: Doubleday.

Maritain, J. (1971 [1943]) *Education at the Crossroads*; New Haven, CT: Yale University Press.

Marx, K. (1976 [1867]) *Capital: A Critique of Political Economy: Volume 1*; London: Penguin.

Massignon, L. (1994) *The Passion of Al-Hallaj: Mystic and Martyr*; Princeton, NJ: Princeton University Press.

Maynard Smith, J. (1972) *On Evolution*; Edinburgh: Edinburgh University Press.

Merton, T. (1966) *Conjectures of a Guilty Bystander*; New York: Random House.

Mingers, J. (2009) 'Discourse Ethics and Critical Realist Ethics: An Evaluation in the Context of Business', *Journal of Critical Realism*, 8:2, pp. 172–202.

Mitscherlich, A., and Mielke, F. (1949) *Doctors of Infamy: The Story of the Nazi Medical Crimes*; New York: Henry Schuman.

Montaigne, M. de (1991 [1595]) *On Solitude*; London: Penguin.

Neill, A. S. (1985 [1960]) *Summerhill: A Radical Approach to Child-Rearing*; Harmondsworth: Penguin.

Neumann, A. (2009) *Professing to Learn: Creating Tenured Lives and Careers in the American Research University*; Baltimore, MD: Johns Hopkins University Press.

Neumann, A. (2012) 'Research as Thought and Emotion in Researchers' Learning', *Research Intelligence*, 118, pp. 8–9.

Newton, C., and Tarrant, T. (1992) *Managing Change in Schools: A Practical Handbook*; London: Routledge.

Nixon, J. (2008) *Towards the Virtuous University: The Moral Bases of Academic Practice*; New York: Routledge.

Noddings, N. (2012) 'The Caring Relation in Teaching', *Oxford Review of Education*, 38:6, pp. 771–781.

Noddings, N. (2015) *A Richer, Brighter Vision for American High Schools*; New York: Cambridge University Press.

Oakeshott, M. (1991) *Rationalism in Politics and Other Essays*; Indianapolis, IN: Liberty Fund.

Organisation for Economic Co-operation and Development (OECD) (2007) *OECD Glossary of Statistical Terms*; Paris: OECD.

Osborne, P. (ed.) (1996) *A Critical Sense: Interviews With Intellectuals*; London: Routledge.

Oxford English Dictionary (OED). *See* Simpson 2005.

Palmer, P. J. (2007) *The Courage to Teach: Exploring the Inner Landscape of a Teacher's Life: 10th Anniversary Edition*; San Francisco: Jossey-Bass.

Pavitola, L., and Latsone, L. (2015) 'Giving Voice to the Outcomes of our Research', *Value and Virtue in Practice-Based Research: Fifth International Conference: The Significance of Our Research: Influence and Impact*, York, June 2015.

Pieper, J. (1966) *The Four Cardinal Virtues*; Notre Dame, IN: University of Notre Dame Press.

Pirrie, A. (2003) 'Spoilsport: On Sport and Attainment', *Educational Research*, 45:2, pp. 181–188.

Pirrie, A. (2010) 'Notes from the Exclusion Zone: Critical Reflections on Educational Inclusion', *Scottish Affairs*, 71, pp. 78–94.

Pirrie, A. (2015) 'Icarus Falling: Re-Imagining Educational Theory', *Journal of Philosophy of Education*, 49:4, pp. 525–538.

Pirrie, A., and Head, G. (2007) 'Martians in the Playground: Researching Special Educational Needs', *Oxford Review of Education*, 33:1, pp. 19–31.

Pirrie, A., and Macleod, G. (2009) 'Travels with a Donkey: Further Adventures in Social Research', *Power and Education*, 1:3 <www.wwwords.co.uk/POWER>.

Pirrie, A., and Macleod, G. (2010) 'Tripping, Slipping and Losing the Way: Moving Beyond Methodological Difficulties in Social Research', *British Educational Research Journal*, 36:3, pp. 367–378.

Pirrie, A., MacAllister, J., and Macleod, G. (2012) 'Taking Flight: Trust, Ethics and the Comfort of Strangers', *Ethics and Education*, 7:1, pp. 33–44.

Pirrie, A., and Thoutenhoofd, E. D. (2013) 'Learning to Learn in the European Reference Framework for Lifelong Learning', *Oxford Review of Education*, 39:5, pp. 609–626.

Pring, R. (2004) *Philosophy of Education: Aims, Theory, Common Sense and Research*; London: Continuum.

Rawls, J. (1972) *A Theory of Justice*; Oxford: Oxford University Press.

Salmon, P. (1988) *Psychology for Teachers: An Alternative Approach*; London: Hutchinson Education.

Salmon, P. (1992) *Achieving a PhD: Ten Students' Experience*; Stoke-on-Trent: Trentham.

Seabright, P. (2004) *The Company of Strangers: A Natural History of Economic Life*; Princeton: Princeton University Press.

Sen, A. (1992) *Inequality Reexamined*; Oxford: Oxford University Press.

Senechal, D. (2012) *Republic of Noise: The Loss of Solitude in Schools and Culture*; Lanham, MD: Rowman & Littlefield.

Serres, M. (1997) *The Troubadour of Knowledge*; Ann Arbor, MI: University of Michigan Press.

Simpson, J. A. (chief editor) (OED) (2005) *The Oxford English Dictionary: Third Edition*; Oxford: Oxford University Press <http://www.oed.com> and <http://dictionary.oed.com/>.

Sink, C. (ed.) (2005) *Contemporary School Counseling: Theory, Research, and Practice*; Boston, MA: Lahaska Press.

Sink, C. A. (2011) *Mental Health Interventions for School Counselors*; Belmont, CA: Brooks/Cole.

Sink, C. A., and Bultsma, S. A. (2014) 'Psychometric Analysis of the Life Perspectives Inventory and Implications for Assessing Characteristics of Adolescent Spirituality', *Measurement and Evaluation in Counseling and Development*, 47:2, pp. 150–167.

Sink, C. A., Cleveland, R., and Stern, J. (2007) 'Spiritual Formation in Christian School Counseling Programs', *Journal of Research on Christian Education*, 16:1, pp. 35–63.

Sink, C. A., Rondeau, L., Seo, M., and Cho, H-I (2010) 'Assessing Spirituality in American and Korean Adolescents: Initial Psychometrics on the Life Perspectives Inventory', *6th International Conference on the Social and Moral Fabric of the School: Meaningful Education*, March 2010.

Sink, C. A., Seo, M., and Kim, D. H. (2013) 아동청소년을 위한 긍정상담 *[Child Adolescent Counseling and Spirituality: School Counseling in Positive Psychology]*; Seoul: Hakjisa Publishing.

Smyth, J. (2006) '"When Students Have Power": Student Engagement, Student Voice, and the Possibilities for School Reform Around "Dropping Out" of School', *International Journal of Leadership in Education: Theory and Practice*, 9:4, pp. 285–298.

Smyth, J., and McInerney, P. (2012) *From Silent Witnesses to Active Agents: Student Voice in Re-Engaging with Learning*; New York: Peter Lang.

Spinoza, B. (1955) *The Ethics*; New York: Dover.

Spivak, G. C. (author) and Harasym, S. (ed.) (1990) *The Post-Colonial Critic: Interviews, Strategies, Dialogues*; New York: Routledge.

Steele, C. M. (2010) *Whistling Vivaldi: How Stereotypes Affect Us and What We Can Do*; New York: W. W. Norton.

Stenhouse, L. (1975) *An Introduction to Curriculum Research and Development*; London: Heinemann.

Stern, L. J. (1982) *Sociobiology and Social Philosophy*; BPhil Thesis, University of Oxford.

Stern, L. J. (1997) *Homework and Study Support: A Guide for Teachers and Parents*; London: David Fulton.

Stern, L. J. (1999) *Developing as a Teacher of History*; Cambridge: Chris Kington.

Stern, L. J. (2001) *Developing Schools as Learning Communities: Towards a Way of Understanding School Organisation, School Development, and Learning*; PhD Thesis, London University, London: London University Institute of Education.

Stern, L. J. (2006) *Teaching Religious Education: Researchers in the Classroom*; London: Continuum.

Stern, L. J. (2007) *Schools and Religions: Imagining the Real*; London: Continuum.

Stern, L. J. (2008) 'The Virtue and Value of Research in Spirituality', *British Educational Research Association*, Edinburgh, September 2008.

Stern, L. J. (2009a) *The Spirit of the School*; London: Continuum.

Stern, L. J. (2009b) 'Monologue or Dialogue? Stepping Away from the Abyss in Higher Education', *London Review of Education*, 7:3, pp. 271–281.

Stern, L. J. (2009c) *Getting the Buggers to Do Their Homework: Second Edition*; London: Continuum.

Stern, L. J. (2010) 'Research as Pedagogy: Building Learning Communities and Religious Understanding in RE', *British Journal of Religious Education*, 32:2, pp. 133–146.

Stern, L. J. (2012) 'The Personal World of Schooling: John Macmurray and Schools as Households', *Oxford Review of Education*, 38:6, pp. 727–745.

Stern, L. J. (2013a) 'The Influence of Research Within Religious Education: The Westhill Seminars, RE Professionals, Pupils and Schools', *British Journal of Religious Education*, 36:1, pp. 1–21.

Stern, L. J. (2013b) 'Martin Buber, Empathy and Research Practice: A Response to Rachel Cope', *Journal for the Study of Spirituality*, 3:1, pp. 67–72.

Stern, L. J. (2013c) 'Surprise in Schools: Martin Buber and Dialogic Schooling', *Forum: For Promoting 3–19 Comprehensive Education*, 55:1, pp. 45–58.

Stern, L. J. (2013d) 'Virtue and Value in Educational Research', Chapter 10, in J. Arthur, and T. Lovat (eds) *The Routledge International Handbook of Education, Religion and Values*; Abingdon, Oxfordshire: Routledge, pp. 114–123.

Stern, L. J. (2014a) *Loneliness and Solitude in Education: How to Value Individuality and Create an Enstatic School*; Oxford: Peter Lang.

Stern, L. J. (2014b) 'Dialogues of Space, Time and Practice: Supporting Research in Higher Education', *Other Education: The Journal of Educational Alternatives*, 3:2, pp. 3–21.

Stern, L. J. (2015a) 'Soul-searching and Re-searching: Action Philosophy Alone', *Educational Action Research*, 23:1, pp. 104–115.

Stern, L. J. (2015b) 'Children's Voice or Children's Voices: How Educational Research Can be at the Heart of Schooling', *Forum: For Promoting 3–19 Comprehensive Education*, 57:1, pp. 75–90.

Stern, L. J., and Backhouse, A. (2011) 'Dialogic Feedback for Children and Teachers: Evaluating the "Spirit of Assessment"', *International Journal of Children's Spirituality*, 16:4, pp. 331–346.

Stern, L. J., Grant, T., and Ward, P. (2015) 'How Solitude Will Bring Us All Together', *Professional REflection: The Journal of NATRE*, 33:1, pp. 54–57.

Stern, L. J., and James, S. (2006) 'Every Person Matters: Enabling Spirituality Education for Nurses', *Journal of Clinical Nursing*, 15:7, pp. 897–904.

Strauss, A. L., and Corbin, J. (1990) *Basics of Qualitative Research: Grounded Theory Procedures and Techniques*; London: SAGE.

Sunstein, C. R., and Thaler, R. H. (2008) *Nudge: Improving Decisions About Health, Wealth and Happiness*; New Haven, CT: Yale University Press.

Troman, G. (2008) 'Primary Teacher Identity, Commitment and Career in Performative School Cultures', *British Educational Research Journal*, 34:5, pp. 619–633.

Trotman, D., Willoughby, R., and Lees, H. (2016) *Education Studies: The Key Concepts*; Abingdon, Oxfordshire: Routledge.

Unger, R. M. (2004) *False Necessity: Anti-Necessitarian Social Theory in the Service of Radical Democracy*; London: Verso.

Universities UK (UUK) (2012) *The Concordat to Support Research Integrity*; London: UUK.

Walford, G. (ed.) (1991) *Doing Educational Research*; London: Routledge.

Wegerif, R. (2008) 'Dialogic or Dialectic? The Significance of Ontological Assumptions in Research on Educational Dialogue', *British Educational Research Journal*, 34:3, pp. 347–361.

Wenger, E. (1998) *Communities of Practice: Learning, Meaning, and Identity*; Cambridge: Cambridge University Press.

Whitehead, J. (1989) 'Creating a Living Educational Theory from Questions of the Kind, "How Do I Improve My Practice?"', *Cambridge Journal of Education*, 19:1, pp. 41–52.

Wilson, E. O. (1975) *Sociobiology: The New Synthesis*; Cambridge, MA: Harvard University Press.

Winnicott, D. W. (1986) *Home is Where We Start From: Essays by a Psychoanalyst*; Harmondsworth: Pelican.

Wittgenstein, L. (1958) *Philosophische Untersuchungen: Philosophical Investigations: 2nd Edition*; Oxford: Blackwell.

Wittgenstein, L. (1961 [1918]) *Tractatus Logico-Philosophicus*; London: Routledge & Kegan Paul.

Woolf, F. (2004) *Partnership for Learning: A Guide to Evaluating Arts Education Projects: Second Edition*; London: Arts Council England.

Woolf, V. (2014 [1929]) *A Room of One's Own*; Adelaide: eBooks@Adelaide <http://ebooks.adelaide.edu.au/w/woolf/virginia/w91r/index.html> accessed January 2016.

Index

Religion, Education and Values

Debates about religion, education and values are more central to contemporary society than ever before. The challenges posed by the interaction between these different spheres will continue to increase as the effects of globalization and cultural pluralization impact on educational settings. Our radically changed and rapidly changing environment poses critical questions about how we should educate individuals to live in increasingly diverse societies.

Books in this series offer the most recent research, from a variety of disciplinary perspectives, on the interface between religion, education and values around the world. The series covers such themes as the history of religious education, the philosophies and psychologies of religious and values education, and the application of social science research methods to the study of young people's values and world-views.

Books within the series are subject to peer review and include single and co-authored monographs and edited collections. Proposals should be sent to any or all of the series editors:

Professor Stephen G. Parker (s.parker@worc.ac.uk)
The Rev'd Canon Professor Leslie J. Francis (Leslie.Francis@warwick.ac.uk)
Dr Rob Freathy (r.j.k.freathy@ex.ac.uk)
Dr Mandy Robbins (mandy.robbins@glyndwr.ac.uk)

Vol. 2   Stephen Parker, Rob Freathy and Leslie J. Francis (eds):
          Religious Education and Freedom of Religion and Belief.
          286 pages. 2012. ISBN 978-3-0343-0754-3

Vol. 3   Ann Casson:
          Fragmented Catholicity and Social Cohesion: Faith Schools in a
          Plural Society.
          198 pages. 2013. ISBN 978-3-0343-0896-0

Vol. 4   Sylvia Baker:
          Swimming Against the Tide: The New Independent Christian
          Schools and their Teenage Pupils.
          259 pages. 2013. ISBN 978-3-0343-0942-4

Vol. 5   Nuraan Davids:
          Women, Cosmopolitanism and Islamic Education: On the Virtues
          of Engagement and Belonging.
          195 pages. 2013. ISBN 978-3-0343-1708-5

Vol. 6   Julian Stern:
          Loneliness and Solitude in Education: How to Value Individuality
          and Create an Enstatic School.
          224 pages. 2014. ISBN 978-3-0343-1733-7

Vol. 7   Stephen G. Parker, Rob Freathy and Leslie J. Francis (eds):
          History, Remembrance and Religious Education.
          423 pages. 2015. ISBN 978-3-0343-1720-7

Vol. 8   Trevor Cooling with Beth Green, Andrew Morris and Lynn Revell:
          Christian Faith in English Church Schools: Research
          Conversations with Classroom Teachers.
          205 pages. 2016. ISBN 978-3-0343-1938-6

Vol. 9   Julian Stern:
         Virtuous Educational Research: Conversations on Ethical
         Practice.
         258 pages. 2016. ISBN 978-3-0343-1880-8